WITHDRAWN

# Wittgenstein: a Critique

*International Library of Philosophy*

---

*Editor:* Ted Honderich

A catalogue of books already published in the
*International Library of Philosophy*
will be found at the end of this volume

# Wittgenstein:
# a Critique

## J.N. Findlay

*Bowne Professor of Philosophy,*
*Boston University*

# ROUTLEDGE & KEGAN PAUL

London, Boston, Melbourne and Henley

First published in 1984
by Routledge & Kegan Paul plc
14 Leicester Square, London WC2H 7PH, England
9 Park Street, Boston, Mass. 02018, USA
464 St Kilda Road, Melbourne,
Victoria 3004, Australia and
Broadway House, Newtown Road,
Henley-on-Thames, Oxon RG9 1EN, England
Set in Times
by Columns, Reading
and printed in Great Britain
by Robert Hartnoll Ltd, Bodmin, Cornwall
Copyright © J.N. Findlay 1984
Library of Congress Cataloging in Publication Data
Findlay, J. N. (John Niemeyer), 1903-
Wittgenstein, a critique.
(International library of philosophy)
Includes index.
1. Wittgenstein, Ludwig, 1889-1951. I. Title.
II. Series.
B3376.W564F56     1984      192      84-6969
British Library CIP data also available
ISBN 0-7102-0330-6 (C)

# CONTENTS

# I

# INTRODUCTORY

## I

The aim of this book is to offer a comprehensive critique of the thought of Wittgenstein from a standpoint which recognizes him to be, both in his earlier and his later thinking, a systematic philosophical thinker of immense consequence and originality, however much this may seem to be belied by the disjoined, aphoristic manner in which his main theses are set forth, like a series of brilliant *aperçus* that spring from no central body of doctrine. Like the founder of Buddhism, to whose deeply negative forms of mental enlightenment and liberation his own forms of linguistic enlightenment and liberation have often been likened, Wittgenstein professed to have no doctrines, no deep-going theories regarding the world and what may lie behind it, such as earlier philosophers had canvassed, but rather only a method that would lay all such deep enquiries to rest, enabling the mind to take repose in the recognition of plain facts ordinarily expressed, and in inferences of the most banal ordinariness and obviousness. But though thus regarding the deep-going doctrines of the earlier philosophers in such a light, Wittgenstein's accounts of the situations in which doctrines arise, and the expedients by which they can be laid to rest, themselves involve a definite doctrine regarding what can and what cannot be said, and why it can or cannot be said, and this has profound implications for all the last things commonly recognized by philosophers. Like the Great Vehicle school of Buddhism, which

1

turned the doctrinal abstentions of early Buddhism into an elaborately argued for, many-sided doctrine of emptiness or nullity, credited with as many facets and emotive attributes as the doctrines which it demolished, so what we may call the deliberate unphilosophy of Wittgenstein became a profoundly philosophical treatment of the relations of the universal to the particular, of frames of mind to what they assert or refer to, of complex wholes to their ultimate constituents, of a man's self to the other selves whom he recognizes and with whom he converses, as well as his relations to all the unspeaking, unthinking things that he speaks about, whether to himself or others. This treatment, in view of its deep desire to abolish what it itself is, a deep doctrine ranging far beneath the surface of things, exposes it, however, to deep criticism at almost every point, although its tactics of aphoristic evasion make it very hard to pin it down or to shoot it down. Such a pinning down and shooting down must, none the less, be attempted in this book, for in neither its earlier nor its later phases is there anything in Wittgenstein genuinely unassailable and definitive. We shall now, however, seek to destroy its ideal of a philosophy which builds on the ultimate obviousness of assertion and conception, except that we continue to hold to the presence of an element of the immediately unordinary and unobvious, as itself a persistently ordinary and obvious feature of all that we have to handle and come into contact with, and which we can demystify, not by identifying it with something that it is not, but only by recognizing it for just what it is. The thoughts that cannot be identified with images or words, while standing in the closest and most necessary relation to these, the other persons whose experiences we intimately enter without ever having them, the infinity we exhaustively understand without being able exhaustively to illustrate it, the powers that contain all their expressions within them but not in actuality, the relationships which modify things profoundly without modifying anything in them, the deep affinities which lead things to act in concert without concerting to do so: all these matters appear queer, and requiring explanation ~~and demystification, when we try to~~ conceive them as something they are not, and become wholly obvious and ordinary when we recognize them for just what they are. For well or ill, we would seem to live in a world like that of the ancient patriarchs where unordinary visitants are always dropping in upon us: what we should learn is to treat them as ordinary, and make of them our friends. What Wittgenstein often arguably does is to treat them as phantasms, and to try to scare them away, thereby impoverishing his discourse and his vision of the world.

What, however, shall we say was the slant upon the world and its facts and objects, and on the persons who comment on it, and react to it, in all that they do, that is especially characteristic of Wittgenstein as a philosopher, and that distinguishes him from most other philosophers? It is a slant which concentrates on the world, and on all the things and persons in it, and on all the possibilities and desirabilities and whatever else is in the world, from the pervasive standpoint of significant speech and language: it considers whatever is in the world in the role of something to be talked about, all matters of possible worldly fact in the role of things that may be verbally asserted, or denied, or hypothesized, or questioned, or otherwise dealt with linguistically, and all persons as speakers that can be talked with and talked about, and that can range over the whole world with their discourse, and also at times venture beyond the limits of the world in specially sanctioned, unordinary forms of speech, or in pregnant silences that are, in a way, the limiting form of all speech. The governing slant of Wittgenstein's philosophy may further, as Stenius and many others have recognized, be compared with that of Kant, and may be called 'transcendental', in one of the many senses of that obscure, somewhat tendentious term. The philosophy of Kant is 'transcendental' in that it does not try to deal with anything in the world, including the thinking subject, as it may be absolutely or in itself, but only as it can be given in experience, or in the acts of judgement and inference which build upon and extend experience, or in the acts which set limits to experience and knowledge, but which also range beyond them in thought-stances which, while they never have a claim to achieve knowledge, none the less inspire and direct the progress of empirical knowledge. The philosophy of Wittgenstein is similarly transcendental, in that it sees the world, and its personal and impersonal contents, not as something which, in some un-mentionable sense, merely is there, but in a context of the symbolic activities which in some manner indubitably reach out to things and situations, and pronounce truly or falsely upon them, and which also, by a reflex, are able to reach out to their own acts of so reaching out, and are thus in some measure able to clarify their own nature. And, while Kant merely takes it for granted that a plurality of conscious subjects can cope with the problems of the empirical world in much the same manner, Wittgenstein becomes increasingly insistent, as his thought develops, that the reachings out to the possibly true or false face of things, that are characteristic of speech-symbolism, *must* be shareable: one speaker must be able to make the same symbolic reference or assertion as another, and must be able to communicate it to others, and it is in fact only in so far as there is such communicability that symbolic references and assertions are possible at all. Reference and assertion are further, both for Kant and for Wittgenstein, necessarily governed by intrinsic rules of some sort, and rules which are capable of being understood and followed by other thinkers and speakers as well as by a given one. And for Wittgenstein, as for Kant, the interior thought which does not display itself in overt symbols has none the less the same articulate structure as overt speech, and is directed to things, persons and facts in the common empirical world, in the same general fashion, and is accordingly communicable in principle, even if not always in the detail of practice.

Like Kant, further, Wittgenstein believes that speech and interior thought lend themselves to transcendental illusion, in regard to both what is objective and what is subjective: we can be deceived into imagining that we are dealing with substantive things and issues when we are merely projecting the forms of our speech- or thought-reference outwards into an imaginary objective realm, or inwards into a subjective one, in a wholly vacuous and pictorial manner, and not really dealing with substantive things and issues at all. In Kant we have the mental activities of synthesis and analysis leading, on the one hand, to the transcendental ideas of absolutely all-inclusive wholes, to which nothing in experience can do justice, and hence we form the notion of souls which underlie all possibilities of inner experience, or of the cosmos or world, which includes and unifies all forms of spatio-temporal existence, and, finally, the idea of a God, who includes in himself all possibilities, and hence exists of necessity. These ideas correspond to nothing that we can know or know of, but they inspire us to articulate our experience in the most highly unified, yet most richly differentiated and continuous system of natural kinds that can be reconciled with the empirical appearances. In Wittgenstein we have, in similar fashion, the unified distinctions of our language objectivized into properties which are treated as real ingredients into many objects, having much greater simplicity of character than the affinities of objects would rightly warrant: our language also subjects them to general laws which are mistakenly treated as generating and explaining the phenomena we range under them. All our experience is similarly regimented by a series of acts of expectation, belief, volition, approbation, etc., which really only reflect words covering widely varied types of behaviour and inner feeling, and not the invariant mental acts that are supposed to underlie them. In the same way, complex readinesses for varied forms of speech and action, in relation to certain objects, are pictured as containing all these varied forms of speech and action in some obscure, unrealized manner, and not only these, but also the objects with which they are connected, which are present in experience in some surrogate, spectral form. Wittgenstein's transcendental illusions are different from those of Kant, and spring from linguistic uses rather than thought-tendencies: their explanatory sources of influence, and the manner in which these can be resisted, have, however, many analogies. The thought of Kant and Wittgenstein developed, however, in a somewhat different manner. While Kant in his later thought mitigated his view of the ideas that transcend experience as wholly illusory, Wittgenstein became stronger in his insistence on the illusory, pictorial character of most of the concepts of the inner life, and their supposed source in private self-observation or introspection. The realm of interior acts of thought, imagination, belief, etc. became for him a realm well-founded in a language and its uses, but having no status beyond these. And the simples which Wittgenstein had in his earlier work located behind the complex objects, watches, tables, etc., of the world as we ordinarily speak of it were later subjected to criticisms which left nothing of them standing.

Wittgenstein, like Kant, is further open to important internal criticisms springing from his own critical norms: if, in the case of Kant, these have mainly centred on his vacillating attitude towards what, in its completion of the incompletable, transcends possible experience, Kant showing himself willing, in his transcendental psychology, to conceive acts of the productive imagination and other faculties, which are certainly not objects of possible experience, such criticisms, in the case of Wittgenstein, must mainly centre on his failure to apply his own criticisms of his original atomization of the world into unanalysable, independent simples, to his later atomization, of universals into a vast class of overlapping affinities, and of experiences which present a front of unity into a vast number of independent feelings, images and other mental minutiae which vary from occasion to occasion, and from subject to subject, and have no stronger bond than a word. The whole approach, further, which would try to understand the organized unity of discourse in terms of a set of artificially isolated, simple language-games is arguably an error of the same type as his earlier resolution of the world into simple objects picked out by simple names. All these points of criticism will, however, only become alive when we dwell in detail on the sinuous contortions involved in Wittgenstein's aphoristic method of philosophizing, with its constant attempts to persuade us that something or other, usually very negative and pulverizing, describes a wholly obvious, evident fact of experience, though this is often, in fact, neither obvious nor evident at all. Philosophy by rhetorical question, backed up by vividly pictured experiences and accounts of imagined tribal usages, is not easy to counter: often the only possible response to an appeal framed by Wittgenstein in such words as 'But aren't you always experiencing something different when you say $X$?' or 'Do you know of an experience characteristic of pointing to $X$', etc., is simply 'Yes' when the answer 'No' is expected, and 'No' when the expected answer is 'Yes'. Wittgensteinian argument consists largely, it is regrettable to say, in the putting across of a set of ungrounded atomistic prepossessions by a vivid series of insinuations, persuasive pictures and leading questions, when a thoroughgoing search for unifying concepts, covering all alternatives and consequences, would better deserve consideration and acceptance.

## II

This book will not attempt to dig deeply into the historical and biographical facts regarding Ludwig Wittgenstein and his works. These have been authoritatively set forth in a number of studies and memoirs, including those of Lord Russell, Professor G.E. Moore, Professors von Wright and von Hayek, Norman Malcolm and Mr W.W. Bartley. It can be taken as well-established that Wittgenstein was born in Vienna in 1889, in one of those immensely gifted, highly cultivated, public-spirited, half-Jewish families which were among the glories of the last age of the Austro-Hungarian monarchy. It is also clear that his interests were at an early stage turned towards the physical sciences, and that, after finishing school at Linz, he studied at the Charlottenburg Technische Hochschüle in Berlin from 1906 till 1908, acquainting himself profoundly with such a foundational work as Heinrich Hertz's *Principles of Mechanics*, which provided him with a clear conception of a fully elaborated deductive system, and also showed him how something so ethereally abstract could yet mirror the facts of experience. With such interests, it was natural that Wittgenstein should have become interested in the foundations of arithmetic and mathematics in general, and that he should have been induced to visit Gottlob Frege at Jena in 1911, and been sent on by the latter to Bertrand Russell at Cambridge, where he remained during 1912 and 1913. The two great thinkers had certainly been in touch with one another since early in the century. Russell had studied the writings of Frege in preparation for his own great work, The *Principles of Mathematics*, published in 1903, and had discovered a contradiction, requiring extensive revisions in his own and Frege's procedures, with which he acquainted the unhappy Frege in 1902.

Frege and Russell were both elaborating a purely logical theory of arithmetic, holding that numbers, and all that can be said about them, or in terms of them, could be analysed in terms of notions present in *all* our propositional assertions, and that their truth rested on axiomatic principles governing all such assertions, which were not confined to a special arithmetical or mathematical sphere. The most complex truths of arithmetic and the higher mathematics, if formally purified, became lineal descendants of truths as poor in significance as that, if anything is the case, either it or anything whatever is the case, or that, if one has something together with something else, and also has something other than either, then one will have something and something else and something else. Wittgenstein's insight into the self-returning emptiness, or pure tautology, of all purely logical and mathematical truths has its origin here, as also his views as to the nature of propositions, and of the elements incorporated into them, which were implied by the symbolisms and introductory discussions which these great analysts had produced.

It is also an established fact that Wittgenstein at some early age had acquainted himself with the semi-Kantian, semi-Buddhist teachings of Arthur Schopenhauer in his *Die Welt als Wille und Vorstellung* (*The World as Will and Presentation*), and that from this he had derived his belief that the world of sense-experience and science, with all its causally connected material objects and conscious subjects, only existed in and for the sensuous intuitions and conceptual elaborations of conscious subjects, but that there was also a single transcendental substrate lying beyond or beneath all these subjective shows, and that this substrate was nothing other than the will which we recognize as present in ourselves, a voluntary aspect that operates in a wholly blind manner in the physical and chemical phenomena of external nature, in a more dimly conscious manner in the activities of organisms, and in an increasingly lucid and reasoning manner in the activities of men. Schopenhauer further held that this transcendental will could achieve some sort of a dim awareness of itself, and that this awareness could lead it from a subservient identification with finite, personal ends and objects, which necessarily involved it in struggle and misery, to a comprehensive renunciation of all such personal ends, and to a mystical self-naughting in which it might achieve an incomprehensible final peace and blessedness. The norms of ethics, with their refusal to regard one's personal interests as in any way taking precedence over those of others, and the ascetic, sacrificial practices of religion, were ways in which the Absolute Will sought to outwill itself, and to seek a liberation from finite interests which is also willed for all. And finally, also, the unutterable joys of art and beauty, and particularly those of music, in which everything becomes a disinterested enjoyment of pure sound or spectacle, which cannot be externally frustrated, these are for Schopenhauer precursors of that last liberation *from* self which is also, from another point of view, the liberation *of* self. It will be plain to those who have studied the writings of Wittgenstein that these Schopenhauerian doctrines are much in evidence in the background of his first work, the *Tractatus Logico-Philosophicus*. And they are also in evidence in various acts in the course of his life, in the renunciation of wealth inherited from his parents, in his glad acceptance of various humble and menial jobs, in his attempt to join a monastic order, and so on. They are also in evidence in his deep respect for the ethico-religious writings of Augustine, Pascal, Kierkegaard, Tolstoy and others. Plainly Wittgenstein was a man in love with poverty, chastity and obedience, whether or not he was always able to achieve them. Of Kant, as opposed to Schopenhauer, he seems to have had a limited knowledge – Wittgenstein had in general a limited acquaintance with the great classics of philosophy – but it is related that he once read the *Critique of Pure Reason* aloud in a prison-camp in Italy.

It may further be surmised, with some degree of reason, that the transcendental subject, whose will underlies all the phenomena of external nature, was not for Wittgenstein something *equally* present in himself and in all other conscious beings (though this is not the sort of thing that can be confidently asserted). It was, there is reason to think, for Wittgenstein, something primarily present in himself, and by him projected upon other beings. This becomes particularly clear from certain passages in Wittgenstein's *Notebooks* for 20.10.1916 and 17.10.1916, where he says: 'Only remember that the spirit of the snake, of the lion is *your* spirit. For it is only from yourself that you are acquainted with spirit at all', and also

> This is the way I have travelled. Idealism singles men out from the world as unique, solipsism singles me alone out. . . . And in this sense I can also speak of a will that is common to the world. But this will is in a higher sense *my* will. As my idea is the world, in the same way my will is the world-will.

Wittgenstein was therefore not only an idealist but in some sense a solipsist, and this would appear not only to be asserted in the *Tractatus* (§§5.62–5.641) but also, less plainly, in the *Blue Book* (pp.58–60). But the fact that Wittgenstein had no use for any transcendental subjectivity but his own, also makes it clear why he could not meaningfully refer to the latter, at least not in any ordinarily accepted notation. As the *Tractatus* puts it in §5.64: 'The self of Solipsism shrinks to a point without extension, and there remains the reality coordinated with it.' But Wittgenstein as a bodily presence endowed with speech obviously does not differ from other speech-endowed bodily presences in his world, and the language in which he talks about this world is in no sense private to himself, but is shared by all the other speaking presences in that world. All this will concern us more fully later, when we consider the relevant passages in the *Tractatus* and later writings.

Another matter of importance in Wittgenstein's first stay at Cambridge was the fact that he became interested in experimental psychology, and undertook studies of rhythm as a foundation for further investigations into aesthetics. Experimental psychology was in those days largely Wundtian, and regarded conscious experience as a continuous stream of mental elements, among which sensations, images and three pairs of simple feelings were distinguished: mental syntheses only agglutinated these elements into complex wholes, and determined their emphases and their succession. This view of mental life had no place for any special mental acts of meaning and reference: a place for these had to be found in the complex context in which mental elements were assembled, in the associated complexes which they induced, as also in the stimulus-situations in which they occurred, and the behavioural reactions which accompanied them. This Wundtian psychology had its most remarkable development in the 'existential' psychology of Edward Bradford Titchener, who, unable to found a psychological school at Oxford, was not satisfied till he had founded one at Cornell, where he continued to teach till his death in 1927. Titchener's existential psychology professed to study mental life for what it *is* (hence the term 'existential'), and not for what it means, and what it *is* is merely a stream of variously combined, contextually interrelated, duly successive mental elements, each exhibiting characteristic attributes and dimensions, and all falling under the three headings of sensations, images and feelings. In the rigorous existentialism of Titchener even attention merely amounted to an attribute of 'clarity' attaching to certain elements. For this psychology it was a great mistake to import anything referential or logical or meaningful into the description of the conscious stream: what psychological complexes meant, or what they objectively signified, was not to be taken as part of their psychological content, and we were further committing the 'stimulus error' if we imported anything belonging to their physical sources, or to our reactions to such sources, into this psychological content. This existential psychology is admirably expounded by Titchener in his *Text-Book of Psychology* of 1910, his *Experimental Psychology of the Thought-Processes* of 1909, and his Lectures on the *Elementary Psychology of Feeling and Attention* (1908), and in other works. There is no reason to think that Wittgenstein was acquainted with any of the works of Titchener, but the Wundtian character of the experimental psychology he met with in Cambridge must have driven him in a similar direction, which became more and more emphatic in his later writings. Wittgenstein cannot imagine that a real psychologist would envisage an experience as consisting of anything but sensations, images and feelings: its reference to this or that, and the manner of this reference, can only, by an abuse or a confusion, be reckoned as an experience.

> Try not to think of understanding as a mental process at all. In the sense in which there are processes (including mental processes) characteristic of understanding, understanding is not a mental process. A pain's growing more or less; the hearing of a tune or a sentence: these are mental processes. (*Philosophical Investigations*, §154)

Titchener's gross elementarism further led him, in the early years of the century, into an embittered struggle with the psychological school at Würzburg, one of whose members, Ach, brought into experimental psychology the new categories of the *Bewusstheit* and the *Bewusstseinslage*, consciousnesses which concentrated in themselves a detailed wealth of content (e.g. remembering that one discussed the matter before, without coming to any conclusion) which was not spelled out in anything sensuous or imaginal or verbal or overtly reactive, though it might on demand give rise to an introspective protocol half a page long. There is no reason to think that Wittgenstein knew anything of the work of this important German psychological school, and he therefore treated all accounts of 'nutshell' experiences, which contained in a flash a wealth of interrelated contents, as wholly mythic and

11

imaginary. Hence, just as his solipsism had to transform itself into a pure realism, so his elementaristic Wundtianism had to transform itself largely into a behaviourism of action and speech. The statements here made will, of course, have to be substantiated in detail by a close examination of the relevant texts and a great deal of further argument. Here we are only concerned with the historical roots of his thought. We may note, incidentally, that some of the Würzburg psychologists have a neural basis to their nutshell consciousnesses by the hypotheses of the *sub*innervation or *sub*excitation of many neural pathways, a notion perhaps of interest to those who desire explanatory *mechanisms* in these fields.

During the First World War, in which Wittgenstein fought for his country on the eastern front – I remember him describing the infinite weariness of repeatedly dragging his booted feet out of the thick bogs of Galicia – and was later a prisoner of war at Monte Cassino in Italy, he consolidated the thoughts that he had been working on in Cambridge and after Cambridge. The result was the *Logisch-philosophische Abhandlung* or *Tractatus Logico-Philosophicus*, published in German in 1921, and in an English translation in 1922. This work is undoubtedly one of the major masterpieces of philosophy with a roundedness of structure, and aesthetic finish of statement, which makes it inexhaustibly interesting. Nothing that Wittgenstein later wrote can bear comparison with it, and appears rather as the project for a philosophical work than a finished production. In the *Tractatus* Wittgenstein attempts to conceive of significant speech as in some manner reaching out, beyond the vastly complex objects, properties and possibilities of ordinary discourse, to objects of ideal simplicity, absolute uniformity and complete mutual independence, whose interconnections are likewise simple, uniform and wholly contingent. And, as so reaching out, significant speech also by implication reaches out to an ideally simple, wholly uniform, entirely external pattern of linguistic references and assertions, which is, or can be, perfectly correlated with the structures in the world. In conceiving of such an ideal pattern of possible references and assertions, Wittgenstein must not be conceived as thinking of our actual speech as being wholly wide of the mark, and non-representative of the ultimate structures. The complex objects and intertwined complexities of ordinary fact and diction, on the one hand, and the uniformly simple objects and wholly external connections which underlie them, on the other, are alike projected by the same single, transcendental self, and the one necessarily points to its completion in the other. The statements of what can be called macro-diction, those that deal with the complex objects of ordinary experience, and assert their interconnections, must thus all be felt to point back to a set of statements of what must be called micro-diction, which refer to the simple objects out of which all complex things are compounded, and whose truth or falsehood as statements depends on the micro-connections which obtain among these objects. It does not matter that micro-diction is not anything that can be actually achieved by human speakers: the success of macro-diction presupposes its genuine possibility, whatever this may be thought of as involving. Our ordinary speech therefore has transcendent implications which go beyond the limits of our actual utterances, and among the most important of these implications are the logical laws which connect complex statements with the more fundamental statements on which their truth or falsehood depends, and ultimately on the not further analysable, wholly uniform connections of independent simples, on which the truth or falsehood of all statements of micro-diction must be taken as depending. These logical laws in a sense say nothing about the world: they do no more than co-ordinate one way of stating the facts which make up the world with another. The *Tractatus* further teaches that all the value-judgements of ethics and aesthetics, as also its own statements in regard to the transcendental foundations of language, really say nothing about the world as it actually is put together, but merely reflect the general reaching-out procedures which govern all our references and assertions to matters of fact, and to the effects of these upon our whole practice. All these doctrines, with their many analogies with the teaching of Kant and Schopenhauer, will be discussed more fully later, and our controversial interpretations be given a better justification. The *Tractatus* further criticizes many of the views of meaning, reference and logic held by Frege and Russell. It may be said on the whole to be working out a philosophy of significant speech which conceives of the latter as in an inadequate manner mirroring, or trying to mirror, the ultimate things and matters of fact which are in some manner reached out towards by our diction.

After publishing the *Tractatus*, whose teaching he regarded as 'unassailable and definitive', Wittgenstein retired into various Austrian villages, where he became a somewhat unsuccessful primary-school teacher. One of the most remarkable stories from this period is that of the 'miracle' which he performed when he induced a certain installation to work by simply knocking it about rather vigorously. The charisma of Wittgenstein's personality, even in that setting, accorded well with miracles. But the *Tractatus* had meanwhile attracted the attention of Schlick, Carnap and others in Vienna, who were afterwards to become leaders of the vastly influential Logical Positivist movement. The members of this movement interpreted the atomic simples of the *Tractatus* as being elementary sense-particulars and their simple sense-qualities, and its elementary facts as what can be stated in elementary sense-protocols. This view seemed to accord with the solipsism taught in the crucial *Tractatus* passages we have referred to, and a methodological solipsism accordingly figures in the original form of Logical Positivism, though it was later abandoned for a form of physicalism in the 1930s. The Logical Positivists built largely on a slogan sometimes countenanced by Wittgenstein at this period, which identified the meaning of a proposition with the manner in which it might be verified. This slogan was taken by them as according with the sensationalism of Ernst Mach's influential positivistic theory of science. But the slogan did not have for Wittgenstein the meaning that the Logical Positivists read into it, and it is clear that the sensationalistic interpretation of the *Tractatus* is quite wide of the mark. There is nothing in sense-experience that exhibits the colourless diversity, and the quite unlimited combinatorial possibilities, of the simple objects of the *Tractatus*. Wittgenstein was present at various gatherings of the Viennese Logical Positivists during the 1920s, the record of which is to be found in Waismann's book entitled *Wittgenstein und der Wiener Kreis* (1967). Wittgenstein's new views of the basically arbitrary, rules-of-the-game nature of logic and mathematics began to be expounded at these meetings. The subsequent history of the Logical Positivists does not concern us. It was Wittgenstein's view that they distorted and vulgarized his conceptions, particularly in regard to the deep perplexities of traditional philosophy: these were profound puzzlements, which were not to be dissolved by superficial criteria of scientific verifiability. Wittgenstein in the 1930s was so disgusted by what he held to be the distortions of his teaching by the Logical Positivists that he could not endure their names to be mentioned in his presence.

Meanwhile, in the 1920s, some younger philosophers at Cambridge, and in particular Frank Ramsey, had been wooed away from the analytic realism of Russell, Moore and Broad by the sweet tones of Herr Wittgenstein's flute, and were endeavouring to woo the flautist back to Cambridge. In this endeavour they succeeded towards the end of the 1920s, and Wittgenstein became a highly singular, but vastly sought after, teacher at Cambridge, where he remained till his resignation in 1947. When Moore retired from his philosophical chair at Cambridge in 1939, Wittgenstein succeeded him. During the 1930s and 1940s he then developed a wholly new philosophy of speech, whose governing slogan, afterwards superseded, was 'The meaning of a word is its use in the language' (*Investigations*, §343). The reference of our utterances to the unknowable simples, beyond the complexly constituted objects of ordinary experience, was at this stage subjected to ruinous criticism, and entirely dropped from Wittgenstein's philosophy of significant speech. Simples were whatever counted as simple in the language-performance of the moment. The unique, transcendental speaker likewise vanished from the picture, together with his acts of world-transcendence and world-devaluation, having nothing left that could be set in opposition to himself. It may, however, be doubted whether he ever really vanished from the inner, unuttered, metaphysical persuasions of Wittgenstein, and the passage already cited from the *Blue Book*, p.59, perhaps shows that he did not.

But the vanishing of the unique transcendental speaker had the advantage that with him there vanished any thought of a plurality of private worlds in each of which one speaker alone lived, which would give rise to grave philosophical difficulties in the relations of such speakers to one another, and to any world that might be common to them all. The vanishing of the one transcendental speaker left behind him a single public world, lived in and talked about by an indefinite number of speakers among whom Ludwig Wittgenstein, as a speech-endowed bodily presence, enjoyed no special prerogative. The language or languages used by all these speakers was primarily linked to the objects and situations in their common world, and their public reactions to these. In so far as private aspects were present in their performances, these were essentially linked, whether by words or other forms of correlation, with what was public and common. There certainly were such language-performances as saying what one had been thinking, or describing what one had been imagining, or relating one's dreams and one's memories, and so on. All of these were, however parasitic upon references to ordinary public objects and public reactions to these. There might be situations in which something not publicly manifest might be spoken of as going on, but such privacy could only be accidental: the significantly unmanifest must always be *possibly* manifest. A whole life spent among private phantasms, as was conceived by Descartes and others, was therefore totally unmeaning. The irony of all this is of course that a life of perpetual isolation among private phantasms, and spoken of in a private language, is precisely the state in which Wittgenstein, on an arguable view, believed that he lived, though he was also persuaded that he could not significantly express this belief in an ordinary notation. Our suggested view of Wittgenstein's private metaphysical persuasions will, however, have to be argued for far more thoroughly in the light of all he says.

Wittgenstein's vision of the shared language of the inhabitants of his one common world is characteristically abstract and surrealist. If the simple objects and relationships of the *Tractatus* are remote from the concrete complexities of the empirical world, so too are the simple villagers or tribesmen who inhabit his model cosmos. Their speech likewise falls into a vast number of separate performances, each complete in itself, and by no means necessarily involved in some total, coherent scheme of diction. The villagers would seem to have no science, no logic or mathematics, no ethical codes, no religion, no economic system, no canons of architecture, agriculture and what not. They while away their time in giving orders and obeying them, describing the appearances of objects or fixing their measurements, reporting events or speculating about them, making up stories or reading them, play-acting, singing catches, guessing riddles, making jokes, solving problems in applied arithmetic, and translating from one language to another: they also know how to ask, thank,

16

curse, greet and pray (*Investigations*, §23). By dwelling on these strangely abstracted performances, wholly denuded of any normal context or sense, Wittgenstein believes that we can disperse the mist that clings to our use of more complex expressions in our common life, e.g. the mist which clings to our talk about numbers. We shall, in this work, question the whole use of language-games to illuminate the activities of ordinary, scientific and philosophical speech, despite the immense poetry and beauty in Wittgenstein's descriptions of some of them. They have captured the minds of many through their aesthetic rather than their philosophical appeal.

Wittgenstein's analyses of speech through simple language-games are further related to his later treatment of logical and mathematical principles that were given such an unquestionable, if tautological, status in the *Tractatus*. Logical principles like the Law of Contradiction can, he later holds, be subverted or modified in novel schemes of diction, and so can such an arithmetical truism as that 2+3=5. There are, in fact, countless situations in which 'It is and it isn't' is a legitimate form of expression, a concession that might give great happiness to a Hegelian. And by simply determining that we shall count three twice over after counting two, and before counting four, one can readily become entitled to say that 2+1=4. One cannot then, according to Wittgenstein, even have recourse to the escape that in so speaking one is not using one's expressions in the same sense as is usual. For whether an expression is being used in the same or a different sense is a matter of the language-game one is playing, so that if one's rule is to make 'plus one' yield the same result twice over (i.e. the result 3) if one adds it twice to 2, then this rule is part of the sense of 'plus one' which is accordingly the *same* in this as in other cases. In the same way, if one so uses negation that the Law of Double Negation holds in one type of case and not in another, then it is possible to say that one is not using negation in a different sense in the two sorts of case, but obeying its fixed rules unchangingly. What we shall object to in all this Wittgensteinian arbitrariness is that it ignores the fact that sameness or difference or affinity of sense or character are matters that in some sense *shape*, and should shape, linguistic conventions, and are not wholly shaped by the latter, and that, while it is perfectly possible to run counter to their shaping in one's speech, and may for certain purposes be legitimate – either for special emphases or in response to the unusual, borderline character of certain situations – it is profoundly wanton and linguistically immoral to violate them when there is no such reason. To make every addition of one yield a new number except in the case of the powers of seven, would be, not only arithmetically confusing, but ethically wrong. To call everyone a man except in the case of certain otherwise highly similar beings, merely because one happened to despise them, would likewise be, not only scientifically confusing, but linguistically immoral. The good, with its strict canons of relevant affinity and disparity, presides over discourse as well as over all other spheres, and there are manners of talking which, by their failure to do justice to the important affinities of things, are, except for very special reasons, linguistically censurable and corrupt.

Among the most interesting works of Wittgenstein's later period are the so-called *Blue Book* and *Brown Book*, which were dictated or circulated to the members of certain classes in the 1930s, and published in 1958. These have a vigour and freshness comparable to that of the *Tractatus*, and in some respects superior to the long, often tired divagations of the *Philosophical Investigations*. If one wishes to understand the later workings of Wittgenstein's mind, these works provide invaluable materials. Other works from much the same period are the *Philosophical Remarks* (published 1965 and translated into English in 1975), the *Philosophical Grammar* of 1874, the *Lectures on Philosophical Psychology*, the very important *Lectures on the Foundations of Mathematics*, given in 1939 but published in 1966, and a work *On Certainty*, published in 1969, which shows some reversion to ideas of Moore. We shall comment on some of these works in ensuing chapters of this book.

The *Philosophical Investigations*, the monumental, aphoristic work on which Wittgenstein was working when he died in 1951, was published posthumously in 1953. We shall devote the last chapter of this work to its consideration. It contains a very interesting Second Part in which a psychology of 'aspects' is considered, and the possibility is canvassed that, for certain persons at least, every familiar word carries an atmosphere with it in our minds, a 'corona of lightly indicated uses' (*Investigations*, §181). The *Bewusstheiten* or nutshell consciousnesses of Ach and

Külpe and the Würzburg psychologists are at least recognized as regular objects of report, though Wittgenstein underrates their pervasive presence, and believes also in their total analysability into more elementary processes.

It will be suitable to end this introductory chapter with a brief account of my own encounters with Wittgenstein, and of the extent to which I was able to achieve some closeness of acquaintance with his thought. I had become estranged from idealistic philosophy when I left Oxford in 1927, and had become deeply interested in the thought of Russell and the Wittgenstein of the *Tractatus*. This conversion to Cambridge ways of thought did not conduce to my philosophical preferment at Oxford, and I was therefore forced to teach philosophy in my native South Africa, and afterwards in New Zealand. But at the end of 1929 I was in Europe, and paid my first visit to Wittgenstein early in 1930; he himself had only recently returned to Cambridge, on the insistence of his friend Ramsey, who had, however, died tragically only a short time before my visit. My first visit to Wittgenstein can only be described as a transporting experience. Not only was his reception of myself, on the mere introduction of a common friend, quite dizzying in its informal friendliness and charm, but I also found him, at the age of 41, of a quite unbelievable personal beauty, such as might be attributed to the Apollo one visits at Olympia, or to the Norse Sun-god Baldur. This personal beauty went with an austere aestheticism in his surroundings, possessions and personal ways, which was, of course, also reflected in his philosophical style. As the extreme beauty of Wittgenstein is not often spoken of, it seemed fit to mention it here: certainly it contributed, even if unconsciously, to his immense influence at Cambridge. Our conversation on this first meeting ranged over many topics. Most memorable was his advice to immerse myself in a study of Russell's *Principles of Mathematics*, then out of print. It was, he said, a much more important work than *Principia Mathematica*, and of course infinitely more important than Russell's many subsequent 'pot-boilers'. Wittgenstein himself had, after long years, exhausted all that it had to teach him, though he had not as yet exhausted what could be learned from Frege: I could obtain his own copy of the *Principles* at Heffer's, to whom he had recently sold it. I indeed found it at Heffer's, but his inscribed name had been rubbed out by the bookseller, and only emerged when one raised the page to the light.

I did not see Wittgenstein again till 1939 when I was spending a year of leave in America and Europe. I had been with Russell and Carnap in Chicago, and with Quine and Sheffer in Harvard, and then saw Wittgenstein for a short time in Cambridge at the end of the Summer term, when he was just concluding a memorable seminar on the Foundations of Mathematics. Later on, in the autumn term of 1939 when the war had already started, I regularly attended the seminars in his rooms in Whewell's Court, Trinity College, which dealt with the theme of Memory. I walked up the stairs to his rooms through all the dislocations and blackouts of those first months of the phoney war, and also had many personal discussions with him. I also meditated continuously on what he had said or written throughout this entire period, and, though my reactions were often critical, they were also very profound. I meditated particularly on his solipsism and on his treatment of the problem of other minds, and also on his view of different philosophies as different fundamental notations which affect the whole way in which we speak of, and see the world. Wittgenstein had a much greater intellectual charisma than any other philosopher I have ever encountered. Only Moore, in his very different way, was similarly impressive. One could not listen to Wittgenstein's least pronouncement, however falteringly expressed, without feeling that it sprang from a mind of supreme integrity and the most penetrating insight. This impression did not diminish, however long one reflected on what he had said. And one certainly had to rebuild the whole structure of one's thinking to accommodate what one had learned from him. It will be plain to readers of this book that I am deeply critical of almost anything Wittgenstein said on almost any topic whatsoever. I have, in fact, systematically used him to climb on to contrary, rather traditional opinions, which have seemed to me truer and better. But without the stimulus of his teaching I should not have arrived at these contrary opinions at all, nor at my general view of metaphysics as being quite fairly describable as the most exciting and richly various of all language-games.

There are many other things that can be said about the personal make-up and impact of Wittgenstein. His pervasive aestheticism certainly displayed a character that, I believe, is technically describable as 'schizoid': there was something queer, detached, surreal, incompletely human about it. His colourless, simple objects are not things that one can touch and handle and look at, and his villagers who sell apples taken one by one from a drawer, and then ritually count them as they are taken out, or who assure themselves that something is red by taking a named sample of red from their pockets, are plainly the inhabitants of a dream or a nightmare, and not of a possible village. Wittgenstein further had a certain deep egocentricity which made his dalliance with solipsism understandable, though this does not mean that he could not be supremely benevolent and beneficent to the other speaking presences in his world. Like the sun he illuminated them all, and one felt in his presence all the happiness of being a satellite that lives on borrowed light. He treated me with extraordinary graciousness, perhaps principally because he saw in me an inconsequential unbelongingness akin to his own. He gave me his then only copy of about the first 150 sections of his *Philosophical Investigations* to read, and asked me also to help on the conduct of his courses by raising any objections or criticisms that I might feel. It is in the light of his many kindnesses that I should wish this present, highly critical book about his teachings to be regarded, not merely as a critique, but also as a tribute.

# II

# THE CONTEXT OF
# WITTGENSTEIN'S THOUGHT:
# THE INTENTIONALISTS

I

In the next two chapters I shall try to expound, with necessary sketchiness, four systematic standpoints, contemporary with Wittgenstein, which had some relevance, whether direct or indirect, to his thinking, and in terms of which the total achievement of that thinking can be best assessed. The first is the intentionalist philosophy of mind represented by the three great continental thinkers Franz Brentano (1838–1917), Alexius Meinong (1853–1920) and Edmund Husserl (1859–1938). There is no reason to think that Wittgenstein was either directly or deeply acquainted with the work of any of these thinkers, though he seems to have glanced at some of the earlier works of Husserl on the coffee-tables of Vienna and once asked me, in regard to Husserl's *Logical Investigations*, why I concerned myself with 'that old work'. They had, however, a great influence on Russell and Moore, and many of their opinions filtered through to Wittgenstein from these and other Cambridge sources, and became targets of criticism at many points in his work. We shall also devote some time to their philosophy of mind, since it provides an illuminating contrast to many views of Wittgenstein, and one which we shall sometimes see reason to rate as superior to his views. The second systematic standpoint we shall have to consider will, of course, be that of Russell, and we shall do so with particular reference to the *Principles of Mathematics* of 1903, which Wittgenstein rightly regarded as one of the great masterpieces of philosophy. The third standpoint is that of G.E. Moore, whose approaches to philosophical truth through common sense and ordinary language must have had an influence on the earlier phases of Wittgenstein's thought, though they were themselves profoundly influenced by Wittgenstein's thought at a later stage. Lastly, we shall consider the contributions of Gottlob Frege (1848–1925) to the philosophy of logic, language and mathematics, contributions which were given an extremely high rating by Wittgenstein himself, and which are similarly rated by many of our contemporaries, but which, to the present writer, seem narrow in philosophical scope, and technically ingenious rather than philosophically profound. Such assessments may, however, be left aside for the present.

Turning to the intentionalist philosophy of mind, this was, of course, reintroduced into European thought, from reinterpreted Aristotelian and Scholastic sources, by Franz Brentano, in his immensely important *Psychology from the Empirical Standpoint*, first published in 1874. This work is rather a set of conceptual prolegomena to an empirical psychology than an empirically conducted work, and is mainly an attempt to contrast what Brentano calls a 'psychic phenomenon', i.e. a mental state or attitude, to what he calls a 'physical phenomenon', a state of things which in no respect deserves to be called 'psychic' or 'mental'. It is a conceptual and also a grammatical exercise, basing itself on what we say, mean and understand when we call something 'mental', and is not a setting forth of the empirical things or properties to which the term has been applied. The first thing that it is important to note is that *reference, direction* to something, which may be wholly other than or unlike the act or process of referring or being directed, is essentially a psychic or mental condition: it is not sufficient that something should exist or be there, it must exist or be there *for* someone's activity, it must be an object of notice, of concern, or awareness, whether clear or dim, if there is to be anything mental in the whole matter. There must, if one likes, be that so objectionable and perplexing mirroring of something in another medium, if anything of a mental or a psychic sort is to be there, which does not however mean that we are forced to reify the mirror in which, as we say, the mirroring takes place, or the 'reflections' that are metaphorically said to appear in it. What is mental is simply the reaching out, to employ another metaphor, to something or other, which as so reached out to, bears the pregnant name of an 'object', and which reaching out can be further distinguished both in terms of what it reaches out to, its direction of reference, and also in terms of the different *manners*, presentative, believing and so forth, in which it thus reaches out to its objects. Mental phenomena are said by Brentano to be 'intentional': they refer to or intend objects, which may be entirely different from or beyond themselves, and wherever such an intending or referring is absent, there can be nothing of a psychic or of a mental nature present. Thus if there are tones or colours which simply are there, and not there in the pregnant sense of having something like a presence *for* someone, then there is nothing mental about them: they are purely physical phenomena, physical existences. And if there is a whole world of mountains, trees, plants, suns, electrons, molecules, cells, organisms, etc., and nowhere do we have that peculiar directed-ness to them, or presence of them, or reference to them, which makes them themes of intentional discourse, then they are all purely physical existences, even if some of them, highly organized and articulate, were to respond to things and states in the physical world by noises regularly correlated with the latter. And even if they are able to trigger off responses in other highly organized, articulate existences of the same sort as themselves, there would be nothing mental or psychic, in Brentano's sense, in the existences and responses in question, impossible as it seems that they should exist in the imagined circumstances.

All this does not mean that there is, for an intentionalist of Brentano's persuasion, anything irremediably mysterious or dubious about psychic phenomena, whether in ourselves or in others. To be aware of the non-psychic things around us is to be able to be aware that they are there for ourselves, for our intentional, psychic life, in a variety of manners, and the 'inner perception' which mediates the latter awareness is for Brentano inseparable, though also distinct from, the outer perception which mediates the former. To see mountains and hear sounds is, by a shift of attitude, to become aware that they are present to ourselves in a variety of manners on different occasions, confident or doubtful, attentive or inattentive, pleased or displeased, etc. That we saw the front side of the mountain but only knew that it had a rear aspect, that we noted that there were trees on it up to a certain height, but did not note any absence of houses, are matters on which we can often report with complete confidence, however much there may, particularly with lapse of time, be obscurity in some cases. And Brentano does not in practice doubt that our intentional acts also reveal themselves in our uses of language, and can be studied by way of such language. The whole intentionalist mental philosophy is in fact based on a study of the forms of language, without, however, reducing intentional stances to verbal usages and inclinations, and while admitting that these require considerable modification and enrichment when one tries to be wholly accurate as to the way things really looked to one, or were really felt by one, or were really thought of by one. Inner perception is not for Brentano the same as inner observation, and there would be no objection, from his point of view, to the elaborate protocols of the Würzburg psychologists, which range far beyond ordinary introspective reports, and yet achieve, after some training in the questions that can and should be asked, considerable agreement as to the general character of what is reported. Nor is there, from Brentano's point of view, any irremediable obscurity and unclarity regarding the intentional acts of others and their reports upon them. Brentano, like Kant, simply never saw the problems regarding other minds which have in our century yawned upon all of us philosophers. There would, for him, be something of a problem in correlating the way things look to one man, with the way they look to another, but so would there be in correlating the ways they look to the same man on different occasions, even when separated by small intervals, and problems in correlating the ways in which physical objects appear or behave in one stretch of their being to the manner in which they appear or behave in another. All knowledge involves going beyond what one can observe, to what one cannot observe, according to principles seeking maximum continuity and uniformity. It is irrational to posit immense undiscoverable differences where extrapolations from discovered continuities will fill these in, and there is no more fundamental problem in knowing how things are regarded by someone *who* one isn't, than at some place in the universe *where* one isn't. For short of being a God, one cannot be everywhere or everywhen or, after a fashion, everyone, and one's normal certainties regarding other places, times and persons do not depend, in any obvious manner, on any final, divine solution. The difficulty of being at other places and times than where and when one is, are, in fact, as irresoluble as the difficulty of being someone that one isn't, since there is no absolute identity of one space – or time – location with another. The difficulty is, however, cogitatively surmountable in both cases, whether by scientific extrapolation, or sympathetic projection, or however: these modern epistemological issues are not, however, much considered by Brentano. Brentano does not, further, hold to the sensible presentation over the noetic or cogitative one, nor to the belief that only the former really confronts an object, and that all noetic or cogitative reference derives its justification and validity from actual or possible sensible confrontation. Brentano certainly believes in an inner evidence which distinguishes knowledge from mere belief, but this inner evidence attaches to the cogitative certainties of logic and mathematics as much as to the Cartesian certainties of internal perception.

What is, of course, most memorable in Brentano is his attempted division of all mental intentions into the three basic classes of presentations, judgements and the phenomena of love and hate, with its companion doctrine that all judgements are built upon presentations, whereas the phenomena of love and hate are built upon the possibilities of *both* presentations and judgements. Presentations are mental atitudes which set objects before us, whether sensuously or cogitatively, or in a combination of both, without taking up any further position towards them. Judgements, in Brentano's wide sense, are reality-attitudes, in which some content is taken as real or factual, or dismissed as unreal or non-factual, or regarded in some manner intermediate between these, while the phenomena of love and hate are attitudes of a conative or affective type, sometimes actively practical, sometimes quiescent and unpractical, in which some presented object is approved as good, or rejected as bad, setting off a trend to realize it in the former case, and to exclude it from realization in the latter. Brentano further believed, as we have said, in a unique inner experience of evidence which guaranteed the correctness of judgements in certain cases, and a unique inner experience of *Berechtigung* or justification which guaranteed the validity of certain acts of affective-conative acceptance or rejection. We need not here enter into the intricacies of these conceptions, since they have little relation to Wittgenstein, who certainly did not accept anything like an interior criterion of validity. The threefold doctrine of presentations, judgements and acts of approval, is, however, important: one cannot have complex attitudes of belief or disbelief, approval or disapproval towards something, unless one had some idea, whether clear or confused, of what it is, and one cannot have an attitude of approval or disapproval towards something without some concern with its realization or non-realization in the world. So much is entailed by the proprieties of language, and of the intentional activities which, on Brentano's view, underlie language. Brentano's classification is true to the structures of mental activity and to the grammar of mental terms, whatever deeper structures one may choose to see beneath these.

We may note here, in passing, that there is nothing in Brentano's analyses to exclude an overflow of intentionality into overt behaviour, as well as into the use of language: it is obvious that there must be such an overflow, and not a merely contingent one, if we are to interpret behaviour and the use of language as we confidently do. Brentano took an Aristotelian view of the psyche of man, and there is nothing in his doctrine to exclude a governing intentionality from the bodily activities of the organism as well as from its inward, non-corporeal activities. There have, in fact, been behaviouristically oriented psychologists, e.g. Tolman and Brunswik, who have found intentionality as fruitful a concept in *their* treatments of men and animals as Brentano did in his. A *purely* behaviouristic treatment of intentionality would, however, on views like Brentano's, be unacceptable, since the orientation of behaviour to specific objects is always problematic, and in some cases indefinitely problematic. The problem of reference comes up at every turn, as it did for Wittgenstein: how can we be absolutely sure, in default of the speech-act which confesses an *inner* direction, that a man is oriented precisely to *this* or to *that*? It is only because we are in possession of a direct intentional route to objects that we can postulate the presence of such a route in cases where we are not ourselves treading it. Hilary Putnam's problem of reference here emerges in full strength: what magical bond relates the words 'The cat is on the mat' to the relations of a pussy to a floor-covering, rather than to the relations of a penguin to an ice-floe, or of Mardi Gras to New Orleans? Causality will not do the connective work in most cases, and the appeal to behavioural dispositions only constitutes an infinite draft on the bank of credulity. Plainly we must directly know what it is to be intentionally directed in *some* cases if we are to extend such directedness indirectly or analogically to words and behaviour.

An all-important point must here be stressed: that the concept of intentionality does not entail that the object of an intentional orientation must be a *real part* of that orientation, or that it must have a real existence anywhere at all. The objects of intentions necessarily enter into the descriptions of those intentions, since we cannot say what sort of an intention we are having without saying what it is directed to, or is *of*, even if its object be so vaguely conceived as to be no more than a 'something'. But though intentional objects thus enter into the description of an intention, they will not have an actual existence *in* it, nor need they have an actual existence anywhere. Linguistic usage rejects the inference: I am thinking of a perfect wife: therefore there is somewhere a perfect wife of whom I am thinking. As Brentano teaches in the first Appendix to the 1911 edition of his *Psychology from the Empirical Standpoint*, the intentional relationship is not a relation in the proper sense (*im eigentlichen Sinne*) at all, since a relation in the proper sense can only subsist if all of its terms are actual – one cannot have a relation of sitting upon a non-existent chair: it is rather to be described as relation-like (*Relativliches*), as being a relation towards something which need not be actual at all. The intentionalist has therefore no need to postulate an infinite limbo of non-existent objects, as Meinong, a follower of Brentano, was later to postulate, and as Wittgenstein, in so many condemnations of ghostly duplicates in the mind, was to deprecate. One had simply to be clear as to the grammar of intentionality, whether verbally expressed or left unexpressed, that one may quite well be mentally oriented to something that does not, and perhaps cannot exist, or to what is wholly indeterminate, or to what exists elsewhere, and only partially agrees with one's conception of it, without its following that there must be something which is as one conceives it, except in the attenuated sense that one is undoubtedly oriented towards a certain sort of

28

object, and that this object has to be 'brought in' to any adequate description of one's mental state. To the further problems of forms of diction and intentional experience in which there are relations obtaining between real objects and objects with a merely intentional inexistence we cannot here address ourselves. Geach and others have dealt very interestingly with them.

Brentano, it may be further noted, was Aristotelian in placing all *entia rationis*, all universal qualities and relations, all propositional and factual unities, all classes and numbers, etc., in the realm of purely intentional objects. We need not suppose that there really *are* such objects in the full sense in which only the concretely individual can *be* at all. This does not mean that it may not be convenient, for many purposes, to talk *as if* there were such objects, and as if they entered into reality in some fuller manner.

There may be an impression that the tendency of Brentano's intentionalism is idealistic, and it can certainly be developed in such a direction, as it was in the phenomenology of Husserl. The use of the word 'act' lends acceptability to the view that every object whatever is in some sense a *product* of subjective activity, and Husserl has, in fact, tended to speak of every object as 'constituted' by an appropriate intentional act. In general, however, the suggestion is disowned that the term 'mental act' should carry any connotation of activity or creativity: a mental act may be a wholly passive experience, and its object may have a being that is wholly independent of it. There is, in fact, no reason why the doctrine of intentional acts should not be developed in a wholly realistic direction, as it was by Meinong, Ingarden and others. That an intentional act has a direction to a perfectly specific object, and that this direction is part of its essential description, does not entail that there may not also *be* an object which satisfies the intention in question, and be just such an object as the intention is directed upon. And it may exist quite independently of the intention directed upon it, perhaps some-where remote in space or time or in the experience of someone other than the referring subject. Thus I can refer without difficulty or perplexity to the thought of Julius Caesar as he debated within himself whether to cross or not cross the Rubicon. Remote reference indeed involves obscurity, for how can anything here and now and in me, 'reach out' to something that is there and then and in someone else? And for the reaching out to be meaningful, there must be meaning given to the coincidence of our intentional object, which enters into, without being an existent part of, our intentional reference, with something 'out there', which would exist whether I intended it or not. The problem is insoluble on theories which try to reduce reference to the use of a word, while dispensing with the 'meanings' or 'senses' which in some fashion inform *words*, form the content of *thought*, and can also be realized or fulfilled in *things*. What these difficulties show is that we cannot indeed dispense with a concept which acts thus mediatorially and amphibiously. It is, we may say, part and parcel of every intentional reference, whether verbalized or not, that there may in fact be something, either exactly, or perhaps more or less as we conceive our object, and that there may be a complete or partial coincidence of content between the one and the other. The notion of existence, as well as the Tarskian notion of truth, entails just this, and the only problem is not to see it as a problem at all, but as simply part of the ontology or, if one likes, the grammar of intentionality. Coincidence between what we conceive and what really is, is further not to be taken as a miraculous falling together of two quite disparate things, but a coming together which represents the completion of either. We have no difficulty in conceiving of a close resemblance between two remotely situated entities which have, as we say, nothing to do with one another. Why not a similar fitting into one another of the intentional target of a reference and a real target which is just as what the intention aims at? An even happier metaphor would be that of a pattern of coloured light which falls precisely on a surface whose pattern coincides with it, and is brought out by it. These are not idle pictures, but useful likenesses which bring out what is clearer than a picture and which only becomes puzzling when we picture it in terms of spatially separate parts. The notion of such coincident fulfilment is given further strength by undoubted cases of perfectly experienced adequation of a thought with a reality. If I opine regarding a book of poems, kept on the top shelf of my bookshelf, that it will be delightful to reread one of its poems, my opinion may be perfectly fulfilled by finding the book there, and a poem in it, and taking delight in my reperusal of the poem. It is not obscure, in such a case, how my unfulfilled anticipation strains towards the target of a fulfilling coincidence, even if we cannot be sure, in some cases, that we have actually hit our target, or even that it *can* be hit by anyone. Only a God can be conveniently credited with the property of being able to fulfil all the references that have true or real targets at all. It is important here to argue that only an intentional act can perform the sort of reaching out to objects of which an actual fulfilment is possible: words, bodily gestures, behavioural trends, etc. must borrow their intentional targets from the intentions in terms of which we interpret them, and which are themselves the intentional objects of such interpretations. It is by postulating the existence of such intentional acts, or by conceiving non-intentional acts, upon some sort of analogy with them, that we can arguably give a quasi-intentionality to acts and states in which intentionality is not evident, and perhaps not actually present.

## II

We have given a sketch of the main points in the intentionalist mind-theory of Brentano, stressing those points on which his views had an indirect influence on Wittgenstein, mainly through Russell and others at Cambridge, and also those points which help in the criticism of Wittgenstein's opinions. In the case of Meinong and Husserl, our treatment may be much more cursory, as the details of their systems derive from the basic positions of Brentano, and have little relation to the details of Wittgenstein's thought. Of Meinong we may say that he developed the intentionalism of Brentano in the direction of a comprehensive realism called *Gegenstandstheorie* or object-theory, the most important feature of which is perhaps the doctrine of Objectives, i.e. of objective structures embodying the sense of true or false, or of possible or impossible propositions, which are also the appropriate objects of judgements or assumptions. Such objectives in some cases enjoy a timeless being called *Tatsächlichkeit*, factuality or Being-the-case, though they retain their status as objectives even if they are not facts. The doctrine of objective propositions had its remoter origins in the Stoic doctrine of λεκτα or things said, and in the doctrine of *Sätze an sich*, or propositions-in-themselves, of Bernhard Bolzano in the early nineteenth century. Meinong was undoubtedly the philosopher who gave greatest emphasis to this doctrine of objective propositions and facts, and from him it passed on to Russell and Moore, and thence on to the Wittgenstein of the *Tractatus*. Frege was independently interested in propositions as *entia rationis*, and gave them ontological priority over the objects and concepts in them. Propositions and states of affairs are arguably quite as good, as candidates for prime ontological status, as are the concrete things of common persuasion: they at least fill up all the corners of being better than Things manage to do.

The belief in objectives as being genuine entities, whether they were facts or not, led to Meinong's further belief in objects that were objects, and that had a definite so-being (*Sosein*), a descriptive characterization, even if they lacked *Sein* or being. A golden mountain, a round square, had a definite *Sosein*, and could be subjects of propositions, even though they lacked *Sein*, and they also had a wider status called *Aussersein* which pertained to all objects equally, whether they enjoyed being or non-being. They had to be something even for it to be the case that they did not have being. Thus the round square was round and square, even if this entailed that it did not and could not exist. Russell adopted a variant of this doctrine in his 1903 *Principles of Mathematics*, where all entities, whether existent or non-existent, were said to have being, e.g. the Homeric gods had it. Later on, however, in *Principia Mathematica*, he repudiated this Meinongian doctrine, holding that true propositions that seemed to be about non-existent entities (e.g. 'The round square does not exist') were so analysable that non-existent entities ceased to figure in them. 'Round squares do not exist' was not really about round squares, which are nothing, but about all the things in the world, which are comprehensively declared to be in no case both round and square. Whether this down-to-earth analysis is to be preferred to the manful intricacies of Meinong's arguments, which successfully pluck the jewel of consistency from the nettle of antinomy, may, however, be questioned. The present writer, at least, continues to have the deep persuasion that the absence of golden mountains and round squares from the world is not to be identified with any fact about anything that *is* in the world, and that intentional references to non-existent targets are not to be so analysed that they have real targets. The disposal of inconvenient entities by analysing them away, or by calling them 'logical constructions', was, however, a device that Wittgenstein took over from Russell, and the status of non-existent objects comes up rather frequently in his writings. Meinong, however, to revert to our present subject of discourse, posited the being of many other sorts of objects, beside objectives and existent or non-existent objects. There were dignitatives that were apprehended through our evaluative and affective attitudes, and that were in some cases authentically and independently there and knowable as such. There were also desideratives that were apprehended through our strivings, and that were in some cases certifiable as objective cases of *Sollen*, or of what objectively ought to be. This proliferation of objects was further matched by a proliferation of attitudes: there were, for instance, non-serious judgements called *Annahmen* or assumptions, and there were non-serious feelings and desires through which we apprehend the real or imagined feelings and desires of others. This is not the place to enter into all these Meinongian intricacies: suffice it to say that there is no question that they do not also illuminate, and that the present author found the time he spent in studying them one of the most philosophically rewarding in his life.

## III

If we now turn to Husserl, we have the intentionalism of Brentano developed in an idealistic manner. Husserl may have rejected idealistic or psychologistic treatments of logic and mathematics in the *Philosophy of Arithmetic* of 1891, and in the *Logical Investigations* of 1900–1, but his later thought arguably reduces the being of anything objective to its 'constitution' by an intentional act, or by a developing series of such acts. To the Husserl of the *Ideas towards a Pure Phenomenology and Phenomenological Philosophy* of 1913, we may say that *Esse* – in all cases other than that of intentional activity itself – amounts to a *Constitui*, a being constituted by intentional activity, despite frequent denials of any kinship with Berkeleyan thought. This dependence of what is objective on intentional activity applies not only to all abstract *entia rationis*, but also to the whole natural world in space and time, and to the psychic constituents of that world, in so far, that is, as they are constituted by a subjectivity other than their own. The solipsistic implications of such a constitutionalism are, however, resisted by Husserl, though it is not clear how he would hope to evade them: this is not a matter on which I wish to pronounce in this book. In my opinion, Husserl should have been content with a constitution of nature and of intersubjective life, which left unaffected the independent being of the objectivity thus constituted, since it is, as we have seen, a great merit of the concept of intentionality that it allows us to hold that things may independently *be* as they also are constituted by our intentionality, and that they may absolutely transcend our intentional constitution of them, as well as being constituted by us as having such a transcendence. An intentional object is not a real part of an intention but merely a specification of its objective direction, and it may therefore coincide or suffer an identification with an object which transcends the intention: things may *be* precisely as they are given, or seen as being.

It is not, however, our purpose to enter into a controversial discussion of the idealism or realism, the solipsism or the monadic pluralism, of Husserl's view of intentional activity, even though this would not be irrelevant to the treatment of similar issues by Wittgenstein. What is important and great about Husserl is the intricately worked out detail of his intentional descriptions, which no one else has ever carried so far. Of many of his analyses of sense-perception, or 'appresentation' as the awareness of intentional life in others, and above all of the phenomenology of our ever-present consciousness of the passage of time, we can only say, dumbstruck with admiration, 'This is indeed the inner life, as it really goes on in everyone.' What is remarkable about Husserlian descriptions is that they are nearly always dynamic, and show us the stream of conscious intentionality working towards certain consummations while yet keeping hold of what it has so far gone through. Thus our perception of physical objects is always by way of sensuously fulfilled, one-sided adumbrations (*Abschattungen*) of their infinitely many-sided nature, and always keeps its hold on a whole horizon of sensuous adumbrations that are now lapsing into the past, and looks forward to a similar horizon of sensuous adumbrations that will accrue in the future. William James, a true phenomenologist, had much to say on these lines, and an obscure awareness of a similar dynamic obviously inspired many of the crabbed accounts of conscious syntheses that we read in Kant. Obviously an impressive aspect of our intentional life is that it is always pressing onwards towards a fulfilment in terms of the clear picture, the fully-framed utterance, the precisely fitting practical response, and so on, and it is also, for the most part, holding a great wealth of other pictures, utterances and responses in reserve, but not in that merely dispositional manner, which amounts merely to a possibility that they could be present, but rather in a manner which constitutes a far more living and intense presence than any narrowly one-sided fulfilment. A man in whom a sequence of symphonic phrases lives on, as Lotze puts it, as an abiding mood in the soul, has a much more fully actualized awareness of those phrases than one to whom they are merely successive fragments: the so-called fringe of consciousness, what we have on hand, or *im Griff*, is arguably its true centre and substance, and always ranges beyond the clear image, the articulated word and the accomplished act.

Husserl further makes use, in his phenomenological descriptions, of the notion of an *empty* intention, which does not mean an intention which is *without* an object, but an intention whose object is not present in a completely intuited or fulfilled manner, whether sensational or imaginal or inwardly experienced. Even the carpet which is seen as going on invisibly under a piece of furniture, involves such an empty intention, and one without which we should not see our familiar room as it is, and the condensed understanding of what takes quite a time to articulate embodies the same pregnant emptiness. The emptiness of an intention is, of course, intrinsically related to a possible fulfilment, and it is the source of a disposition which becomes fully actualized when we pass on to an appropriate set of sensations, pictures, utterances, gestures and overt acts. And the step by step fulfilment of the empty intention is, of course, the standard way of becoming clear, as we say, of what we are thus emptily intending, and reinforces our sense of its complex content. The life of conscious intentionality consists, in fact, in an ever-repeated passage from an empty to a fulfilled form of reference, and back again to the latter, but much more of its substance lies in the empty than in the fulfilled sector.

The constant passage from what is focally present to what is only marginally so, and vice versa, are likewise conscious movements which interlace with the constant passage from the fulfilled to the empty reference and vice versa, and these two are essentially modes of conscious intentionality that can be regularly before us and distinguished from their objects. Those who doubt whether they can introspect conscious references as such should be asked to note, in immediate retrospection, the passage from a focal to a marginal reference, or from a fulfilled to an empty one. These can be as palpably phenomenal as is the waxing or waning of a pain, or the hearing of a tune or a sentence, in which objective rather than subjective differences are emphatic. It would therefore, we may say, have been a good thing if Wittgenstein could have had a closer acquaintance with phenomenological description as practised by such as Husserl, and not merely as practised in the Cambridge psychological laboratory. It would have made him less eager to look for such things as images, feelings and specific performances in each conscious experience, and, when these proved to be absent or randomly variable, lay stress only on words and their uses, forgetful that these too are frequently absent and randomly variable.

One of the most significant later doctrines of Husserl is his importation of the basic logical constants into the phenomenology of what he calls the life-world, the world as it appears to the non-analytic, and even verbally inarticulate, conscious person. This doctrine puts him in with such as Chomsky who see something built-in, innate in the categories of general grammar. Husserl's ideas on this point are principally developed in his *Erfahrung und Urteil*, a book based on lecture-material which was posthumously edited and published by Ludwig Landgrebe. In this work Husserl makes it understandable how negation, disjunction, implication, quantification, modalization, as well as all the varieties of tense, should enter even into the pre-linguistic life-experience of the most unsophisticated men. We may even extend them to animals, since they certainly rest on processes native to all conscious beings. Thus negation, or the absence or lack of some content from the life-world, is projected in every case where an intentional anticipation is frustrated, disappointed, by what is intuitively there. We look for a continuance of what is going on before us in a familiar manner, and are confounded by the non-fulfilment of our projection. Things are *not* as we anticipated. The experience of affirmation likewise springs up from the experience of fulfilment: things indeed *are* as our intention would have them. In the same way the disjunction in which our intentionality hovers between two or more anticipated fulfilments is frequent in the life-world: we are curious whether something in the distance is a man or a penguin or a scarecrow, whether a fabric is wool or cotton, etc. The behaviour of men, and sometimes even of animals – the rat, we are told, has many hypotheses – shows this same hovering between alternatives which the use of the connective 'or' illuminates not at all, since it must be interpreted in terms of just such a hovering. In the same way the life-world of men, and doubtless of animals, is full of *kinds* of things of which certain fulfilments are expected: even in the absence of *names* for such things, we have regular expectations in regard to them. Possibilities and probabilities are likewise constituents of the life-world, which is full of promises and perils: something or someone is about to descend upon us, to attack us, to caress us kindly, etc. We do not require language for unfulfilled possibilities and probabilities to be part of the surrounding appearances. And all the modalities of tense are thus displayed: something is there as having just ceased to be palpably there, or is just what we encountered a few moments ago, etc. It is only because all these categories are woven into the fabric of the life-world that the uses of words can be learned so easily: in the right situation, a well-directed gesture suffices. The learning of a language is thus largely the acquisition of an ability to translate the phenomenological language of the life-world into the less perspicuous language of words. But the learning of language, of course, further affects, and feeds back into, the phenomenology of the life-world, in a most thoroughgoing manner: verbal classifications colour everything, and everything we see in the world may well seem to have something to *say* to us. The instantaneous translation of our own experiences concentrated into words, and our similar performance in interpreting the attitudes of others, is all-pervasive: words with their grammatical connections are ready to crop up everywhere. Language-games are indeed forms of life, and they enter into the life of phenomenal things as well as of persons. It would, however, have been well if Wittgenstein had been able fully to acknowledge these pre-linguistic intentions and meanings, and the colourings they lend to phenomena, instead of seeing only in the Word the absolute beginning of all logical and phenomenological structure. The delicate perception which can see a whole range of readinesses as surrounding the use of a word, might well have seen similar readinesses surrounding the appearances of the life-world, whether objective or subjective, even when words were not present at all. The world as it primitively appears to us, in all its fulfilled and unfulfilled, physical and psychic dimensions, is plainly the foundation of the world of verbal discourse, however much the extensions added by the latter may be taken back into the former.

One topic remains for comment and regret in this section, though we have already referred to it in our last chapter: Wittgenstein's total ignoring of the work of the introspective school of Würzburg under Oswald Külpe in the early years of this century. Here we have a whole school which practised introspection with the utmost rigour, and never reported anything as having been *erlebt* which had not been experienced in the almost immediate past, and commented upon immediately after, that they were always having experiences perfectly definite in content and permitting of a long verbal explication, in which a sensational or imaginal or verbal element was entirely missing, or only irrelevantly present. They established thereby, what countless untrained speakers have declared on countless occasions, that it is possible to have experiences which permit of a complex imaginal, verbal and behavioural unpacking, without the slightest hint of unclearness and dubiety, even though such an unpacking is in no way achieved or attempted, or only achieved in a grossly inadequate, irrelevant, minimal way. One can have the consciousness 'He is fooling me', 'One may as well pretend to listen to all this', 'That number is not a prime', etc., and even the completion of a musical or other sensuous pattern, in a condensed manner which involves no vestige, or no more than a vestige, of an actual spelling out in images or words, and that, in fact, most of our interior life is at all times conducted in this manner. What Kant says about the necessity of synthesis is in fact mainly a recognition of this fact. To have recourse to dispositions in such cases serves no legitimate purpose. Dispositions are an

38

important class of *entia rationis*, indispensable in ontology, but they are not forms of life that can be consciously lived through, any more than can, for example, the relations of numbers. Wittgenstein makes persistent mention of cases where people describe their inner states in the Würzburg manner, but sees in their testimony merely a determination to use words in a certain pictorial manner, of which he personally disapproves. It is odd that Wittgenstein should be thus prejudiced against an introspective language-game which has been actually practised by very scrupulous persons, and prefers one that bases itself on mechanistic and other irrelevant models.

# III

# THE CONTEXT OF
WITTGENSTEIN'S THOUGHT:
RUSSELL, FREGE AND
MOORE

I

In the present chapter we shall expound those doctrines of
Bertrand Russell that may be reckoned to have had a great
influence on Wittgenstein. Some of these are now little known,
since the *Principles of Mathematics*, to which Wittgenstein
accorded vast respect, and which is a far more philosophical work
than *Principia Mathematica*, is no longer much read. We shall
also briefly expound the teachings of Frege, whose relevance to
the interpretations of Wittgenstein, and whose general philosophical importance is now fully, perhaps a little too fully,
recognized. And we shall finally say something about the teaching
of G.E. Moore, who, though it has been contested, approached
philosophical problems from the angle of what we ordinarily say,
just as Wittgenstein did, and must unquestionably have influenced Wittgenstein profoundly, even if the influence of Wittgenstein on the later thought of Moore may have been even more
profound.

Russell, like Wittgenstein, passed through a period of logical
realism, almost Meinongian in his case, which was succeeded by a
period of linguistic reinterpretation and constructivism, in which
the true sense of sentences and expressions was not always what
their outer form suggested. The period of logical realism was that
of the *Principles of Mathematics* of 1903: the period of linguistic
reinterpretation that of the *Principia Mathematica* of 1911, with
its important Introduction, revised or replaced in 1926. Both

40

works had an immense influence on Wittgenstein, particularly the former, and he also became fully acquainted with such popular Russellian works as *The Problems of Philosophy* (1912), *Our Knowledge of the External World* (Lowell Lectures at Harvard, 1914), the *Introduction to Mathematical Philosophy* of 1919, and *The Analysis of Mind* of 1921. Wittgenstein spoke of all these popular works as potboilers, and thought little of them, but *The Analysis of Mind* had unquestionably a great influence on his later, language-oriented thought: it too teaches a doctrine of meaning as use, and has critical views, similar to Wittgenstein's later ones, of intentionalistic and psycho-analytic views of mental life. Its brightly written accounts of the latest imagistic, non-imagistic and behaviouristic views of psychology may likewise have affected Wittgenstein's views of what contemporary psychologists were up to. There is, however, little reason to think that Wittgenstein paid much attention to any of Russell's works subsequent to 1921, though he continued to discuss his own work with Russell.

Russell's philosophy from 1900 to 1910 all revolved around mathematics, of whose notions, principles and methods he was attempting to give a philosophical analysis and justification. General treatments of epistemology and ontology only proliferated after 1910. Russell worked on the grandiose project of reducing all mathematical notions and principles to purely logical ones, a project which arose naturally out of the development of logistic, or symbolic or mathematical logic, during the nineteenth century. Prior to the nineteenth century there had been attempts to give logic a purely symbolic form, e.g. in the use of variables by Aristotle in his treatment of syllogisms, in the proposed *calculus ratiocinator* or universal symbolic language of Leibniz, a philosopher much admired by Russell, and in the work of Lambert and others in the eighteenth century. The beginnings of an algebraic class-logic date from Boole's *Laws of Thought* of 1854, and were carried on further by de Morgan, Venn, Jevons, Schröder and others, while relational arguments were formalized by Peirce and some others. The deduction of all arithmetic from a small number of primitive propositions by Peano in 1895 was likewise an important preliminary to the development of Russell's thought. These primitive propositions were '0 is a number', 'Every number has a successor', 'The successor of a number is a number', 'No two numbers have the same successor', '*0* is not the successor of any number', 'Whatever is true of *0*, and of any successor to a number of which it is true, is true of all numbers.' The task of Russell was then to restate these principles, and their indefinitely burgeoning consequences, in terms of a few notions expressed by 'logical constants', which occurred in all discourse and not solely in mathematics, and which were listed in the *Principles* as implication, class-membership, relation, being such that something is true of one, and the general notion of Truth itself, together with all further notions involved in the general notion of propositions involving such logical constants. *Principia* gives a different, much more workable list. Russell's task was further to deduce all true propositions involving only these notions, and for the rest only variables, from a limited number of basic axioms – about twenty in the *Principles*, and still fewer since then, in the improvements of Sheffer and others – among which we can cite as examples from the *Principles*: 'If *p* implies *q*, then *p* implies *p*', '*p* or *q* is equivalent to *p* implies *q*', 'Every relation has a converse.' We also must in such deduction employ principles which are *rules* of deduction rather than premisses, e.g. 'A true hypothesis in an asserted implication may be dropped, and its consequent asserted.' These principles are much more satisfactorily set forth in *Principia* than in the *Principles*, and the distinction kept clearer between principles which are premisses of deduction, and principles which are rules of deduction, and also the distinction between principles which can be treated as mere definitions of certain meanings in terms of others, and principles which can be treated as expressing non-definitory connections. *Principia Mathematica* is also clear as to the great amount of the arbitrary in some of these distinctions, as in that between axiomatic principles, on the one hand, and theorems which are merely consequences of these, on the other. The axioms could, in many cases, be de-axiomatized and demoted to theorems, and the theorems contrariwise elevated to axioms.

## II

Russell's work in the early years of the century is extremely interesting because it is ontological and realistic, and in this respect parallel to Husserl's contemporary *Logical Investigations*, which also seeks to depsychologize the matters talked about by logicians and mathematicians. Russell at this time also regards the axioms and theorems of mathematics as stating substantial truths about the world, and about all possible worlds, and not as being merely the tautological reflections of the workings of our language, or of the workings of our minds. In asking what mathematical statements mean, philosophy must never bring in the 'totally irrelevant notion of mind' (*Principles*, §3), for the propositions of mathematics are only illuminated by enquiring into their objective constituents, and considering how these constituents function and are unified in the propositions in question. Our subjective apprehensions of such constituents, and our apprehension of their constitution into propositional unities, are totally irrelevant to such objective enquiries. Conscious intentionality, in the first decade of the century, took for Russell the prime form of direct intuitive acquaintance, the objects of which were either immediate data of experience, or universal concepts culled from these, and likewise conceived as objects, and also objective propositions in which all these entities were assembled. In so far as our minds reach out to anything *beyond* objects of direct acquaintance, they do so in virtue of the denotative capacities of the objective concepts which enter into propositions with whose sense they are acquainted, and can thereby be enabled to refer to, or know by general description, entities with which they are not acquainted at all. Man, for example, is an objective concept which enables us to refer to all cases of humanity, and even to such as are individually unknown to us, or perhaps merely possible (see *Principles*, §56 and *Problems of Philosophy*, ch.5).

Not only, therefore, are subjective attitudes irrelevant to mathematical and other propositions, unless such propositions concern these as constituents or denotata, but the words which express such propositions are likewise irrelevant, except in so far as they enable us to form conjectures as to the objective propositional structures which underlie them. Russell, however, assumes that grammar is capable of throwing far more light on these objective propositional structures than is commonly supposed, and that every grammatical difference is *prima facie* evidence of a genuine philosophical, i.e. ontological, difference. 'Grammar, though not our master, must yet be taken as our guide' (*Principles*, §46). All these opinions are relevant to the doctrines of propositions and Facts in Wittgenstein's *Tractatus*, as is also Russell's view that propositions are essentially *unities*, and that, when analysis has destroyed such unity, no mere enumeration of constituents can restore it (*Principles*, §54). This view is capped by the further view that propositions are the only unities of distinct constituents that there are or can be, and that a unity is always a proposition, even if an unasserted one (*Principles*, §135). This view implies the conclusion, not clearly stated by Russell in the *Principles*, that every proposition must consist, in the last analysis, of wholly simple constituents, since every complex thing, e.g. a man or a mountain, can be complex only in virtue of the objective propositions which bind its elements together.

Russell, therefore, in this early ontology, believes in objective propositions, which will have being whether they are true or false. Being, he further says in *Principles*, §428, belongs to every conceivable term or object of thought,

> to everything that can possibly occur in any proposition, true or false, and to all such propositions themselves. Numbers, the Homeric gods, relations, chimeras and four-dimensional space, all have being, for if they were not entities of a kind we could make no propositions about them. This being is a general attribute of everything . . . while existence, on the contrary, is the prerogative of some only amongst beings.

This Meinongian opinion was, of course, criticized, both as regards non-existent things and false propositions, in Russell's post-1910 writings, and such criticisms inspired Wittgenstein to further acts of ontological demolition.

The early ontology of Russell accordingly believes in the being of all the constituents and denotata of objective propositions. These he calls *terms*, and are said by him all to be unitary and single, all identical with self, and other than terms other than themselves, all utterly immutable in their being, whether they exist or not, and all capable of functioning as logical subjects of propositions. These Terms are then divided into things, on the one hand – particulars such as those designated by 'this' or

'Socrates' – and concepts, on the other, the former being capable of occurring in propositions *only* as subjects, whereas concepts can occur in propositions in a curious dual manner, *either* as part of what is asserted in a proposition, or as the logical subject that a proposition is about. Thus 'Humanity pertains to Socrates' is about the concept of Humanity as well as about Socrates, whereas 'Socrates is human' is not about humanity as such, but only about Socrates (*Principles*, §48). The temptation here arises, Russell notes, to say that concepts functioning as terms in propositions cannot be quite the same entities as concepts functioning as part of what is asserted, i.e. 'human' and 'humanity' must somehow stand for different entities. Russell, however, resists this temptation, to yield to which would lead to inextricable difficulties. For we should have to speak of *both* of them and distinguish them from one another, and this would mean that a concept functioning as a mere part of an assertion could also occur independently, and so differ from itself (*Principles*, §49). As Plato might have put it, the very same Eide, which can be considered in and for themselves, are also present in the things that participate in them, and need not merely be represented by copies. Russell argues, accordingly, that concepts are quite as self-subsistent as things, but can occur in more than one way in propositions, as terms that the proposition is about, or as mere parts of what is asserted in such propositions. Things cannot occur in propositions in such a twofold manner.

Concepts further differ from things in yet another remarkable manner, as we just have noted. They can *denote* their actual or possible instances, as things, having no instances, cannot. They therefore enable propositions containing certain concepts to be about entities and classes of entities that are not among the constituents of such propositions, and they thus enable minds, that know or believe or entertain such propositions, to have 'knowledge by description' of countless entities with which such minds have no acquaintance at all. Russell's view of cognitive intentionality therefore reduces it to the single relation of direct acquaintance, but this acquires a second dimension of descriptive reference in virtue of the denotation which is present in all concepts. Concepts have therefore something like a built-in, *objective* intentionality, which serves as a kind of support and extension to our subjective intentionality. We mean objects which are not directly *there for us* in virtue of the objective denotation of concepts which are present in such objects. Such a view is cumbrous, but by no means unilluminating. Plainly it is of the essence of universals to be capable of instantiation, and the awareness of universals must therefore include an awareness of their actual and possible instances.

Russell, we may further note, regards the sense of quantifiers as being part and parcel of the concepts to whose symbolization theirs attaches: there are thus six distinct concepts expressed by such words as 'all men', 'each man', 'any man', 'a man', 'some man', and 'the man'. Russell is not sure whether to say that these six distinct concepts also represent six distinct types of object or are merely distinct ways of denoting the same objects, and attempts to illuminate the question by devising a charming logical exercise in which Brown and Jones are *all* paying court to a given lady, or in which *any* of them can be said to paying court to her, or in which *each* is paying court to her, or in which *some* of them are, or *one* of them is, doing so, etc. The logical relations of all these quantifiers, wholly neglected in modern logic, are taken to reflect nothing arbitrary, but to be part and parcel of the objective relations of universal concepts.

Russell further defers to the deep linguistic chasm between predicative concepts, on the one hand, which can apply to terms taken singly, and relational concepts which can only be said to proceed, like the Holy Ghost, from one term to another, or to others. Verbs, with the aid of prepositions, are generally used to express relational concepts, whereas adjectives mainly express predicative concepts. Russell in the *Principles* builds on the view, also argued for in his *Critical Exposition of the Philosophy of Leibniz* of 1900, that it is quite wrong to try to reduce relations to predicates, or to reduce all forms of proposition to the subject-predicate form. There are innumerable forms of proposition whose sense runs from term to term, or from numerous terms to one another, and which are not correctly analysable as predicating a concept of a single subject. To hold otherwise is to give an unwarranted fillip to philosophical monism or monadism. Russell, in fact, gives countenance to the view that *all* propositions can be seen as implicitly relational, since even a subject-predicate proposition can be regarded as relating a term to a concept (*Principles*, §53). This opinion may have been one of the sources which led Wittgenstein in the *Tractatus* to make all his basic, atomic facts relational rather than predicative. Relations further have an externality to their terms which is not the case with subjects and predicates: in the class of ultimate, and therefore simple terms, this is desirable.

Propositional functions are further regarded by Russell in the *Principles* as an important class of universal concepts which cover whatever is left of a proposition when we disregard the definite terms which occur among its constituents, or the denotata of its concepts: we express such a function by replacing the expressions which stand for such constituents or denotata, by symbols of variable meaning for which symbols of constant, definite meaning can be substituted. The difficulty about propositional functions is that they do not always seem to yield a separate factor which characterizes or relates the terms to which they are applied in propositions. In 'Socrates is a man' we can readily distinguish between Socrates, on the one hand, and being a man, on the other, which latter can be asserted of others, and which can be expressed in functional fashion as '$x$ is a man'. But, if we consider 'Socrates has a wife implies Socrates has a father' it is hard to distinguish a conceptual factor applying to Socrates here but applicable to others, since if we leave out Socrates, we only have the expression ' . . . has a wife implies that . . . has a father' where there is no clear identification of the subjects denoted by . . . in its two occurrences (*Principles*, §82). None the less, Russell denies that a variable is merely a symbolic convenience, but holds that it represents a very important *logical entity* which is very hard to analyse convincingly, since it does not denote an assemblage of terms, nor yet one particular, definite term, but quite different terms in different contexts. Variables therefore have a kind of individuality, corresponding to that of the definite entities which could replace them in propositions. The situation is therefore different when the same variable occurs more than once in a propositional function, or when different variables are substituted for this one. The order of the variables, and which variable is taken to govern which, also make a difference. What Russell here says is deeply interesting, quite obviously there is illumination in treating a variable as having an ontological as well as a symbolic side, and we neglect the resources of our language in failing to develop the former as well as the latter.

### III

Very important among the constituents or denotata of propositions are certain ontological structures known as 'Classes' in the time of Russell, but now usually referred to as 'sets'. These structures are important since they can be regarded as the subjects of which numbers are predicated, or as the members of classes of higher type which are identified with numbers. Thus the class consisting of Plato and Aristotle is two in number, and is a member of a class of classes, each of whose members consists of something and something else. The class of finite integers, on the other hand, has a transfinite membership, while the class of round squares, or of integers between four and five, has no members at all, and is numerically null or nought. Classes occur enumeratively in propositions when their members are actual constituents of such propositions, and are mentioned in its verbal expression: thus Socrates and Plato occur enumeratively in the proposition that Socrates and Plato are two. Classes, however, can occur denotatively in a proposition when their members are not actual constituents of those propositions, but merely denotata of concepts occurring in them, such concepts, for example, as 'all Greek philosophers', 'some great Greek philosophers', 'the greatest of Greek philosophers', etc. It is obvious that very large, or infinitely large, classes can only enter into propositions in this second, denotative manner, unless perhaps for the non-successive apprehension of a God, which Russell does not think worth considering. Denotative class-concepts are, however, to be distinguished from the classes they denote, and the same class might be denoted by several distinct class-concepts, e.g. by man and by featherless biped. Russell does not, however, say that every class could be determined extensionally or denotatively as well as conceptually, only that, in the case of transfinite classes, 'death would cut short our laudable attempt at a complete enumeration' (*Principles*, §71).

Russell goes on to an interesting ontological consideration of the logical connective 'and' – not the conjunctive, propositional 'and' – which occurs in such enumerations as Socrates *and* Plato *and* Aristotle. Is this 'and' a concept distinct from the concepts it

48

unifies? If so it would seem to add an element to those terms, and so to turn their connection into a proposition. The meaning of the purely enumerative 'and' is, however, such that it implies no concept other than those of the items it connects: it would seem, therefore that it represents a contentless or meaningless addition. It is, however, plain that, if it induces no sort of unified combination of Socrates, Plato and Aristotle there will be nothing in these to be three in number, since each is in isolation only one. 'Thus it seems best', Russell says, 'to regard "and" as a unique sort of combinatory factor, not as a relation connecting *A* and *B* and *C* into a whole which could be one' (*Principles*, §71). The notion of 'and' does not, however, enter into the meaning-content of *every* class since it is absent from the concept of a unit-class, of a class with only a single member.

The ambiguous behaviour of classes further leads Russell to bifurcate them into two groups: that of classes as many and of classes as one. Classes as many are the more fundamental of these logical groups, since classes have to be pluralities if Numbers are to be predicated of them. 'In a class as many, though they have some kind of unity, they have less than is required for a whole. They have just as much unity as is required to make them many, but not enough to prevent them from remaining many' (*Principles*, §70). We have, however, to distinguish classes as one from classes as many, since classes as One exemplify Concepts which their members do not exemplify severally, and are members of higher Classes which their members do not exemplify at all. Thus the human race is a member of a class of races, whereas its members, individual men, are not members of this class, since they are not races. Russell infers that there is an ultimate distinction between a class as many and a class as one: they are really different, but logically related entities. When we talk about a class as many we are not therefore talking about any single entity, but only about a plurality of such entities. The class as one, e.g. the human race, is quite a different, single entity (*Principles*, §74). Russell has some interesting things to say about the null class. Though symbolic logic finds it convenient to treat a class without members as a genuine class, Russell doubts whether, on an extensional view of classes, its concept can be held to denote anything at all. He solves his problem by holding that a Concept may be a genuine denotative concept even when it actually does not denote anything, when '$x$ is a case of p' is false for all values of $x$. The significant and true proposition that 'Nothing is not nothing' can then be understood as saying that the concept of nothing is not itself nothing, though it denotes nothing. If we desire the concept of a class which will include all denotative concepts which do not denote anything, then the class of all such concepts will itself provide such an extensional referent. There always *is* a class of all the denoting concepts which do not denote anything. All in all, Russell's discussions of the ontology of classes could well have found a place among the discussions of the Platonic *Parmenides* or of certain parts of the dialectic of Hegel. This will not endear it to some, but it remains admirable none the less.


IV


We turn finally to consider Russell's treatment of certain important connective features in and among propositions: those expressed by the 'logical constants' which represent the 'form' of the propositions in question. These are not 'constituents' of most of the propositions they contribute to, but are rather qualifications of such propositions as wholes, or relations among them as wholes and are only 'constituents' of higher-order purely logical propositions. Such a logical constant is the notion of truth, or objective assertion, for it makes a difference whether a proposition occurs as an independent assertion, e.g. 'Plato was younger than Socrates' or as a mere element, not independently asserted, in another proposition, e.g. in 'If Socrates was older than Plato, Plato was younger than Socrates.' The 'assertion' here referred to is not, Russell tells us, assertion in a psychological sense, but full-strength, unqualified being-the-case, a notion which also plays a part in the symbolism of Frege, to which Meinong also gave the name of the modal moment, and of which Wittgenstein was unable to make sense. All the axioms and theorems in a logical system are assertions in this sense, but not the hypotheses which may occur in apagogic proofs and other like contexts. (This sense of 'assertion' is not to be confused with the sense of 'assertion' which highlights the purely predicative or functional aspect of a proposition, e.g. being younger than

Socrates, that is asserted of Plato.) It may be further noted in this connection that Russell's notion of truth in the *Principles of Mathematics* has no connotation of logical necessity. All truths are mere truths for the purpose of the *Principles*: logical truths, like empirical generalizations, are merely general implications in which any antecedent of a certain form is not true without a consequent of a certain related form also being true. It is true, of course, that the antecedents and consequents belonging to pure logic will contain only variables and logical constants, and not any constants with an empirical content or provenance, but this makes no difference to the sort of truth they embody, whose remoteness from the empirically factual is simply irrelevant.

Of the constants, besides truth, which Russell enumerates in the first paragraphs of the *Principles*, we have explicitly mentioned only Implications, the relation of a class-member to its class, and the notion of 'such that', i.e. a notion equivalent in most cases to the relation of a class-member to its class, or of the *value* of a propositional function to the function in question. To these may be added 'such further notions as may be involved in the notion of propositions of the above form'. Our initial stock in trade therefore amounts to the notion of implications, taken in the 'material', non-necessary sense, i.e. the relation which holds between two propositions when the former is not true without the latter, and the notion of being a value of a propositional function, which is, to all intents and purposes, the same as being the member of a class. Why Russell chose implication as his basic logical constant, rather than negation or conjunction or disjunction, or some notion based on these, is explained in the Introduction to the Second Edition of the *Principles* (p. vii, 1938). He desired to include in pure Mathematics, as the offspring of pure Logic, such principles as can receive a treatment, not as axioms, but only as hypotheses. All systems of geometry and rational dynamics require such principles: given certain hypothetical premises, certain conclusions are logically entailed, and there were countless disciplines in which such hypothetical logicization and mathematicization might prove possible (*Principles*, §4), a hope not unlike that which inspired Plato's later project of reducing Ideas to Numbers, and all dialectical to mathematical principles.

*Principia Mathematica* does not, of course, make the notion of implication primitive, but defines it in terms of negation and disjunction. A system which made implication primitive would, in fact, have to be very strange. It would have, as Russell says in *Principles*, §19, to equate not-*p* with the assertion that *p* implies any and every proposition. We do not, in fact, know what apparatus of primitive propositions Russell would have used in the second volume of his 1903 *Principles*, had he managed to complete it at the time. The *Principia Mathematica* of 1911, in whose development the simplifying influence of Whitehead was prepotent, was to make the whole deductive development more perspicuous. What was, however, abundantly brought out, even in the imperfectly worked out *Principles*, was that all the truths of the mathematical sciences, whether based on unconditional or merely hypothetical principles, could be developed out of a set of propositions of such consummate triviality, e.g. 'If *p*, then either *p* or *q*' etc., as at a later date to deserve the Wittgenstein designation of 'tautologies'.


V


The ontological logic of the *Principles* was however, from the very start, pregnant with antinomic difficulties which led to the replacement of its realism with a nominalistic doctrine of 'incomplete symbols' and 'logical constructions'. This new attitude is taken up in the system of *Principia Mathematica*, as also in Russell's popular works in the second decade of the century, which all accept a slogan of 'Constructions *versus* Inferences'. This may be taken as saying 'Try to show how certain speech-forms do not, if properly analysed, require the postulation of certain sorts of entity, but only misleadingly prompt us towards such a postulation.' Symbols and symbolic combinations seem to stand for certain entities, but, if they are replaced by other symbols and symbolic combinations of a more perspicuous, uniform kind, this appearance can be made to vanish. There is nothing that is hard in the world, for Russell at this period, but the short-lived data that impinge upon our senses, and the short-lived images and feelings that they arouse in us, and everything else can be regarded as a 'logical construction' out of these. Wittgenstein, in his early work, was to borrow this onstructive atomistic programme, but the atoms he postulated, eing such as rather fitted in with Hertz's *Principles of Mechanics*, were quite different from Russell's.

The passage from a burgeoning logical realism to a thoroughgoing logical constructivism, was mediated, as we have said, by the intolerable emergence of serious logical contradictions when certain concepts were manipulated in what seemed a logically unexceptionable manner. The dangerous manipulations in question always involved reflexivity or possible relation to self, coupled with negativity: assertive forms that could not relate something to itself, or to something of the same type as itself, or which only did so positively, did not give rise to antinomies. Thus one had to deal with Propositions that concerned a range of propositions, among which these Propositions themselves could be included, and concerned these in some negative fashion, or again with concepts that were concepts of concepts and also covered a range in which they themselves might be found, and which were then further negative in their content. One also had to deal with classes of classes which were such as to have a range of members in which they themselves might be included, while also being negatively related to such members. In all such cases, and in many others, hopeless contradictions arose: if certain propositions were supposed true, their content rendered them false, and if they were supposed false, their content rendered them true. Thus if a Proposition can directly or indirectly 'say' of itself that it is false, as it can quite legitimately say this of countless other propositions, then it is false if it is true, and true if it is false. In the same way if a concept can be *the* concept of not applying to itself – which concept quite legitimately applies to countless concepts, e.g. the concept of humanity does not apply to itself, since Humanity is not itself human, only man being such – then, if one raises the question whether the concept of not applying to itself applies to itself or not, one gets the sphinx-like answer that, *if* it applies to itself, it does not apply to itself, since this is what it makes its cases be, whereas, *if* it applies to itself, as unity applies to itself, being single, and as goodness applies to itself, being good) it also does *not* apply to itself, and for the very same reason as in the previous case, that this is what it makes its cases be. And, in the case of the class of all the classes that are *not* members of themselves – there are many such: e.g. the class of integers less than five is not one of its own component integers – it is the case that, if it is a member of itself, it is not a member of itself, since its membership consists of classes that are not members of themselves, and also that, if it is not a member of itself, then it *is* a member of itself, since it itself fulfils the condition necessary for membership in itself. These cases resemble the thin ice which occurs in the corners of a beautiful skating-field, from which skaters have to be warned off by special notices. Perhaps it would have been a good policy to put up similar notices only in the special cases where paradoxes impended, and to leave the rest of the field unimpeded. The later Wittgenstein would seem to have been sympathetic to such a policy. It would at least have carried the message that perfect generality is hardly ever safe. Such a policy did not, however, seem acceptable in a discipline in which all things non-logical had been replaced by variables, and hence Russell felt forced to construct a general type-theory in which there were lowest type propositions which concerned only entities which were not themselves propositional, first-type propositions which concerned only lowest-type propositions and entities not themselves propositional, second-type propositions which concerned only first-type and lowest-type propositions and entities not themselves propositional, and so on indefinitely. Similar hierarchies could be constructed for Concepts and for Classes, and the outcome would be that all the peccant utterances which led to insoluble antinomies could be declared to be the 'meaningless' violations of such type-restrictions. Unfortunately the remedy proved worse than the disease, since countless indispensable utterances, not at all negatively reflexive like the antinomic ones, had now to be rescued from the dire threat of non-significance. This was done by introducing an Axiom of Reducibility into whose implausible intricacies it is happily not our duty to enter. What emerged from these difficulties was a new doctrine that made language responsible for all the paradoxes and conundrums of logic and philosophy. If we could only translate all we said into a way that would represent the simple ways in which simple things fit together to form the simplest facts, all such difficulties would disappear. The present writer has no faith in such ultimate simplicities, whether they be those of ordinary discourse, or of sophisticated and sophistical forms of diction, but believes that the language of true philosophy, if there is one, will rather be one that is always willing to jump from seeing things in one complex light to seeing it in quite another: it will thus achieve a juster understanding of the way everything fits into everything. The resort to ultimate simples was, however, the resort of a great period in the history of philosophy, to which Russell, Moore and Wittgenstein alike belonged, and has to be seen in the light of its major merits.

There were three types of logical entity that suffered decimation or destruction in the constructivist revolution that followed the brief heyday of Russell's logical realism: these were propositions, non-existent objects and classes. All became more or less logical fictions, things that it was useful to treat as entities in some forms of talk, but which had to be made to vanish when talk became truly penetrating. Objective propositions could not be tolerated since they could as readily be false as true, and there are grave difficulties in treating a false proposition, which says how things are *not*, on the same level as a proposition which says or is how things actually *are*. Moore underwent a similar conversion from propositions, in which he had devoutly believed: one can see this if one reads his *Some Main Problems of Philosophy*. Russell's solution was traditional and psychologistic: the so-called terms of propositions are cemented together by the believing or judging mind, which combines a subject with a predicate, or a relation with the terms among which it is to hold, or effects some more complex combinatory operation. This cementing is not, however, dyadic, but always polyadic: what we have in it is not the mind confronted by a single propositional complex, which has an independent unity, but the mind confronted by a plurality of objects, particular and universal, which are, in and by the mind's action, connected with one another. The mind does not believe the unified proposition that apples grow on trees, but rather should be said to believe growing on trees *of* apples: just as giving demands a giver, a gift and a recipient, so believing involves a believer, an object of which one believes something (i.e. a logical subject) and the something or predicate that one believes of it. This is so whether the entities are independently combined or not: in both cases the situation is the same for the believing mind. But if there is such an independent combination of the entities other than the believer, his belief is true, whereas otherwise it is false. This naive theory is not very different from Aristotle's in *De Interpretatione*, though Russell later decorates it with images, belief-feelings and other modern trappings. It entails that there are no such entities as propositions, which can as readily be false as true, though it may be convenient to talk as if there were. The only genuine combinations in such situations, apart from believing minds, are the factual combinations which make some of our believing true, and whose elements then recur in a more complex, polyadic interrelation with our minds. if our believing is false, there are no such objective combinations, only combinations in which a subjective factor is always one element. The present author, like Wittgenstein, is, however, unable to regard this as a satisfactory analysis of false belief, which seems to involve a unified intentional objectivity which enters into the description of our believing, although it may not be an existent part of it, nor of anything. Othello was not distressed by a connection of his wife with Cassio which was only in his mind, but by a connection which was, for him at least, objective. It is not, however, my task to discuss this ancient problem, but only to express my sympathy with the view that what isn't the case enters ineluctably into whatever is the case, even if only by being excluded by it, and so has a more than merely intentional role in the world.

If Russell was so willing to dissolve false propositions, it was natural that he should be equally willing to dissolve non-existent objects. The existence of objects was taken to mean simply that certain concepts had application to instances, whereas non-existence meant simply that certain concepts were not exemplified in any of the objects in the world. The true logical subject of a statement of existence or non-existence was therefore the totality of objects in the world, and what we were predicating of them was that a certain description, or set of propositional functions, had application to *some* of them, or could be negated of *all* of them. There could be no such thing as existence predicated of a given individual: if it was there, given, named, there could be no question of its existence or non-existence which could really only cover descriptions which applied or did not apply to it or to something. This view is open to objection: we can always recognize as a fact that this thing *before us* exists and that it might very well *not* have existed. It is also clear that, when we *wish* that something existed, e.g. a child of our own, we may not wish that any of the *actual* things in the world should be our child, but only that another, quite different child, that exists nowhere, should exist, and be our own. Judgements of existence and non-existence therefore plainly have reference beyond the limits of the actual world and its contents, and cannot be satisfied merely by rearranging or modifying those contents. Wittgenstein was to take over this Russellian view: his *Tractatus* regards it as nonsense that there *could* have been other ultimate simple objects than there are. To suppose the existence of other objects than there are is only to suppose that the simples in the world should have been otherwise arrayed and compounded. It is further understandable that the collapse of all propositions in true propositions, and the latter into facts, should lead to the elimination from the realm of logical entities of all those higher-order propositions whose expression involves negation, conjunction, disjunction, and implication, as well as all the modalities. Russell in the *Principles* had tried to define all the logical connectives in terms of implication and universal quantification, and *Principia* had substituted disjunction and negation for the latter. Whatever logical connectives one's diction employed, one only reached truth-functions of elementary propositions, of propositions whose structures involved no such connectives or quantifications, but were such that the truth or falsehood of all non-elementary propositions depended wholly upon *their* truth or falsehood, so that, if one knew *their* truth and falsehood completely, one would know the truth or falsehood of all non-elementary propositions. If one knew all the elementary matters of fact that were the case, one would be able to determine the truth-status of all the implications, conjunctions, disjunctions, negations, quantified generalizations, etc. of these elementary matters of fact, and hence all such implications, conjunctions, generalizations, etc., became merely an interlacing tangle of symbols through which all those elementary facts must peep in those elementary facts themselves, those complexities would not be represented. This view is, of course, not acceptable to those who believe that many logical functions apply *beyond* what exists to what merely *might* have existed, and also that a disjunction or implication, for example, may have components that have some sort of a necessity of connection, whether formal or eidetic or nomological, and so be capable of truth in worlds other than our own. That if a man is thwarted he will tend to grow angry, or that a human being is either male or female, has a basis stronger than what happens to be the case in regard to particular men. We need not, however, develop the fundamental objections to a purely truth-functional interpretation of the higher types of proposition. Russell himself had objections to such a view. Thus he argued that a generalization covering *all* cases could only be achieved if we knew that we *had* all the cases, i.e. that there were no others. Hence there must be at least one primordial negative generalization presupposed by all others. He also had difficulties with propositions concerning belief and other mental attitudes to propositions. Thus '*A* believes *p*' is plainly not a truth-function of *p*, since some men believe almost anything, whether true or false. But if one can then substitute a sentence for a proposition, and analyse belief in terms of a confident readiness to assert sentences, one can be rid of this inconvenient case, a convenience of which Wittgenstein later availed himself.

Russell's view of propositions and facts as the only true unities of elements, led further to the view that the basic facts about the world must have analysably simple components, and that all propositions about complex entities must permit of an analysis into elementary or atomic propositions about wholly simple ones. This view, not greatly stressed by Russell, was of course further developed by Wittgenstein into a doctrine of unknowable, simply connected simples as in some obscure manner referred to in all our discourse. Russell did not develop this opinion in such an obscure direction, but opted for a theory in which the ultimate atoms of discourse, whose interconnections create all ultimate atomic facts, were simply very short-lived experiences: sense data, images and some feelings, and various not further analysable qualities and relations that they might exemplify. In his two popular works, *Our Knowledge of the External World* (1914), and *The Analysis of Mind* (1921) he worked out a theory in which both mind and matter were analysable into varying arrangements of these ultimate components. When Wittgenstein published his *Tractatus*, Russell wrote an Introduction to it that interpreted it in this sensationalistic, psychologistic manner which was subsequently taken up by the Logical Positivists

Wittgenstein, who had come to philosophy from physics rather than psychology, repudiated this interpretation: his simples had a simplicity transcending anything sensed or imagined. They were 'colourless', i.e. quite without quality, and their relations were likewise colourless and uniform. Whatever the differences of Wittgenstein's analyses from Russell's, and their much greater austerity, they all nevertheless have their roots in the latter.

We turn to the last casualty in Russell's demolition of logical entities: the casualty of classes. Classes had proved particularly refractory in the special case of the class of all classes not members of themselves, and it was obvious, if logical truth was to be sustained, that there could not *be* such a class. But, if it was impossible to assemble classes together in one unexceptionably conceived case, it was reasonable to treat them *all* as suspect: their 'names' must be incomplete symbols, definable only in context, and they themselves must be 'logical constructions', mere shadows of symbolism that would vanish when symbolism was completely analysed. What all this really meant was that Russell was taking a step in the direction of intensions, of formulable *Concepts*, and away from the mere ranges of cases which in most cases defied complete enumeration, and were often barred from being entities by their latent contradictions. The limited intensionalism which Russell thus tried to import into his interpretation of class-symbols was, however, not without its cost. One had, for example, to suppose, as in Zermelo's Axiom of Selections, that there always would *be* a one-one relation connecting the members of one Class with those of another, in order to give significance to their numerical equality. And one had similarly to believe that there *were* properties which applied to a transfinite range of cases, in order to give meaning to statements about infinite classes. Classes, thus summarily dismissed by Russell, continued, however, to prosper in his thought, and he may perhaps be said to have rejected classes as unities, in favour of classes as many, i.e. classes as indefinite multitudes resembling the great and small of Plato. Certainly Russell's later analyses continue to be class-analyses: a mind is only a class of sense-data, images and feelings linked together by mnemic causation, while mountains, people, motor-cars, and all the *things* of common sense are only immensely scattered classes of sense-data which belong to different minds, or perhaps not to mind at all, and whose causal relations are of what we call a physical rather than a mnemic type. This was the Logical Atomism which Russell argued for in a famous Monist article in 1918–19, and which he tried also to foist on Wittgenstein, though the latter refused to accept it. Classes like propositions, etc., were therefore banished from the ultimate bricks of logical building, but they none the less remained the headstone of Russell's corner, the category in terms of which he continued to think of everything. It will be seen, from our account, to what extent the thought of Wittgenstein's *Tractatus Logico-Philosophicus* was merely a carrying further of thought-trends present in Russell's *Principles*, his *Principia* and his various popular works.

## VI

Wittgenstein's admiration of Frege was immense, and has prompted an immense interest in Frege among analytic philosophers, particularly in Oxford, where it has practically amounted to a cult. This cult may have some of its roots in an unwillingness to acknowledge intellectual indebtedness to the richer and deeper thought of Russell, who was, however, only a Cambridge man. Jesting apart, the thought of Frege revolves around a few very minute conceptual and symbolic issues, which remained problematic despite all of his explanations: possibly his greatness consists in having shown the utterly problematic character of the simplest forms of meaningful discourse. Wittgenstein, despite his admiration for Frege, shows little of the latter's penetrating minuteness of approach: his doctrine of meaning as use has its roots in the incomplete symbols, logical constructions and other simplifying devices of Russell's later work, rather than in the objects, the concepts, the senses, the references and the other linguistic and ontological devices of Frege. Frege's work indeed deserved the characterization of *Spitzfindigkeit*, i.e. unprofitable scholastic exactitude, with which his colleagues at Göttingen saddled him: such a characterization could at no time, and in no degree, have applied to Wittgenstein. The writings of Frege, long inaccessible to many in the German, have now happily, in their main sections, been translated into English, the *Grundlagen der Arithmetik* (*Foundations of Arithmetic*) of 1884 by J.L. Austin, and portions of the *Begriffschrift* (*Language of Concepts*) of 1879 and of the *Grundgesetze der Arithmetik* (*Basic Principles of Arithmetic*) of 1903, together with many important translations of articles, by Peter Geach and Max Black. There is also a complete translation of the *Begriffschrift* (*Conceptual Notation*) by T.W. Bynum (Oxford, 1972). Frege's logical symbolism, with its strange horizontal and vertical strokes, and occasional concavities, may carry suggestions of Stonehenge or Easter Island, but it certainly deserves study, if not adoption. (The Russellian symbolism is much more perspicuous.) In general there is little in the detail of Frege's teaching which Russell did not independently arrive at: only a few all-important questions concerning Meaning and Reference were importantly illuminated by Frege.

Frege holds, against Kant, to the purely analytic character of arithmetic, and to its complete development by a use of the transparent structural forms and constants, the axioms and rules of deduction of pure logic. In this respect he is at one with Russell, and also with Wittgenstein. But he also adheres to an ontology of objective logical entities in many ways reminiscent of Meinong, and of the Russell of the *Principles* (who, of course, borrowed much from him). He not only believes in objective things or objects, but also in objective concepts that characterize or relate them, some of which are illogical and absurd. He also believes in a wholly objective distinction of sense and reference in all such characterizing and relating concepts, and also in propositional unities, and he also believes in a truth or falsehood which is wholly independent of thought or symbolism, and finally in, an objective domain of classes which are the value-ranges of concepts, of the cases in which they apply, and which are always wholly distinct from their membership, which may be finite or transfinite or unitary or null. All these entities of reason are distinct from the gross things that they structure, and which they enable us to talk about. They are, further, entities as much real, and 'out there', as is the North Sea, and are by no means closely related to the personal pictures we form of them, or the inner signs and procedures through which we deal with them, nor yet to the words through which we speak of them. There is nothing in Frege more emphatic than his repudiation of any view of logic and mathematics as mere ways of manipulating symbols, or the assimilation of their objective necessities to the arbitrary rules governing a game like chess. *Grundgesetze der Arithmetik*, §§86–137, disposes very thoroughly of the games-analogies which were later to fascinate Wittgenstein so profoundly.

But though Frege may thus favour an objective view of the logically relevant entities of reason, and may deprecate any psychologistic or nominalistic resolution of them, there is another side to his thought in which his whole approach to them is transcendentally psychologistic, and has many affinities with the thought of Kant, and with the later thought of Husserl. The entities which Reason explores, and which stand in relation to reason as ineluctably objective, are also entities essentially accommodated to the ideals and aim of reason: they are its own, proper objects, and therefore utterly transparent to it (*Grundlagen*, p. 36). In being aware of concepts, sense, references, value-ranges, truth-values, etc. and their interrelations, reason, a subjective human faculty, is aware of matters that are essentially such as to be clearly apprehended and understood *by itself*, just as Reason is essentially such as to be also able to apprehend and understand all things through them. We would seem, in short, to have here a relation of mutual fit which is as much idealistic as realistic: it accords with the Platonic view that what is most completely real is also most completely knowable, and vice versa. The ground of objectivity is therefore, Frege says, to be sought in reason alone, but the reason in which it is to be sought is as much for him an ontological as a subjective principle. This reason has nothing about it which ties it to the varied approaches of individual minds, their pictures, their feelings, their personal thought-transitions, etc.: it is essentially something which pertains to mind as such (as also, doubtless, to the objectively real as such). Logic as opposed to psychology, Frege later said, was a study of *Mind* rather than of minds. These profound reflections had unfortunately no influence on the earlier or later teachings of Wittgenstein.

We shall now dwell briefly on a few important points in the general views of Frege, which we have so far only summarily sketched. The first point is the primacy of the articulated proposition, to which, though it is objective, Frege gives the name of a *Gedanke* or thought. It is in the propositional unity that all other entities of reason perform their part; the domain of reason is a domain of articulated propositional unities, not of detached things or objects. Wittgenstein's view in the *Tractatus* that the world is everything that is the case, the totality of facts, not of things, here had its inspiration. As in Russell, however, the articulated propositional thought has *two* sorts of constituents, whose logical role is very different: it consists, on the one hand of concepts, *Begriffe*, which are essentially unsaturated (*ungesättigt*), incomplete, and which require a supplement of cases, whether directly referred to or generally indicated, to yield a complete propositional unity, and of objects, on the other hand, which have no such inherent incompleteness, but which can count as entities in their own right. Such unsaturated concepts, are, in the most evident cases, what Russell called 'propositional functions', in which the objects that might complete them, whether into true or false propositions, are in their expression represented by variables. These variables do not represent entities, but rather significant gaps in propositional structure, which require a filling up, or saturation with appropriate objects in order to yield complete thoughts or propositional unities. Thus being a philosopher who is the pupil of a greater philosopher – the sense, in Russellian terms, of the function '$x$ is a philosopher, and for some $y$, $x$ is a pupil of $y$ and $y$ is a philosopher greater than $x$' – is an unsaturated function which yields a true proposition if, say, its gap is filled by the individual object Aristotle. In believing in objectively incomplete entities Frege is in company with Meinong, one of whose most interesting doctrines is that of incomplete objects (*unvollständige Gegenstände*), e.g. a cube *qua* cube, whose further character is left indeterminate, but which can mediate references to wholly complete objects. It may, however, be doubted whether Frege is quite as resolute in accepting incompleteness as is Meinong, for he holds that, when a concept is taken out of a propositional unity, and directly referred to, or is made the logical subject of a proposition, it loses its essential incompleteness, and is therefore not a concept at all. Thus if I talk of the concept horse I am not really dealing with the concept horse as I should be dealing with it if I said that Bucephalus was a horse. (See *Über Begriff und Gegenstand*, 1892, pp. 54–5.) Frege does not, however, give any adequate account of his transformed concept which is no longer a concept, nor how it meets the demands of the Law of Excluded Middle, which is for him an objective law for all objects. He does not, like Meinong, have recourse to a widened sense of negation, in which *not* having a property is extended to cover being undetermined in respect of that property, and is not limited to definitely *lacking* that property, this lack being only a special form of negation. Frege therefore fails to clarify the use of his brilliant notion of non-saturation, which is essential to the understanding of the manner in which thoughts, symbols and ontological aspects require one another in order to make sense. It may also be doubted whether Frege has been loyal to his own doctrine of the primacy of propositional unities: surely, if predicates, relations and concepts require complements in order to yield propositional unities, the same must be true of those individual entities which are the preferred logical subjects of ordinary assertions, and which we dignify with the name of concrete things? Frege's ontology has often been characterized as Platonic, but nothing is less Platonic than his according of fully saturated status to some of those transient, incompletely determined, half-understood something-or-others that we dignify with the name of particular things. The last cough of Edmund Husserl is arguably as much an incomplete something-or-other as the courage which characterized his demise.

Very prominent in Frege's treatments of the entities of reason is his distinction, in the case of each species of them, of their sense or *Sinn* on the one hand, and their reference or *Bedeutung*, on the other. There is a strong temptation, which has to be resisted, to make this a two-sided distinction in the use of *words* or *signs*. Words and signs, however, only have a sense and a reference in virtue of the objective thought-distinctions that they express, and which in some sense lie behind or beneath them. Thus the concept of being the philosophical husband of an unphilosophical woman occurs in various propositional unities, true or false, and has a reference to each of the instances of which it is true, e.g. Socrates, John Stuart Mill and Edmund Husserl. But it also has a sense which distinguishes it from other concepts, and which might be instanced by precisely the same range of cases, e.g. distinguishes it from the concept of being that range of entities which are all referred to in the previous sentence. It is an all-important property of the sense and reference of concepts that countless concepts which differ in sense may none the less have precisely the same reference, and so provide a truly informative content to the concept of identity or sameness, while it is also the case that a concept having an invariant sense may enable us to refer to countless *different* cases to which the concept applies truthfully, and can also, in a higher-order Sense, be said to refer to the whole class of cases, or whole range of values (*Wertverlauf*) of which it is true. Frege further does not believe, as Russell believes, that quite uncharacterized individual entities, even if given in direct acquaintance, can ever enter in propositional unities: their entry must always be mediated by a concept of some sort, though each may be the only entity to which this concept truly applies. Thus Socrates, however much he may figure in propositional unities, always figures in them as exemplifying a conceptual circumscription of some sort, which may, of course, differ widely, but unimportantly, in the thought of different persons. There can, of course, be higher-order concepts of concepts as well as of instances which are not concepts, and such higher-order concepts will have reference to the puzzlingly hypostatized Concepts – the hypostatic concept horse which is said not to be a concept – of which they may truthfully be predicated, as well as a sense which is quite distinct from that of the hypostatized concepts in question.

The *Spitzfindigkeit* natural to Frege led him, however, to try to apply the sense–reference distinction to propositional as well as to other Objective Unities, and to hold all the propositional Unities which were true, and which could be asserted in a non-psychological sense symbolized by his stroke-notation, ⊢ had reference only to a single unique object called the true, to which all true assertions were divergent references, and which approached their unique object of reference through a different mesh of concepts. Just as there are infinitely varied descriptions of Socrates, or the planet Venus, or the virtue of chastity, or whatever, which do not prejudice the identity of the object on which they converge, so also there are infinitely varied statements of the true which are unaffected in their reference by the variety of their content. There are likewise infinitely many statements of the false or untrue, e.g. that Socrates was a teetotaller, or that Socrates was a prime number, may be counted as such. Frege's astonishing decision to make the true and the false be the objects referred to by all propositional unities, rather than the concepts or subjects which conditioned their truth or falsehood, has occasioned much bewildered comment. The matter becomes less puzzling when we consider the difficulty of parcelling out truth and falsehood into innumerable independent truths and false-hoods, and deciding what is or what is not part of a given case of the true or the false. That Antony loves Cleopatra, and that Cleopatra is loved by Antony differ in sense, but do they, or do they not, state the same truth? No satisfactory criterion for propositional identity or distinctness has yet been devised. In default of this, it is perhaps simplest to accept a mass-theory of the true and the false, of a world that is everything that is the case, and that excludes everything that is not the case, and this would seem to be the solution adopted both by Frege and Wittgenstein, though the latter expands the true into a concept of logical space, which includes the possible as well as the true. Frege, with his refusal to take modality seriously, is unable to countenance such an expansion.

The position of classes in Frege's theory is interesting. Frege has no place for the purely enumerative classes permitted by Russell, which would allow us to regard Socrates and Plato and Schopenhauer as a class having three members, and so also, if one were really liberal, Socrates and chastity and the number five. For Frege, classes are always the value-ranges of definite concepts, and mere disjunctions of unrelated determinations, such as those just given, would not count as such. And certainly, for Frege as for Russell, a class could not be determined by an infinite disjunction of truth-functional alternatives, since neither of them had a God who could take in such transfinite ranges and cover them all in one timeless glance. It is, however, to be regretted that Frege did not seriously consider the possibility of enumeratively determined, as well as of conceptually determined classes. Number, above all, is indifferent to the conceptual character of what is counted, and even to its belonging in the same conceptual category. Socrates and chastity and the number five certainly make up a triad. Husserl's theory of number in his *Philosophie der Arithmetik*, which identifies the number three with the mere concept of something and something else and something else, in which no determining concept, apart from objective diversity, is invoked, would seem to have something to be said for it. It has not been refuted by the criticisms of Frege, as is generally held to be the case.

Frege was further much exercised, from what he says in an Appendix to his *Grundlagen*, by Russell's discovery that the *Wertverlauf* or value-range of the concept 'Class which is not a member of itself' has contradictory properties. It is a case of being a member of itself, if it is *not* a case of being a member of itself, and it *is*, likewise, a member of itself if it is *not* a member of itself. Frege's attempts to dissolve these antinomies deserve respect: they all involve an *ad hoc* principle or principle of thin ice, the principle that when generalizations, even logical ones, break down in certain ranges of cases, one must recognize and guard against such antinomic cases, without necessarily looking for some comprehensive principle which will render them generally perspicuous. Frege's whole method in fact encourages us to recognize that there is nothing queer about the exceptional case: it constitutes the necessary limit to the unexceptional one.

A valuable aspect of Frege's doctrine lies in his treatment of intentional objectivity. When one is dealing with reality, everything is extensional: everything that is true of objects considered as instances of one set of concepts, is true of the same objects considered as satisfying another set of concepts. When, however, one is dealing with minds and the way in which they view things, *sense* has a priority over *reference*. That someone conceives certain objects as exemplifying certain concepts, or as entering into certain propositional unities, does not mean that he conceives of the same objects as exemplifying *other* concepts or as entering into *other* propositional unities, even though there is factual equivalence among the pairs of concepts and of propositional unities in question. The man may not even know that the same objects permit of such differing thought-approaches. If we are interested in objects, not as they are *qua* objects, but as they are for variously oriented thought-attitudes, then the identifications possible in thought-indifferent thought vanish: we may use the same words in expressing thoughts about thoughts as we use in expressing straight thoughts, but our orientations are quite different, and what is, *qua* thought of directly, the same, may be quite different when thought of *as* thought of by someone. None the less, there remain interesting logical relations between thoughts directly oriented towards objects, and thoughts oriented towards thoughts oriented to objects even if these are not so simple and uniform as the thoughts which avoid all reference to thoughts. In thoughts which do not avoid such higher-order references, sense as opposed to reference predominates, and we must distinguish clearly between what in ordinary unreflective thought and talk is very confused.

We have indicated something of the wealth of distinctions that emerge in Frege's treatment of sense and reference, and have perhaps made plain that we neglect these at our peril. Wittgenstein was impressed by Frege's differentiations, but did not attempt to deepen them, or to carry them further, thinking perhaps that they were sufficiently overridden by the general slogan of meaning as use, which derives rather from the later potboilers of Russell, than from the profounder discussions of Frege or of Russell in works like the *Principles*. Our task is not, however, to deal with these difficult profundities, but with the bright play of Wittgenstein's less systematic genius.

## VII

We shall conclude our present contextual chapter by dealing briefly with some points in the thought of G.E. Moore, affectionately, and a trifle patronizingly, called 'Old Moore' by Wittgenstein, but by whom we may none the less believe that he was deeply influenced.

Moore was the philosopher who more than any other influenced a whole generation of Cambridge and other intellectuals, by his doctrine, in *Principia Ethica*, of the unanalysable uniqueness of the concept of good, and of its complete disparity from anything naturalistic or factual, as also by his further teaching that the criterion of rightness in action was simply the maximization of what is good, and that the greatest good things were not virtue or knowledge, as then given priority by earnest Victorians, but aesthetic pleasure and personal affection. Wittgenstein's view of the 'transcendental' character of ethics and aesthetics, and his refusal to connect them with anything that merely is the case, probably had its roots in these Moorean opinions, as had also his view that differences in philosophical opinion made no difference to one's principles of right conduct, and that an idealist, a realist or a solipsist might be equally fair and compassionate in his practical attitudes to others. Wittgenstein's mysticism in regard to ethics and aesthetics did not, however, owe anything to the influence of Moore.

Equally inspired by Moore was Wittgenstein's general acceptance of the common-sense picture of the environing world, which we do not ordinarily call into question, and which is taken for granted in our ordinary speech. Moore believed that we were far more certain of a whole body of cosmic facts: that the world and its constituent objects was scattered widely through space and had gone on for a long time, that it contained many extended, corporeal objects that were known through their effect on the senses, but which would exist even when they did not affect anyone's senses, and that there were acts of consciousness belonging to conscious minds that were very different from anything material or corporeal, though closely associated with the latter. We were sure of the existence of our own acts of consciousness by a sort of direct knowledge, but we were also sure of the existence of acts of consciousness connected with minds and bodies other than our own, but sure in a more indirect manner. We were also sure of past events through memory, and of future events through inferences based on past regularities of occurrence. Hume had questioned whether we had any right to infer the character of the future from the character of the experienced past, but we were far more sure of the imminence of certain future happenings thus inferred than we could be sure of any premisses or principles which Hume invoked to discredit such inferences. We were similarly much more sure of the persistent reality of unobserved bodies external to us in space, and having an occasional impact on our senses, than of any sceptical premiss that might make such persistence and impact doubtful. There is, accordingly, a common-sense view of the world, taken for granted in what we ordinarily think or say, that does not admit of serious question. This common-sense view of the world, incorporated into ordinary speech, is throughout presupposed in the thought of Wittgenstein, and even more strongly in his later than his earlier writings. One of his last published writings, *On Certainty*, is thoroughly Moorean in its approaches, but makes the amusing error of holding that we can be sure that men will never be able to travel to the moon.

Moore, however, opens the floodgates of philosophical doubt when he raises questions as to the analysis of common-sense certainties, and of the concepts which enter into them. Those concepts and certainties are firmly in the grip of ordinary thought and speech, but there remain questions as to the more elementary notions that enter into them, and as to how they may be related to one another in them. Thus it is an open question whether the mind-independent reality of material things is that of something not at all sensuous, but in some manner responsible for what is sensuously given to our minds, or whether it consists merely in the regular possibility of such sensuous givens, or whether it may not consist in the reality of something neither spatial nor sensuous, but of the same general nature as our acts of consciousness, or whether it may not be a centre for objective 'appearances' which in some way are not merely there for our acts of consciousness, etc. The whole of traditional philosophy can thus be brought back in the guise of a set of problems of analysis, and idealism, materialism, dualism, sensationalism, scepticism, phenomenalism, etc. can all be resuscitated as offering us alternative analyses of what we indubitably know. Ordinary language, moreover, though it is unquestionably oriented to what we know, is in many cases the seat of misleading suggestions. Sometimes its phrasing seems, in fact, to have been so designed as to bewilder and deceive philosophers. Thus ordinary language seems to accord some sort of real being to false propositions and non-existent objects, and a great philosopher like Meinong has accordingly built a whole system of thought around these misleading suggestions. Some of Moore's most interesting studies in *Some Main Problems of Philosophy* and elsewhere deal precisely with the unmasking of these misleading suggestions, and amount to a demonstration that we need not believe in such questionable entities as propositions which are not Facts, nor correspond with facts, nor in objects which have definite properties and a definite internal structure, but which do not exist in any sense at all. It will be obvious that Wittgenstein took over the analytic approach of Moore in his earlier writings. The *Tractatus* analyses all ordinary statements in terms of facts linking wholly unanalysable objects with one another. Ordinary language is all right, and corresponds with fact

and reality, but what fact and reality ultimately consist in, is
nothing statable in ordinary language, but only in a completely
analysed language that is not at our command. We have, in fact,
only arguments which guide us towards such a language, and to
the Facts and Objects to which it corresponds. These references
to unknowable inaccessibles drop out of Wittgenstein's post-
*Tractatus* thought, but at all stages of his thought he believes,
however, with Moore, that ordinary language can be very
deceptive, if not studied in actual use, and can by false analogies
lead us to suppose that we are dealing with entities that we are
not really concerned with at all. Thus we can readily be led to
suppose that references to the non-existent are references to
something that exists in a shadowy manner, or in some non-
ordinary medium. We can imagine or believe that King's College
is on fire, and this can readily suggest to us that there is a state of
affairs towards which our thought is then directed, even though
King's College is not actually burning. We may similarly form the
impression that we know the complex answer to some question,
or can continue a tune in the appropriate manner, and may then
say that the answer or the tune already lurks in our minds in an
obscure fashion, even though we may find that we do not really
know the answer or tune at all. At all points we tend to locate in
a mysterious mental medium what is really only something that
*could* present itself in circumstances that have not arrived. We
are likewise puzzled by the measurement of time, and, since
measurement in space demands that the measured parts should
all be there together, we find it strange that we should be able to
measure lengths of time whose stages are never given together.
In all these cases language deceives us by its false analogies, and
we think we are dealing with something deep and queer, when
we are merely dealing with a different sort of case. Wittgenstein,
in these treatments, is throughout taking his cue from Moore. We
must analyse what we are really doing when we use certain
expressions, what we really hope to bring out by our use of them,
and what our use of them really amounts to, however much this
may seem to be other than it is. Wittgenstein's attempted
analyses of the uses of expressions, and of the manner in which
they accord with situations and with one another, may seem very
different from Moore's analyses of objectively conceived proposi-

tions and concepts, but they are both essentially analytic. They try to break up the seeming structures which our speech seems to set before us, and to achieve a deeper and truer knowledge of those structures, which will liquidate many of the puzzlements that an incorrect analysis suggests. Where Moore realizes with relief that there is nothing more to the existence of time than such matters as breakfast this morning, lunch now at noon, and dinner later on, that we are not having to deal with something at once vanishing, yet inscrutably presenting its parts together for our measurement, Wittgenstein is able to compass precisely the same solvent insight by considering how we were taught the use of tenses to talk about time, and the use of clocks and other devices to measure it. Both in their very different fashions penetrate beneath the structures which language misleadingly suggests, if considered from an insufficiently analytic standpoint, to the structures that actually govern language in its living use. Wittgenstein has therefore taken much of his characteristic method from Moore, and both end by presenting an account of the world and its contents, including its speakers and thinkers, which both abolishes, as illusions or misinterpretations, many of the unordinary puzzlements and resolutions of puzzlement that philosophers have put forward, and yet also, after a fashion, reinstates them all, by showing that their haunting presence is a necessary feature of our life as thinkers and speakers, and that the mists and miasmata of philosophy can best be transformed by permitting many *alternative* notations or analyses to take their place. It is regrettable, however, that Wittgenstein never developed his insight into the necessity of alternative philosophical notations, instead of simplicistic attempts to eliminate them all, whereas in Moore alternative basic analyses remain undemolished. The influence of Moore on Wittgenstein, and of Wittgenstein on Moore, were alike profound, since they could not but recognize in each other the supreme integrity and clarity of thought to which each passionately aspired. Moore was arguably as close to the Socratic ideal of complete lucidity of speech, even on the most obscure issues, as anyone has ever been, and Wittgenstein, though he passed beyond the whole ideal of such exactitudes to some unduly negative and tentative positions, none the less sketched the whole being of talking man in the world in a more unified and simple manner than had ever before been compassed. If we have grave criticisms to raise against many of his too simple insights, this need not detract from their importance nor from his greatness.

# IV

# LANGUAGE, LOGIC AND PHILOSOPHY IN THE *TRACTATUS LOGICO-PHILOSOPHICUS*

## I

The present chapter will attempt to expound and comment upon the main contentions of Wittgenstein's early masterpiece, the *Tractatus Logico-Philosophicus*, seen, however, in the light of much posthumously published material, whether in the form of note-books, lecture-notes, reported discussions, and various later attempts at comprehensive treatises, which will not be cited in great detail. It will also be seen in the light of a general hermeneutic consensus which has developed after many wholly false starts, e.g. after the Russellian and Logical Positivist misinterpretations of the *Tractatus* as connecting the sense of all forms of utterance with primitive personal reports of sense-data or anticipations of such. The *Tractatus* rather relates significant speech to an ontology or a cosmology: it attempts to sketch the basic pattern of a world in which significant speech will be possible. In certain crucial passages it also connects the world, i.e. the objective world of our common experience, with a transcendental subject which has to make sense of it and to speak of it, and this means that the cosmology of the *Tractatus*, like Kant's metaphysic of nature, may best be regarded as stating how we, as speakers, must construe the world of which we are speaking, rather than as anything that we have independently to posit. This will exempt us from having to take in full seriousness what Wittgenstein has to say about a body of unchanging, simple objects contingently related in a wholly uniform, characterless ashion. The *Tractatus* further relates significant speech to a philosophy of the life of mind which turns the latter into an obscure, ill-developed appendage of the former, rather than, as is traditionally the wont, explaining significant speech in terms of inner, cogitative acts which underlie it, and which *give* it its significance. This great inversion, comparable to the Platonic subordination of concrete things to their characters, rather than the other way round, or to the Berkeleyan inversion which makes mundane objects depend on our perceptions of them rather than the other way round, would be sufficient to make Wittgenstein's work philosophically momentous. The explanatory priority of significant speech over everything in nature, mind and the abstract and normative sciences, is, of course, carried much further in Wittgenstein's post-*Tractatus* writings, and a main concern of this book will be to criticize it as thoroughly as possible. Speech, we shall try to argue, in accord with tradition, should much rather be taken as mirroring the ineluctable patterns of subjectivity and intersubjectivity, and the normative demands of a correlated objectivity, than the other way round. We shall, however, have to make plain that Wittgenstein's new way of words has neither clarified nor dissolved the old problems of philosophy, but merely transferred them to a new medium in which they become questions as to what we say, or ought to say, without laying down wholly clear standards for determining the matter.

## II

The world is held in *Tractatus*, §§1-1.21 to be everything that is the case: it is the totality, not of the things that facts are about, but the totality of the facts that concern anything whatever. Obviously, we should not have the world in its completeness if we merely had before us a list of its component entities that exhausted it completely. We should also have to be informed as to the relational bonds that connected those entities with one another, and also what entities, if any, entered as further components into the entities enumerated in the former list, and how these further components were related to one another. Obviously too, we should not have the world in its completeness if we stopped at any point in the listing of component entities, and saying how they were bonded together, until and unless we arrived at entities, if any, that were not put together out of component entities, but were simple and unanalysable. Wittgenstein will later argue that there *must* be such entities, but, for the time being, we need only say that the world in which we place things and facts cannot solely consist of what we can find in the world of our limited experience, but must necessarily embrace countless things, and facts about these, that transcend such limited experience, and that are at best only matters for whose presence more or less cogent *arguments* can be offered. The world includes not merely the fact that my watch is on the table, but also all the facts about the components of either watch or table, and about their composition to form the objects in question, as also whatever facts help to compose the relation connoted by 'on', etc. Somehow, however, when we locate watch and table and their relationship in the world, we must be making reference to a totality of things and facts that cannot possibly be enumerated or envisaged or made an object of experience. It is well to be clear that so much of the transcendent is involved in introducing us to the world, or the world to us, in *Tractatus*, §§1–1.21.

§1.12 tells us further that there is no need to consider as facts of higher order all the *negative* facts consisting in the absence of certain positive facts from the world: if we have *all* the positive facts connecting entities with entities, then what we have automatically includes the absence of any others, since the notion of *all* involves just this. Russell had, however, already pointed out that to talk about *all* instances in which something is the case, only renders negative facts superfluous by itself being a covert case of negation. To have *all* is *not* to have any more. It is not therefore the case that we can dispense with negation altogether in seeing the world as everything that is the case. Wittgenstein is later to argue that not only are all negations superfluous in conceiving the world as it totally is, but also all facts that involve the logical connectives of conjunction, disjunction, implication and the forms of quantification. Having all positive facts of connection as objects of reference, one not only implicitly has all negations, but also all conjunctions, disjunctions, implications and generalizations, whether universal or existential, that pre

uppose these. The complete tally of the world, therefore, need
involve nothing that is negative, alternative, conditional or
general, or otherwise logically complex: positive, definite,
unconditional, unqualified matters of fact will yield the complete
tally. There are, however, for Wittgenstein, infinite possibilities of
fact surrounding the existent facts which make up the world, for
we can certainly say or think that certain matters of fact obtain in
the world though they do not so obtain, and there may be
nothing more to their not so obtaining beyond the fact that they
fall outside of the privileged totality which makes up the world.
We can therefore legitimately allow ourselves to picture existent
matters of fact as the occupied points in a total space, which has
room for countless other possibilities of fact, which can be
pictured as being the unoccupied or empty points or areas in such
a space. §1.13 thus introduces the highly problematic notion of
logical space, to which there are quite a number of subsequent
references.

A final very significant point is made in §1.21, that the matters
of fact, realized or unrealized, which are under consideration,
must all have *complete logical independence* from one another.
Each could have been realized, or remained unrealized and
merely possible, while all others remained the same. Thus each
of the occupied points in logical space could have been
unoccupied, or vice versa, without affecting the occupation or
non-occupation of other points in logical space. There can be no
built-in connection, positive or negative, among the matters of
fact considered in §1.21. It is plain, however, that Wittgenstein is
here tacitly passing from facts in general to a particular, ultimate
variety of facts, on which all other varieties of fact are held to be
founded, facts which have no inner complexity of structure, nor
are concerned with entities having any inner complexity of
structure, and which therefore, in the sheer simplicity of their
being the case, neither entail that anything *else* is or is not the
case. This is not true in regard to most of the facts that we
ordinarily acknowledge, e.g. that my watch is on the table. Such
ultimate, not further analysable, mutually independent facts only
enter the discussion in §2.

In §2 every matter of fact is said to consist in the existence of
certain *Sachverhalte* or States of Affairs, by which, as we have
said, certain ultimate, not further analysable matters of fact are

meant, having the complete logical independence from other ultimate matters of fact which §1.21 has wrongly suggested belongs to *all* facts in relation to one another. Ultimate facts may concern or be about several entities, but they cannot represent a negation, or a disjunction, or a conjunction, or a generalization, or any other function of more basic facts. They were called 'atomic facts' by Ogden, the first translator of the *Tractatus*, and Wittgenstein was satisfied with the translation. Facts built upon, and presupposing such atomic facts, e.g. the conjunction of two such facts, could, by contrast, be called 'molecular'. But §2.02 goes on to inform us that, not only must an ultimate fact not permit analysis into other ultimate facts – if it did so, it would not be logically independent of these – but it must concern entities or objects that are unanalysably simple, and which cannot be regarded as compounded out of other entities in any manner at all. For if what a fact was about was a compound of separable entities, then it would depend on the fact or facts of their compounding, and could therefore not be ultimate. (This argument leaves open the possibility that an object might be a many-sided unity of inseparable aspects, distinguishable only in the light of differing comparisons. Wittgenstein would probably have regarded such an object as simple, e.g. the transcendental ego with its two distinct aspects of thought and will.)

§2.02 further argues for the simplicity of the ultimate objects that all facts are about, that, in default of such simplicity, we should not be able to give a definite *sense* to any statement of fact. Facts about complex objects only have a definite 'substance' (in the sense of a definite sense) if such complexity depends on the manifold relations among objects which are *not* complex, in facts which are the ways in which such simple objects are put together to form the complex objects in question. If the existence of an object consisted in a combination of objects, which consisted in a combination of objects, and so on indefinitely, no object would have anything substantial to it, and no propositional utterance would have a definite sense. Facts, to be facts, must be the obtaining of something definite among terms which are similarly definite, and this condition is not fulfilled if facts are only an obtaining of relations among things which involve the obtaining of other relations, among things which involve, etc. without any descent to ultimate terms which all these relation directly or indirectly relate. The simple objects which underlie all complex objects and situations are what all facts are ultimately about: they are the unalterable form of the world, in which all its possibilities of fact must be contained (§§2.02–2.033). Wittgenstein's argument for ultimate simples is therefore entirely *a priori*: they are the things that we cannot help thinking of as what underlie all propositional references and assertions as last logical subjects, but of which we can form no further conception and need have no intuitive acquaintance. The resemblance is here to Kant's transcendental objects or things-in-themselves, which in some passages are credited with a monadic simplicity borrowed from the thought of Leibniz. It must here be noted that Wittgenstein's objection to an infinite regress of sense is not an objection to transfinite assemblages as such, since in §4.2211 he says: 'Even if the world is infinitely complex, so that every fact consists of infinitely many States of Affairs, and every State of Affairs is composed of infinitely many Objects, there would still have to be Objects and States of Affairs.' In the situation contemplated, there would still be wholly simple, definite objects and not further analysable facts about them, even if the number of such objects, and of facts about them, was transfinite. Later on, however, Wittgenstein would not have tolerated such an infinity, since *we* certainly could not exhaust it by successive analyses. But in the *Tractatus* there could have been held simply to *be* an infinite series of sets of facts, each set of which was the analysis of a previous set; there would in such a case always have *been* a complete analysis of any set of facts, even though this analysis had no terminal members. That *we*, with our successive methods, could not consummate such an infinite analysis, would not prevent it from being present, just as the transfinite series of cardinals is unaffected by our inability to run through them all. There would therefore seem to be an unwarranted intrusion of the anthropological point of view in Wittgenstein's arguments for ultimate simples: such an intrusion was, of course, to become more and more pronounced in his later work.

III

n §2.01 we are given to understand that each ultimate state of affairs is simply a combination of objects, by which 'objects' we are to understand a set of wholly simple entities, wholly without internal structure, since, if they had such structure, there would be facts as to their composition, which would be more basic than the facts of their external combination with other objects. The incomposite objects, therefore, that enter into ultimate states of affairs, can in one sense be said to be independent of the ultimate combinations into which they enter, inasmuch as they might have entered into *other* factual combinations, but not, however, inasmuch as they should not be capable of entry into ultimate combinations of *some* sort. It is, we may say, of their essence, and not an accidental matter, that they *can* be so combined. The nature or essence of an ultimate object, what it can be said to be in and for itself, must in fact be wholly *constituted* by its possibilities of entry into ultimate matters of fact, and one can only fully know this nature by knowing all of these possibilities (§2.0123). An ultimate object's inner nature, as opposed to its external properties, is thus an ultimate object's permanent possibilities of combination with other ultimate objects, whereas its external, contingent properties are confined to its actual or existent combinations. It is plain from these utterances that Wittgenstein does not conceive of his ultimate objects as having anything irreducibly *qualitative* about them, which might serve to distinguish them from other objects, or to sort them into kinds. The only thing that, in such ultimates, could approach purely qualitative differences, would be their differing *combinatory capabilities* in relation to other ultimate objects. It is not, then, in virtue of any variations in intrinsic quality that there are differing combinatory possibilities among ultimate objects, but that ultimate objects simply *do* differ in combinatory possibilities with objects other than themselves, and that this *alone* sorts them out into objects of the same, or of another kind. And apart from such combinatory possibilities they would be simply and surdly different (§2.0233). The qualitative differences in the world as we find it, must therefore all admit of a final analysis in which nothing unanalysably qualitative will remain, and Wittgenstein inclines to the belief that it was an insight into this necessity which led physicists to seek to explain differences of so-called secondary qualities in terms of differences in so-called primary qualities, i.e. into mere differences in arithmetical multiplicity

xtended into many independent dimensions, with nowhere
1ything irreducibly qualitative about them. The reduction of
1alitative differences into mere differences in combinatory
)ssibilities, among entities in no respect qualitatively distinct,
ems, however, a wholly unintelligible step. It was thrown out of
)urt by Leibniz, by Berkeley, and more recently by Whitehead,
1d it has not been rendered more acceptable by the picturesque
guments of Wittgenstein. A world of unqualified simples
1dowed only with possibilities of mutual combination is plainly
1ly a world of nothings nugatorily related. It is only in a world
entities independently qualified that combination can mean
1ything.

The purely combinatory nature of the intrinsic properties of
e ultimate constituents of the world is also set forth in the
omentous proposition §2.0232: 'Roughly speaking, Objects are
)lourless.' Ultimate objects are without character, and, apart
om their combinatory capacities, wholly uniform. It can only be
hen ultimate objects enter into combination with others that
1aracters like colour, etc., can arise. We can perhaps imagine
em arising inasmuch as highly characteristic shape-characters or
.ythm-characters arise out of selections from wholly character-
ss, uniformly related points in space or instants in time, though
'en there we must have visual, auditory and other qualities to
ve salience and meaning to our selection. The exciting way in
hich the inexhaustible varieties of even, odd, square, prime and
her types of number likewise arise in the wholly monotonous
.ocess of adding unit to unit might also serve to cast light on
'ittgenstein's extraordinary reduction of quality to combinatory
ipacity, but, by and large, it remains a fantastically unillumina-
1g step.

§2.0124 and §2.014 attribute to ultimate objects and their
·mbinations all the possibilities of ultimate states of affairs, and
the complex matters of fact (*Sachlagen*) that are built out of
ese. Each ultimate object is therefore surrounded by the
)ssibilities of combination with other ultimate objects which
·nstitute its logical space. §2.0131 seems, however, to suggest
at ultimate objects might *differ* in type or form, and so be
.rrounded by a distinctive logical space of their own. Thus a
·eck in the visual field is surrounded by a space of colour-
)ssibilities (not, for example, of pitch-possibilities), a note in

the auditory field by a space of pitch-possibilities (not colour-possibilities) and so on. An object is said to have a form which covers its possibilities of combination with other objects but to make this notion of a special form important and interesting we shall, however, have to include all its necessities and impossibilities of combination, as well as its possibilities. Certain ultimate objects must be such that they *must*, or they cannot, be combined with certain other ultimate objects, or combinations involving these. Thus whatever set of ultimate objects underlies what we recognize as being a complex object of a certain colour, *must* be combined with ultimate objects and combinations that we recognize as cases of extension and figure, and *cannot* be combined with combinations that we recognize as being cases of another colour. This notion of a special space is, however, ruinous to the principles of the *Tractatus*, which holds to the unlimited combinatory capacities of every ultimate object with every other. Of course, limitations in combinatorial capacity might apply *only* to complex, non-ultimate objects, but it is hard to see how these could be limited in combinatorial capacities if their ultimate elements were not so at all. Only if what we take to be qualitative differences rest solely on the arithmetical and dimensional differences of ultimate objects, can we begin to understand how certain non-ultimate objects should have different combinatorial capacities from their ultimate elements. These difficulties could, of course, be undercut if we simply held, with interpreters like Russell and Stenius, that there are simple *qualities*, e.g. shades of blue, which are themselves ultimate objects, simple entities with differing capacities for combination or non-combination with other like entities. Such a view would certainly restrict the boundless combinatory openness of the *Tractatus*, and would perhaps represent an improvement. Wittgenstein himself, in his 1930 Aristotelian Society paper on *Logical Form*, as well as elsewhere, asserts that two distinct colour-predications, e.g. of blue and of green, of the same object at the same time, might very well exclude one another, without for that reason involving any complexity of content. Such predications might represent ultimate, simple facts, and what was meant by the words 'blue' and 'green' might not be combinations of any sort, but unanalysable assertions. There would then have to be something like a special logic in the region of colours, and in other similar regions, which would not be reducible to the general logic which ignores quality-differences altogether. A great deal of Wittgenstein's later writing deals with such special logics, and elaborates it, but the main drift of this thought is against it. The necessities and impossibilities of logic are for Wittgenstein empty formal statements of what alone makes sense in *all* statements, or in *no* statements of a certain logical form, and the special necessities and impossibilities, therefore, which obtain in various qualitative regions, must either be empiricized and anthropologized, as Wittgenstein frequently had it, or be believed on faith to be in some manner, and on some analysis, a case of purely formal necessitation or exclusion, which a very deep investigation might somehow manage to reveal to be such. These remarks will be further elucidated as we proceed.

## IV

An important point remains to be considered: how widely is the realm of unfulfilled possibilities, i.e. of empty logical space, meant to extend? Could it extend so far that it passed beyond occupation, to regions where it was at all points wholly empty? §2.013 seems to open the possibility of such an empty logical space, one in which there were possibilities, but no actualities, of objective combination, but it is not clear whether this is a wholly empty logical space in which *no* object is combined with any other, or only a space in which there are *some* combinatory gaps, i.e. combinations of simples which remain unrealized. The latter is probably what Wittgenstein had in mind, since §2.0122 says that ultimate objects cannot occur both independently, and *also* in combination with others, which suggests that all ultimate objects must occur in *some* combinations with others, and cannot exist in total isolation, but also that there are many merely possible combinatory unions, and hence, what is the same, many resultant complexes which do not exist. Logical space thus has many gaps in it, but cannot be wholly empty. It is further important to note that logical space never can include any possibilities of the existence of simples which do not, in fact, exist. Simples, in fact, determine the ultimate form of the world, its complete range of possibilities (§2.0231). Hence we cannot raise any question as to the possibility of their existence or non-existence: they in their totality are presupposed by all significant possibilities. It is only in the case of *complex* objects that questions of existence or non-existence can be significantly raised, since their existence is that of certain combinations, which need not have been realized. The ultimate population of the world, if we can permit ourselves such a phrase, could not be increased or decreased, or be in any way other, since it constitutes the world's unalterable form (§2.023), which is presupposed by any and all of its possibilities. We have therefore in any possible world all the ultimate simples that we find or posit in *our* world, and we could not have any others. In a sense there are not a plurality of possible worlds, but only one world, which embraces all objects and all possibilities of combination among them: the results of such combinations may, however, be so very different, for our unanalysed experience, that talk of a plurality of possible worlds might have justification.

It is hard to know how to react critically to all these fantastic positions. We have postulated ultimate simples, surrounded by ranges of combinatory possibilities with other simples, to ensure that what we assert to be the case, in regard to the vastly complex objects around us, should have a determinate sense, and we now have to ask how the postulation of these ultimate entities, indistinguishable from one another by anything but sheer numerical difference, and linked or unlinked with one another by bonds void of distinguishing character, should be able to assure us that our ordinary assertions about complex, empirical objects *have* a determinate sense. Obviously they do not and cannot do this, and are the fruits of a craving for analytical ultimacy, and purely formal difference, which cannot rest till it has reduced every contentful element in the world to something quite empty and nugatory, to a formal utterance that says nothing at all. Wittgenstein will dwell greatly, in later writings, on the delusive philosophical craving for generality, but he did not, at the time of writing the *Tractatus*, see the craving for exhaustive analysis as similarly delusive. In his posthumously published writings there are, of course, abundant exposures of this delusion, but we shall have reason to argue that these only led Wittgenstein to exchange the delusion in question for several others.

V

In §2.1 a new conception is brought in, that of the *Bild*, the picture or image. This sort of image is of facts, *Tatsachen*, whether simple or complex, and it presents complex factual situations to us in logical space, i.e. the total setting of ultimate states of affairs or matters of fact (§2.11). This must mean that the picture is so organized out of elements that *it is possible* to correlate its elements, and its structure, with the ultimate structures of possible facts in the world, not that the precise manner of this correlation, the rules determining what elements are to be connected with what elements and in what ways, need be clear from the picture alone. The picture so conceived becomes, as it were, a model of reality, of the sum-total of facts and non-facts (§2.12). §§2.13–2.15 then try to illuminate, not with great success, the nature of the correlation that enables a picture to depict or represent certain complex situations, or to represent certain ultimate states of affairs which enter these as components. There must be distinguishable elements in the picture, each of which acts as deputy (*Vertreter*) for some object which enters into the articulated Fact which the picture represents (§2.131), while the picture is a picture because the manner (*Art und Weise*) in which its elements are combined represents that the corresponding things are combined in a like manner (§2.15). The picture is thus a fact just as much as the situation it represents – we must not think of the picture as a thing, but solely as involving a certain sort of combination among its elements – its manner of thus combining its elements is its structure, and this structure points to a possibly identical combinatorial structure among the things or Objects that its elements stand for. This possibility of representing a corresponding structure among correlated things is called by Wittgenstein the representational form (*Form der Abbildung*) of the picture §2.15–151). Being a possibility, such a representational form may exist even when things are *not* combined as the picture suggests.

How the structured picture represents the corresponding actual situation remains, however, deeply enigmatic, since an identity of structure among correlated sets of elements is only a necessary, and not a sufficient condition for representation. The seven last words have the structure of the days of the week, but neither of them can be said to represent the other. We need to be shown why and how the one structure is representative of the other, and how the elements of the one are to be correlated with those of the other. This obscurity is not cleared up by the enigmatic aphorisms §§2.1511–1515, whose metaphors almost savour of superstition. We are told that the picture reaches out to reality as a measuring ruler reaches out to what it measures. Rulers, however, in most people's experience, never reach out to anything: *we* reach out to things *with* them. We are also told that the picture's actual contacts with reality are, as in the case of a ruler, only with the end-points of what is represented. There is really only a correlation of picture-*elements* with fact-*elements*: it is this co-ordination of elements that makes one fact a picture of the other. (Strictly speaking, *either* can be regarded as picturing the other.) The co-ordinations of picture-elements with real elements are further said to be, as it were, the feelers (*Fühler*) of the picture-elements in virtue of which the picture has contact with reality (§2.1515). Most of us, however, have no experience of feelers emanating from a pictorial or verbal assertion which could in some manner bring it into touch with reality. It is *my* acts of meaning or reference, my significant intentions, that alone can provide anything like such feelers. What is needed here is arguably the recognition of mental intentions, specific or unspecific, in direction, which can be fulfilled in observational or introspective encounter, but which remain specific even in default of such fulfilment. Only orientations of mind, which can lend their orientation to lines of action or verbal reference, can throw light on, and give life to, the use of words and symbols, and in attributing such life to the use of symbols we are going beyond them to the acts, endowed with an essential 'ofness', which constitute conscious life. Wittgenstein is keen to demythologize intentionality by making it into a misunderstanding of linguistic reference: we imagine that the objects of our reference are in some ghostly manner present in the queer medium of our minds whereas their only genuine presence is in the uses of our words. Our response is that there is nothing mythic or ghostly in the intentional inexistence of specific objects in our mental intentions: we only need to talk of it unmisleadingly. So-called mental acts are merely the presence to ourselves of objects, their being 'there for us' in a variety of manners, which can often achieve a sort of definite sensuous presence in our understanding and use of words. If intentionality, like all our last concepts, is also conceptually teasing, how much more is Wittgenstein's talk of symbolic elements as capable of putting forth 'feelers' which will enable them to make contact with appropriate elements in reality?

The reason, further, why we do not need special instrumentalities to co-ordinate picture-structure with reality-structure is stated in §§2.16–161. The structure of picture-elements and the structure of the correlated fact are *identical*. The same structure which organizes the elements of our picture also organizes the elements of the fact that it represents, and so has no need to reach out to itself (§2.17). It is, however, only itself *qua* logical with which it is identical, and not itself *qua* spatial, or *qua* coloured, etc. We *can* have a spatial picture of a spatial situation (as in a map), or a coloured representation of a situation involving colours, etc. (§2.171), but such similarity in representative Form is not essential to representation: we may, for example, represent colour-relations by space-relations, as in the colour pyramid, or space-relations by time-relations, and vice versa. In all representation there must, however, be identity of logical structure, in which presumably the number of immediate or ultimate objects is relevant, and perhaps also the manner or manners of their compounding (which manner will only be colourlessly uniform in the case of ultimate objects). Wittgenstein says that any picture is also a logical picture (§2.182): it may import imperfectly analysed qualitative differences into elements or their modes of association, but it will also involve a certain multiplicity and uniform combinatorial capacity in its ultimate elements which will determine their logical pattern. (We cannot allow there to be unanalysably symmetrical, asymmetrical, transitive, etc. types of relational bonding in ultimate facts, without violating Wittgenstein's principle of their total mutual independence.)

§2.172 makes the further, all-important point that combinatory form cannot be represented: it can only be *displayed* in such form (*das Bild weist sie auf*). One cannot talk *about* combinations, which would isolate the unisolable: one can only exhibit them by combining. One might object that Wittgenstein himself is here talking about combinatory forms, but his answer would probably be that he is indeed talking impermissibly, but also helpfully: when a man perfectly understands the situation, he will drop such impermissible talk. The doctrine of display is further rendered difficult by the fact that pictures, in Wittgenstein's wide sense, need not have the same *overt* structure as what they represent, and will sometimes only reveal identity of structure when suitably *interpreted*. That the violent-non-violent crime-ratio is increasing in Massachusetts has, for example, a meant structure which certainly is not overt in its words. And, as Wittgenstein puts it in §§4.014–0141,

> A gramophone record, the musical idea, the written notes, and the sound waves, all stand to one another in the same internal relation of depicting that holds between language and the world. They are all constructed according to a common logical pattern. There is a general rule by which the musician can obtain the symphony from the score . . . And that rule is the law of projection which projects the symphony into the language of musical notation.

Plainly the correlations of picture-elements with fact-elements need not be overt, and the *identity* of their structures only obtains ideally: one has to use rules of interpretation in order to dig down to such structural identities. We shall not here venture into the problems connected with such rules, which are endlessly discussed in Wittgenstein's later writings. Suffice it to say at this point that such rules find a happier home in the realm of intentional acts of mind than in the realm of overt structure however manipulated. Plainly it is simply false in most cases to say that the structure of a sentence or a picture simply *is* the structure of the fact it represents. It is not at all clear, finally, why we should not on occasion *represent* a mode of combination whether by a word or symbolic gesture, rather than by actually showing forth the form of combination in some special case. For we can undoubtedly consider objects exclusively *as* combined in a certain manner, and speech will then enable us to highlight this aspect of a fact without considering anything else, and we do so by making use of abstract nouns like the words 'combination' and 'combinatorial capacity', that we have been using in the foregoing

scourse. Such a form of abstraction does not hypostatize these
mbinatory forms in the sense of treating them as one treats the
*ings* that they organize: it is treating them as being far more
portant and interesting than such things. Platonism can
rtainly be defended as teaching us that one talks more lucidly,
d more substantially, when one treats particular things only as
ses of meanings that are universal, rather than treating the
tter as merely serving to illuminate and describe what is
rticular. Wittgenstein is critical of the philosophical craving for
iversality, but it is arguable that his own craving for
rticularity was a philosophical one, and was therefore itself a
aving for a species of universality that can also at times be
aggerated and perverse.

§§2.21–3 brings in the correspondence theory of truth and
lsehood. What a picture presents is its Sense, i.e. the possibility
a corresponding Fact. This Sense can either agree with reality,
disagree with it: in the former case it is true, in the latter false.
uth and falsehood are therefore essentially extrinsic: a logical
cture or proposition represents a possibility that lies *outside* of
and, because it has this reference to what is thus outside, this
lf-transcendence, we may say, it can be true or false (§2.173).
picture cannot have *a priori* truth, be true because the
ssibility it represents *must* be the case. The appearance of *a
iori* truth in logic, etc. will be shown to be due to voidness of
e content, i.e. *a priori* 'truths' tell us nothing, but merely
ticulate conditions for the Sense of a picture. They have no
ternatives and exclude nothing, and hence also represent
thing that can be the case. These contentions will be critically
amined later on in this chapter. Wittgenstein further says that
is by comparing our logical pictures with reality (§2.223) that
are able to say whether they are true or false. This raises
fficulty when we consider that we are quite unacquainted with
e ultimate Objects and Facts which are, according to the
*actatus*, conditions for the Sense of all pictures and matters of
ct. Almost certainly, however, Wittgenstein is not querying our
owledge of ordinary, empirical matters of fact – my watch
ing on the table, etc. – which make up the world as we find it.
ough we do not, and cannot, know their correct, final analysis,
can and do in some manner reach out to this, stretch out
elers' towards it, anticipate a fulfilment that we cannot in this

case achieve. Our indefinitely general knowledge of complex *Sachlagen* and *Tatsachen*, matters of fact, e.g. that this book has more than 70,000 words, is in some manner an indirect knowledge of the validating relations of simples that ultimately underlie their sense. The same holds, with special strength, in regard to anything apparently qualitative, or qualitatively relational, in the apparent Sense of an element in a verbal picture, i.e. the differences of Sense among predicates and among relations that *seem* not further reducible, but that we hold must depend on ultimate compositional differences. In talking of things as red, or as larger than other things, we must in some manner be reaching out to combinatory differences among simples that are wholly beyond our imagination. The *Tractatus* therefore implies forms of unfulfillable transcendence of meanings, which it cannot further elucidate: it is not our business to help it to do so.

## VI

In §3 Wittgenstein introduces the not very illuminating conception of a *Gedanke* or thought. Such a thought, like the thoughts of Frege, would seem to be an ideal propositional content of some sort, some sort of a picture-fact, embodying what could be the case in its representative, or 'projective' relation to what actually *is* the case in the world. A thought is not a particular image or sort of image, e.g. an interior or private one, which a man uses in his assertions or entertainments of what may be the case: it *may* take the form of such an interior thought or picture in which Wittgenstein is prepared to believe at this stage, but i may equally be a spoken or written or printed sentence, or a diagram or some other similar sign. And, as in Frege, there is no difficulty in conceiving that the same thought should be entertained or asserted by many speakers or thinkers, and should have as definite a relation to objective states of affairs, as do the pictures and the interpretative acts, whatever these may amount to, that pertain to the individual speaker or thinker. But for all these pictures and acts, whether shared or unshared, to count as cases of the same thought, they must all involve element correlated one for one, with the elements of the situation thought of, and a form which is the same, or counts as the same, as the form of the factual situation. Thoughts are therefore merely the types, of which sets of pictures in projective use are the tokens or instances, and will be true or false according as their instances are one or the other. The totality of true thoughts can therefore be said to be a picture of the world (§3.01).

§§3.02–0321 add the new point that there can be no illogical thoughts. If we combine elements in a thought in a manner in which the corresponding objects *cannot* be combined, we shall not be intending anything in logical space, any genuine possibility of states of affairs that might or that might not exist. The difficulty of these contentions is that we shall later be allowed to construct self-contradictory statements which can in no case be true, but which are recognized none the less to be an essential part of our language (§4.4611). They may be without sense (*sinnlos*) but they are not nonsensical (*unsinnig*). They are, in fact, the contradictories of the logical principles which are always true, and to deprive them of sense is likewise to deprive logical principles of sense and dignity. We may here simply regret that Wittgenstein ever identified the logically impossible with the senseless. He would have done better if, with Meinong and Husserl, he had chosen to say the references to the round square and other self-contradictory objects are perfectly significant, since nothing is clearer than the notion of the combination of some property with the lack of some property. It is only in the limiting case where the properties present or lacking are one and the same, that the reference fails to hit any target, is incapable of fulfilment, and it is better simply to say that we are in face of the impossible, than that we are not in the face of anything. It is further important to see that, while the avoidance of the senseless might be a virtue, the total avoidance of the impossible would not be such at all. The logically impossible is the reverse of the logically necessary and normative, and the latter can only redeem us from logical transgressions if we are able to commit them. It is in fact one of the most precious of human properties that we can reach out in talk and thought beyond the limits of all possible fulfilment, and that we can therefore, in full lucidity, see and feel the propriety of avoiding such transgressions. We can perhaps here echo the *O felix culpa* of the Easter liturgy: logic certainly offers us a glorious redemption from the iniquity of realizing possibilities in speech and thought which are not possibilities for being or truth.

It is odd, further, that in §3.0321 Wittgenstein should suggest that the contravention of physical laws can be significantly symbolized, but not the contravention of geometrical laws, which are here strangely ranged beside the laws of logic. Would it not be better, in this connection, simply to recognize a whole family of senses of the necessary, the possible and the impossible, some applying more widely or narrowly than others – e.g. the formally possible is wider in application than the geometrically or chromatically possible – but all permitting significant contravention, which it is the function of normative principles of varying restrictiveness to exclude? §§3.04-05 likewise rule out the possibility of thoughts which have *a priori* truth, and which need not be compared with anything correspondent. But the necessities of logic are arguably in this position since we cannot, and need not, compare them with the infinity of alternative sets of ultimate facts to which they apply. And Wittgenstein's dogmas in regard to ultimate simples certainly savour of the *a priori*, as do the demands for a complete definiteness of sense on which they rest. If all modal concepts are systematically ambiguous, some of their Senses or uses being more restrictive than others, we arguably have many regional cases of the *a priori*, principles which map a given region of discourse or being, and without which we could not study it profitably at all. Wittgenstein in his writings on colour, from 1930 onwards, has certainly recognized a regional *a priori* in this field, and the way was accordingly opened for a great number of *a priori* disciplines of the same sort.


## VII


In §3.1 the verbally expressed thought or proposition (*Satz*) is introduced. This is not the same as the sentence, which Wittgenstein calls the propositional sign. A proposition is a sentence (here implicitly treated as a type rather than an instance) having certain possible projective relations to possibilities of fact, and considered *as* having such projective relations Wittgenstein's proposition is not accompanied by all the fully envisaged correlations which would tie its elements to ultimate objects, but it is essential to its being a proposition that we must view it as capable of being so tied, and so as having a definite sense, though we need not consider, and cannot know, that sense. The proposition is itself a fact, a combination of its elements, and it stands for some immensely complex range of alternative combinations among ultimate constituents (§§3.13–142).

§3.143 tells us that the articulation of the Proposition and the Propositional Sign into their elements may be obscured by its verbal expression: there may, for example, be no distinction between elements that stand for Objects, and elements that stand for Forms of combination among Objects. It would, §3.1431 asserts, be illuminating if for words one used tables, chairs, etc., and expressed their modes of combination by spatial arrangements. The enigmatic aphorism §3.1432 tells us that Propositions are not to be treated as units, but as articulate. 'aRb' means that *a* stands in a certain relationship to *b* only because the name 'a' stands in a relation to the name 'b', i.e. being separated by the sign 'R'. Here one articulate, symbolic Fact is projected on to another non-symbolic one. One cannot simply *name* a fact as one can name an Object.

§3.2 tells us that a thought can be so propositionally expressed that to every element in the propositional sign an ultimate object corresponds. In that case the elements of the propositional sign will be simple signs, and the proposition a fully analysed proposition (§3.201). This is plainly an imaginary or ideal situation. We can only postulate the existence of ultimate objects, and hence cannot correlate simple signs, one for one, with them. The imagined simple signs in such imagined propositions are, however, called 'names', though they are not names of anything *for us*. These names have ultimate objects as their referents: they do duty for (*vertreten*) such objects. It is the configuration of the ultimate names that must correspond, in its logical form, or be logically the same, as the configuration of ultimate objects. A proposition can employ names, and can represent configurations of objects, but it cannot say anything *about* such objects *qua* objects, only name them (§3.221). Obviously one can say nothing about something quite devoid of all intrinsic structure. The names *we* employ are, of course, not names in Wittgenstein's sense, but stand for complex objects, which are logical constructions out of ultimate simples. The propositions *we* utter are therefore, for us at least, of undetermined sense (§3.24): they cover countless alternative possibilities of ultimate states of affairs, without its being clear *which* of these, by their realization or non-realization, render them true or false. The propositions that even we utter must, however, *have* a determinate sense, even if we do not know this sense, and it is this requirement that makes the postulation of ultimate simple Signs a necessary one. A proposition would not be significant – and many of our propositions certainly *are* significant – if it did not in some manner have a complete analysis, even if we cannot formulate this (§3.25). To names of *our* kind, which are not simple in their reference, such definitions ideally correspond. These definitions will enable us to equate propositions using non-simple signs with propositions using only simple signs. These imaginary definitions will not, however, be very useful to us, as we have no use for such simple signs, but the assurance that we *could* use them to name simple objects if we knew any such, will perhaps give us logical and semantic comfort. And perhaps *our* definitions of complex meanings in terms of meanings less complex, does in some manner do duty for these ultimate, ideal definitions. We are in our definitions moving *in the direction* of an ultimate analysis, even if we cannot hope to get there. Russell was therefore correct in holding that Wittgenstein's *Tractatus* postulates an ideal, ultimate language, infinitely more analysed than our actual one, but he was wrong in failing to recognize that the postulation of this ultimate language was not in some sense the actual justifying presupposition of our speech as it actually exists. Ordinary speech is all right because it steadily moves towards the right goal, which it knows must exist, even if it never can reach it. Wittgenstein further stresses that Signs cannot be defined in isolation, but only in propositional contexts (§§3.262–3), in this respect agreeing with the 'context-principle' of Frege.

## VIII

In the paragraphs §§3.3–318 Wittgenstein introduces the notion of an 'expression', and of a propositional function (called by him a 'propositional variable'). An expression is any definite part of a significant proposition – it need not be a separable or an ultimate element – which can be highlighted by replacing everything else in the proposition by variables. Thus the expresson 'Socrates' is highlighted by constructing the propositional function '*F* Socrates' where *F* is a variable covering anything that could be said about Socrates, e.g. that he married Xanthippe, that some do not believe in his existence, etc. Similarly '*x* is between *y* and *z*' highlights 'between', '*x* loves all who love *x*' highlights a complex form of self-love, etc. The expression must always be treated as having a place in a possible proposition. If now *all* our variables are replaced by constant expressions, our expression becomes a proposition, e.g. Socrates loves all those who love Socrates, and if, on the other hand, all our constants give place to variables, our expression becomes an empty logical prototype or *Urbild*, e.g. *xRy*. Wittgenstein here makes the important point that provided we know which propositions are instances or values of our prototype, we need not know exactly what they mean (§3.317). We can live entirely on the symbolic or expressive level of language without worrying about the implications of what we say on the object-level. Obviously this is what we do in a great deal of our talk, but can do so with safety only when the correlations with factual elements are as determinate as they should be. This Wittgenstein proceeds to show is not always the case.

§§3.32–322 tell us that a visible sign is not necessarily the same symbol if it has a different mode of signification (*Bezeichnungsweise*). The word 'is' has several modes of signification, and words like 'exists' and 'identical' have modes of signification quite different from words that superficially resemble them in their use (§3.323 – these examples are inspired by Russell, who said that the ambiguity of the verb *to be* was a disgrace to the human race). To eliminate the confusions due to such differing modes of signification, we must not use the same sign, nor a similarly functioning sign, where the mode of signification is different (§3.325); Russell and Frege, in their symbolism, have gone some distance in this direction. Wittgenstein stresses that the mode of signification comes out in the use (*Verwendung*) of the sign. If, for example, a sort of inference or assertion is allowed in the case of one sign, and not in the case of a superficially similar sign, their modes of signification must differ. Thus 'Some tame lions roar' makes sense, but not 'Some tame lions exist', and 'roar' and 'exist' therefore signify differently.

§§3.326–3.327 make the point that the mode of signification of a sign shows itself in its logico-syntactical use, the combinations it admits, the transformations and translations that it permits, not in its surface form. This logico-syntactical use requires no bringing in of semantics: we can operate purely on the expressional level (§3.33). Signs that have no use, that obey no clear syntactical rules, are syntactically and semantically dispensable: this, says Wittgenstein, is the true meaning of Ockham's Razor (§3.328). On Wittgenstein's view, it is automatically senseless to try to identify a concept or a propositional function with one of its own values: it presupposes these values, and therefore has a different logical form from them. The $F$ that ranges over properties which might pertain to itself, $F$, cannot be the same property, no matter whether we use the same symbol to express both: the modes of signification must differ in the two cases. Hence the Russellian theory of types is unmeaning: expressions whose mode of signification is different simply cannot be the same expression (§§3.331–3.333). Wittgenstein objects to the semantic element in Russell's theory: his talk of properties of differing type as different sorts of logical entity. And he is opposed to talk *about* logical forms except in a carefully guarded manner, which admits that there is something spurious about it. Forms show themselves, and cannot properly be referred to. But it has been pointed out that Wittgenstein has, in fact, adopted his own version of the theory of types in his rejection of all self-reference, which is more severe than Russell's version.

§§3.334–3.3421 stress the importance of digging down to the *essential* features of propositional expressions, which are the same for all propositions having the same sense, and ignoring accidental features, which only *seem* to make a difference. (Some *seemingly* superficial features may, however, involve important syntactical differences.) Translations and definitions bring out the essential as opposed to the accidental features of language (§§3.343–3.3442). §§3.4–3.42 stress the relations of propositions to logical space: each proposition determines a place in logical space. Wittgenstein says *one* place, but only an elementary proposition can do this. A non-elementary proposition rather determines a whole region of alternatives in logical space. The whole of logical space is, however, contextually implied by every proposition, and this includes what lies outside of what it directly determines.

§4.002 dwells on the remarkable fact that our ability to construct languages, consisting of significant propositions and expressions, does not depend on any knowledge as to *how* we thereby manage to refer to ultimate states of affairs, and their constituent objects. The form of our spoken diction is, in fact, such as to conceal, rather than reveal, the ultimate facts which give it reference and render it true or false, and it is owing to this unrevealingness of language that much of the nonsense that occurs in philosophy becomes possible (§4.003). The true form of a language reveals itself in the rules which enable us to translate one way of saying things into another. A comparison may be made with the very different sound of a symphony that we hear, and the same symphony represented in a musical score (§4.0141). The two have, despite appearances, precisely the same logical structure: they can be projected into one another, and both can ultimately be projected into the same region of logical space. The projective rules of logic have the further remarkable consequence that we can always frame *totally new* propositions, and understand their sense (not, of course, know their truth). If we dispose of suitable names and propositional forms, we do not need to have encountered a certain sort of factual situation in order to have a thought of what it is like (§§4.02, 4.027). We can put signs together experimentally and so manage to envisage possible facts that we have never experienced or imagined (§4.031) and which perhaps are realized nowhere.

But Wittgenstein returns to his insistence that the formal aspects of a Proposition – the multiplicity of things it concerns and its mode of signifying them – is not, properly speaking, anything that can be represented symbolically. It has to *be* in the symbols as in the symbolized, and cannot properly be represented by special logical symbols such as the so-called logical constants 'not', 'or', 'and', 'all', etc. and also by the numerals, unless we are prepared to see these symbols as a mere shorthand for a spelling-out that shows, rather than merely points to, a logical structure. On such an approach, a double negation and a simple affirmation would be alternative formulations for the same

Proposition (§§4.061–4.0621). Certain ways of representing fact are, however, more perspicuous than others: the mathematical multiplicity of propositional elements may come close to matching the mathematical multiplicity of objective elements, and may leave few aspects of their mutual tie-up obscure. Thus the functional notation $(x).fx. \vee m.n$ makes plain exactly what element is being universally quantified and that the quantification covers all that occurs after the first dot, and that the *same* element is being universally quantified wherever '$x$' occurs (§4.0411). The Kantian explanation of space as reflecting a form of our intuition is held to be non-perspicuous, because there is no mathematical parallelism between a form of intuition and the three-dimensional structure of space (§4.0412). But if Kant is unperspicuous, Wittgenstein himself is as bad. His parallelism between linguistic structures and the ultimate structures of objects is a sheer matter of postulation: there is nothing in speech which perspicuously reflects the latter, and it is as well that it does not, since a language as complex as the ontology of the *Tractatus* would not be understandable at all. The remaining propositions in §§4.061–4.0641 make subsidiary additions or repeats of such.

## IX

In §4.111 Wittgenstein identifies natural science with the totality of the true propositions which will correspond to genuine States of Affairs. (This restriction to true propositions is probably an oversight, for false propositions, e.g. those about phlogiston, have obviously had a place in science. What Wittgenstein wishes to exclude from science are not plain errors, but pseudo-factual assertions to which no genuine, ultimate states of affairs can correspond.) Philosophy is then held (§§4.111–4.112) not to be a natural science, since it does not aim at establishing factual truths, but a clarification of thoughts and assertions. Only the projective, fact-oriented aspects of our thought are then philosophically relevant: the personal, experiential aspects – what images we form, what feelings we have – are interesting only to the factual science of psychology (§4.1121). Wittgenstein does not here raise the question of a philosophical psychology which will examine the basic categories involved in talking about acts and states of mind, their various dimensions and their relations to neurology and behaviour: it may be taken that his work in the *Philosophical Investigations* does just this. It may here be regretted that Wittgenstein was so inadequately acquainted with the intentional psychognosy of Brentano, and the phenomenology of Husserl. He uses the term 'phenomenology' a few times in his later writings, but for him it was plainly restricted to the description of sensations, images and elementary feelings, the psychological elements of the Wundtian tradition, which must have been influential in the Cambridge laboratory where Wittgenstein made his studies of rhythm. Plainly Wittgenstein at this time conceived of human subjectivity as some sort of obscure interior language where sensation and images (many verbal) and elementary feelings played the part of symbols. A psychology devoted to the study of an interior symbolism could obviously have no close relation to the major perplexities of philosophy. Wittgenstein goes on to say that evolutionary and other theories of the origins of propositional thought are quite irrelevant to the major perplexities of philosophy (§4.1122).

In philosophy a great deal of time must be devoted to eliminating abuses of symbolism, abuses in which we construct what seem to be significant assertions, which can be shown to be not really such. The scientific sphere must be clearly demarcated by philosophy, and distinguished from its own sphere of clarification (§4.113–4.116). The clarifications of philosophy must employ methods which show up the genuine logical forms of propositions, rather than talking about them, and trying to represent them (§§4.12–4.1212). Once we have arrived at a symbolism which shows forth logical form perspicuously, empty and confused attempts at philosophical assertion will cease to be possible (§4.1213). All this is Utopian talk, and how unhelpful it is comes out in the subsequent history of Logical Positivism.

In §§4.122–4.128 Wittgenstein none the less accords legitimacy, 'in a certain sense', to talk *about* the formal features of objects and facts, which can, in strictness, only be *shown* in our speech, not talked about in it. That a formal property or relation (e.g. predication) obtains, should show itself in the working of our symbolism, since it is not a contingent matter that can be represented, but, provided this is recognized, there is no viciousness in talking of formal properties and relations (§§4.122–4.125). The question debated by Bradley, Moore, etc., as to whether all relations are internal or external, resolves itself when one distinguishes between the actual combinations of objects, which are always contingent and external, and the relations of combinatory forms to one another, which are all intrinsic and internal (§4.1251). In §4.1252 Wittgenstein then gives a salient example of an internal logical structure, that of objects connected by *some* power of a relation $R$, i.e. being either $R$ to something, or $R$ to something which is $R$ to something, or $R$ to something which is $R$ to something which is $R$ to something, and so on. The series of integral cardinals is an example of this sort of structure (§4.1452). Obviously the regional logics of colours, pitches, etc., which Wittgenstein no longer tries to reduce to general logic after 1930, will exhibit the same sorts of internal relationships as we find in the general logico-mathematical sphere.

From formal properties and relationships, Wittgenstein passes to the cognate topic of formal concepts: every type of variable which can occur in a propositional function signifies such a formal concept (§4.1271). To object-variables corresponds the formal concept of 'object', to function-variables the formal concepts of a 'property' and a 'relationship', etc. These formal concepts are in a sense pseudo-concepts: they do not correspond to genuine types of entity. Only in propositional or factual structures can they show themselves: we cannot ask if they exist (§§4.1272–4.128). But, as we have observed, Wittgenstein has not shown why we should not reform our speech to fit the great philosophical inversion of Platonism, and treat universal forms as more fundamental than the instances that participate in them. The changed notation which is recommended by Platonism plainly has its merits.

§§4.2–4.2221 recapitulate points previously made. In the analysis of propositions one must ideally come upon elementary propositions consisting of ultimate names in immediate combinations, and corresponding to elementary states of affairs which consist of elementary objects. Non-elementary propositions, on the other hand, do not each correspond to a single ultimate state of affairs, but to vast ranges of alternative possibilities of the existence or non-existence of such ultimate states of affairs. There are vast ranges of such possible existences or non-existences which will make a non-elementary proposition true, and vast ranges that will make it false. In §4.2211 Wittgenstein says that is it not necessary for ultimate states of affairs, and their component objects, to be finite in number for these truth-falsehood relationships to be preserved. If a non-elementary proposition covers an infinite number of elementary possibilities, and these each concern an infinite number of elementary objects, this will make no difference to our power to cover such infinite ranges with our non-elementary references and assertions, which do not, in any case, achieve any full implementation of their sense. Wittgenstein here adopts the Cantorian-Russellian view that there is nothing mysterious and difficult about transfinite aggregates: they merely have a few unusual properties, such as that they can have proper parts which will be equal to themselves taken as wholes. The infinitism of the *Tractatus* here contrasts with the obstinate, Brouwerian finitism of Wittgenstein's later approaches in terms of language-games, and we shall argue that this infinitism represents a better rendering of the open 'and so on' of logic, mathematics and other basic forms of discourse than the finitistic restrictions of his later treatments. References to *all* the cases covered by an open 'and so on' are of such surpassing clarity, even to the quite young, as to make it arguable that Descartes was right in holding the finite only to be intelligible in the light of, and as a negation of, the infinite. Wittgenstein further, in §§4.242–3, stigmatizes symbols of identity as mere conveniences entitling us to perform symbolic substitutions. He will suggest later that, in an ideal form of notation, we should use only one name for one object, and so not require any special symbols of identity.

## X

In §4.26 Wittgenstein states the principle of extensionality or universal truth-functionality. If one formulates all elementary Propositions, and specifies which are true and which false, one can then completely determine the truth or falsity of all non-elementary assertions. There are no higher-order negations, alternations, implications, generalizations, etc., which can add anything to what has thus been specified. §4.27 tells us that if we are dealing with $n$ ultimate states of affairs, each of which can be realized or unrealized, there will be $2^n$ existence-non-existence possibilities for such ultimate states of affairs, and the same number of truth-falsehood possibilities of the elementary assertions which express these. If one now passes to consider the truth-possibilities of *non*-elementary propositions in relation to elementary ones, these will obviously amount to $2^{2^n}$, since each non-elementary proposition can be either true or false in the case of each truth-possibility of an elementary proposition. The number of higher-order assertions involving negation, disjunction, generalization, etc., has therefore a definite ratio to the number of elementary assertions (provided, however, that such higher-order assertions are treated as being the same when their ultimate truth-conditions are the same, e.g. not-not-not-$p$ and not-$p$ will count as the same). The sense of any propositional sign can then be stated by saying, in the case of all elementary truth-possibilities, when it will be true and when false (§§4.44–4.442) and it is further possible to arrange these determinations of truth-conditions in a regular pattern (e.g. $T,T–?$; $T,F–?$; $F,T–?$; $F,F–?$), where elementary truth-possibilities are to the left of the dash, and non-elementary truth-values to be filled in after the dash, where the question-mark is placed.

The principle of extensionality is open to grave objections which can here only be adumbrated. If one refuses to accept Wittgenstein's assumption that a certain body of ultimate simples is common to all possible worlds, then there might be worlds consisting of quite different ultimate objects in greater or less profusion, and hence involving quite different truth-possibilities. In such a world a disjunction or universalization might cover quite different elementary possibilities from those it covers in our world, and its sense would then, in Wittgensteinian terms, be quite different, and yet in view of our rejection of a single possible array of simples, be legitimately looked on as the same. That nothing can be both blue and green in a given part, to take a chromatic example, or that nothing can move more rapidly than light, to take a nomological example, are both propositions whose sense and truth might stay the same in worlds where there were other coloured objects, and other arrays of moving bodies. The sense of higher-order propositions is thus not determined by their lowest order applications, but is wholly autonomous, and might obtain in many different arrays of objects and facts.

§4.46 then bring in a new, all-important point: that there will be two cases of truth and falsehood among non-elementary propositions which do not correspond to any genuine range of elementary truth-possibilities: these are the case, on the one hand, of the Logical Principle or Tautology, which is true in virtue of its own higher-order form alone, and not in virtue of the realizations of the truth-falsehood possibilities of any elementary propositions that it covers. It is either raining or not raining, a case of the Law of Excluded Middle, is a tautology of this sort, for its disjunction of a proposition and its negation will, in virtue of its form, and the governing sense of disjunction, yield true applications whatever constant content we substitute for the variable in its general formula 'Either *p* or not-*p*.' In the same way we have falsehoods in non-elementary propositions which do not depend on the truth or falsity of any elementary propositions of which they constitute the coverage: the simplest case of this is such a self-contradictory proposition as 'It is raining and not raining' which is false whether either of its members is true or false. In these limiting cases of truth and falsehood, only the manner in which the higher-order proposition is constituted out of lower-order propositions decides its truth or its falsity, and Wittgenstein, interested above all in contingent factual truth, says that these limiting cases of truth and falsehood really say nothing. What is always the case, whatever may be or not be the case, and what never is the case in the same circumstances, alike provide no purchase on what is contentful and actual, which always involves an element of the surprising, either what falsifies an expectation that might have been fulfilled, or what verifies an expectation that could not be certain. It must be remembered, however, that these are differences in the manner of signification, which lend meaning and interest to combinations that invariably and necessarily obtain, or to combinations that never can do so. That not-not-*p* entails and is entailed by *p*, or that three times five entails and is entailed by five time three, both connect assertions which, though having like targets, attack them from different quarters, and guide us in much the same way as do contingent identifications. In the same way contradictions unite significant approaches which do not cancel each other out in a wholly *overt* manner – sometimes not clearly at all – and so

103

challenge us to conceive of their overt reconciliation, an endeavour that might lead to an illuminating outcome in some cases – there are many illuminating uses of the sentence 'it is and it isn't', as Moore often pointed out. The most interesting cases of the self-contradictory are those where the conflict, or the reconciliation of conflict, lies quite beneath the surface of what is overtly said, and from this point of view many of the 'contradictions' of such as Hegel can be read as valuable changes in aspect and reference, while many of the seeming consistencies of other philosophers, can be seen to involve the covert use of principles overtly rejected in their systems. Wittgenstein commits this sort of fault as often as do other major philosophers, and is best criticized in terms of it.

## XI

The first half of Section 5 of the *Tractatus* (i.e. up to §5.53) is devoted to interesting, controversial technicalities, on which we shall not comment in much detail. §5.101 considers the numbers of non-elementary propositions that can be conceived as arising out of different numbers of elementary propositions. Thus out of the truth-falsehood possibilities of *two* elementary propositions there arise *sixteen* possibilities for non-elementary propositions. Some of these have received special symbolizations, e.g. $p$ v $q$, others have to be symbolized less simply. If a non-elementary proposition is true in *all* possible cases of the truth or falsehood of elementary propositions, it becomes a tautology or formal logical truth, whereas, if it is false in all such cases, it becomes a contradiction. If we have three elementary propositions, there are 256 possibilities for non-elementary propositions, based on the truth or falsehood of the elementary ones. But unless the number of elementary propositions is infinite, (the number of objects in them perhaps also being infinite) the total number of non-elementary propositions will always be finite.

In §5.11 Wittgenstein explains all cases of logical entailment by the circumstance that the sets of elementary possibilities covered by a set of entailing propositions are also covered by the sets of elementary possibilities covered by an entailed proposition, that the class of the former is included in the class of the latter. This means that there is no magical nexus between entailing premisses and their entailed consequences: the consequence is simply part of the Sense of the entailing premisses, though some notations may make this fact more perspicuous than others (§5.1311). Laws of inference, which tell us what conclusions we may draw from what premisses, are unnecessary: valid inferences will *show* themselves in the forms of the propositions concerned, (or would do so if we could complete a vast and perhaps infinite analysis). This leads Wittgenstein on to the Humean conclusion that there is no relation of logical inferrability in the case of causal connections, which does not, of course, mean that Wittgenstein rejects causal laws as part of the indefeasible pragmatics of human existence. §5.1362 adds the rider that, if causal relations were cases of logical entailment, we should be able to predict what people would do in advance. That we cannot do so merely shows that we do not here have a case of logical entailment, and this is all that is substantive in the belief in free-will. §5.1363 likewise rejects self-evidence as a criterion of necessary truth, since being the case is not part of the sense of being self-evident to someone.

In §§5.15–5.156 Wittgenstein attempts to work out an *a priori* theory of probability, based entirely on the ranges of elementary propositions covered by non-elementary propositions. The basic assumption of this theory is that all elementary propositions, being simple bondings of simples, are as likely to be false as true, and that, since all are totally independent of each other, the truth of any one of them gives a probability of 1/2 to that of any other. If ultimate matters of fact are as Wittgenstein describes them, there certainly is nothing to differentiate them from one another (except perhaps in the number of objects they unite), and Wittgenstein's ruling has an ontological as much as an epistemological foundation. If now we consider a proposition that is *not* elementary, its absolute probability will depend on the ratio of the elementary possibilities in which it will be true to the total range of elementary possibilities. The case, however, in which Wittgenstein is really interested is that of Keynesian relative probability, where we assess the probability of one non-elementary proposition relative to another or to a set of others, which are all assumed to be true. In such cases we have ontological as well as epistemological presumptions: we know that if there are $m$ elementary cases in which $p$ is true, and $n$ elementary cases in which $q$ as well as $p$ is true, then the probability given to $q$ by $p$ will be represented by the fraction $n/m$. The theory of probability here put forward would only be of use if we were acquainted with elementary states of affairs, and could thus formulate elementary propositions. It is, however, conceivable that Wittgenstein means us to use empirical frequencies as non-elementary *indices* of frequencies among elementary possibilities: we certainly proceed as if what happens often springs from more possible sources than what happens rarely. There can, of course, be no logical justification for inferences from empirical frequencies to ratios of ranges of ultimate possibilities, and Wittgenstein cannot have thought that there could be. But, here as elsewhere, he uses his ultimate objects and possibilities of fact as a sort of transcendent basis for our human procedures: we in some manner reach out to ultimates and are rewarded with good predictions. The theory of §§5.15–5.156 is too obscure to be elucidated: it is also too transcendently metaphysical to be philosophically important. It has, however, led to important work by Carnap and others.

## XII

In §§5.2–5.4 Wittgenstein brings in the notion of 'logical operations'. In talking of such, we conceive of non-elementary propositions as constructed by our *doing* something to other propositions, elementary and non-elementary. Thus we can negate an elementary proposition, negate that negation, and so on, negation being an operation that can be again and again performed on its own results. An operation is not quite the same thing as a function: a function has a definite argument, and cannot be applied to itself, whereas an operation is distinct from the proposition or other expression to which it applies, and can be re-applied over and over again to its applications. Wittgenstein devises a general notation for a number of successive applications of an operation to a variable (e.g. $0'0'a$), and also one for the general term of such a series of operations $(a,x,0'x)$. $x$ is here a variable covering *any* term arising out of the successive application of the operation $0$ to $a$, e.g. a negation of a negation of a negation of something. §5.3 now states that all propositions can be regarded as the results of truth-operations on elementary propositions (elementary propositions being the zero terms of such a series). §5.32 tells us that the truth-operations leading to a given non-elementary proposition from elementary ones, are necessarily finite in number: this is clear, since an infinite series of truth-operations has no last member.

In §§5.4–5.5 Wittgenstein gives a new set of reasons for denying that there are specific logical objects, or constant meanings or notions, the basic reason being that logical constants are interchangeable when the propositions in which they function are the same truth-function of elementary propositions (§5.41). Thus $\sim(p.q)$, $p \vee \sim q$, $p \supset \sim q$, $q \supset \sim p$, all say the same. The interdefinability of negation, disjunction, conjunction, implication, etc., shows they are not really distinct concepts, only different ways of pointing to the same ultimate facts. The fact that repeats of logical constants can cancel each other out, and that brackets can be used to show precisely what they apply to, also shows that they are only notational, not direct mirrors of objectivity (§5.461). Wittgenstein further points out that the number of distinct operations we countenance depends on our system of notation. A system which uses only negation and conjunction, or negation and disjunction, or joint negation, etc. can be equally effective (§§5.475–6). There are no pre-eminent numbers in logic (§4.453). Every propositional formulation may be said to contain all its possible reformulations as part of its Sense (§5.47). Another reason for rejecting logical constants as objectively significant is that the tautologies and contradictions in which they occur tell us nothing about the world, add nothing to our information regarding it (§5.43). Wittgenstein also stresses that once a logical system is on the right track, it can be left to look after itself (§5.475). It requires no additional principles not already implicit in it. If the system fails to work, we are either abusing it, or have given no Sense to certain of its symbols (§5.4733).

In §5.5 Wittgenstein decides to consider the operation of *joint negation of a whole set of propositions* as *the* operation by which all non-elementary propositions are successively generated. The operation is first symbolized as $(----T)(z \ldots)$, where T in the first bracket is the final T of a truth-table which obtains when all the propositions of the set are taken as false. The propositions themselves are symbolized by $\xi \ldots$, and may be finite or infinite in number. A more perspicuous notion is given in §5.502: $N(\xi)$. Wittgenstein tells us in §5.501 that the set of propositions jointly negated may be given in three ways: (a) by direct enumeration; (b) by specifying a propositional function of which the set are the values; (c) by specifying a set of operations by which all the propositions in question can be successively generated. The notation just introduced has the merit of combining three features: (1) negation, (2) conjunction, (3) generality. It has long been known that negation and conjunction suffice to generate all non-general propositions, and that general propositions may be regarded either as conjunctions or disjunctions of their whole range of cases. Wittgenstein has combined the notions of conjunction and negation in the notion of joint denial, and he introduces generality by making the conjunctions denied be of indefinite length and be referred to *via* a propositional function.

It is plain how the generation works in the simpler and more complex cases. If we have only one proposition $p$, $N(\xi \ldots)$ is simply its negation $Np$, '$p$ v $q$' is $N(Np, Nq)$, 'If $p$ then $q$' is $N(p.Nq)$. 'Everything is $F$' is $(x).N(NFx)$ while 'Something is $F$' is $N.(x).NFx$. Wittgenstein works his system by conceiving of all the values of a function $Fx$ or $NFx$; universal quantification simply denies all these values or cases, while existential quantification simply denies this comprehensive denial. In this way, all the higher functions and cases of quantification can be covered by a common formula of comprehensive joint denial. Wittgenstein points out that even when we are unable to replace such a comprehensive denial of all cases of propositional function by one that denies a complete enumeration of those cases, we can still refer indirectly to them all (§5.526). This explains how, without being acquainted with all the infinite possibilities of ultimate facts, we can still make a statement which is a truth-function of them all. Wittgenstein says we can describe the world *completely* by these means. This is obviously not the case: our description would have a different ultimate breakdown in another possible world, where we had different objects otherwise aligned But in *our* world, and with *our* alignments of ultimate objects such a description would have a complete enumerative breakdown, even if *we* cannot achieve this. Again we have Wittgenstein reaching out to a consummation that cannot be reached, but which none the less directs and guides his reaching out, a very Kantian situation. Wittgenstein's treatment of truth-functions and truth-operations is based on the work of H.M. Sheffer and J. Nicod, but he has effectively simplified and integrated this work.

In §§5.53–5.534 Wittgenstein proposes a reform of the current notation for identity. He points out that the notion is plainly redundant, and does not cover a genuine relation. For it is nonsense to say of *two* things that they are identical, whereas to say of one thing that it is identical with *itself*, presupposes the identity it is professing to define, i.e. everything is identical with what is identical with what etc. etc. It is already usual to express identity of object by identity of sign: Wittgenstein proposes that we should *refuse* to express identity of object where there is a difference of sign, e.g. $a = b$ (§5.53). He also proposes other conventions that will make plain that only one Object satisfies a certain function (§§5.532–5.5321). Obviously what Wittgenstein is proposing would be inconvenient, particularly in cases where we are not clear whether we are dealing with the same Object or not. He also rejects Russell's attempts to define identity in terms of an identity of indiscernibles, and holds that it is significant to make all the same predications of two different objects (§5.5302). But, whether convenient or not, Wittgenstein seems right in seeing something spurious in the logical concept of identity. (The Hegelian identity-in-difference is something different, and is not considered by Wittgenstein.)

§5.535 attempts similarly to dispense with Russell's Axiom of Infinity, that there is at least one existent class having an infinite membership. Wittgenstein says that this axiom tried to express what should simply be shown by having infinitely many names with distinct meanings. Unless one is satisfied with our actual decimal *rules* for constructing infinitely many cardinal numerals, this is not a practical proposal. Wittgenstein, in fact, agrees with Russell that whether certain propositions about an infinity of cases have a possible application or not depends on the finite or transfinite number of objects and elementary Names actually in the world. And, since for Wittgenstein meaning cannot go beyond the range of objects that there are, infinitist talk will be meaningless or self-contradictory in a finitist world. For us, however, the infinite is a notion of such perspicuity that a system of thought can be reckoned absurd that makes its entertainment contingent upon its having an actual case. And provided we did not try to count an infinite aggregate, but were able to *see* all the finite cardinals realized in the parts of some aggregate before us, and do so in the same sort of single glance in which we can see a five and a four included in an aggregate of nine, there would be no contradiction in our conceiving of an intuition of the infinite. Succession may be of the essence of the Wittgensteinian language-games, but it is not, arguably, of the essence of our conscious intelligence, which can conceive of extensions of consciousness which transcend its actual powers.

### XIII

In §§5.54–5.5422, Wittgenstein deals briefly, but importantly, with Propositions that seem to state relations of minds to Propositions, e.g. *A* believes that *p*, *A* doubts whether *p*, etc. These propositions do not seem to be truth-functions of their propositional objects, since one cannot determine what someone will believe or say or doubt by considering whether what is to be believed or said or doubted is true or false. A given man may believe or say or doubt what is false as readily as what is true, and a given man may fail to believe what is true as readily as what is false. Wittgenstein attempts to deal with these intentional situations by suggesting that we do not have in them a relation between a unitary subject and a propositional complex, but rather a relation between a symbolic fact having a certain logical structure, and a non-symbolic fact having the like structure. Whether the symbols which enter into such a symbolic fact are overtly spoken or written or printed, or are private, personal symbols of some sort, e.g. particular images, is quite unimportant. Wittgenstein further thinks that the necessity of having a complex, articulated set of symbols to mediate a reference to a correspondingly structured possibility of fact, is sufficient to demolish belief in the absolutely unitary soul or subject, which is made the centre of mental life in a superficial psychology. A soul or subject could not, if absolutely unitary, have the internal structure which would render it capable of representing the articulated forms of facts, and, if it had such a structure, it would no longer be absolutely unitary (§5.542). Wittgenstein further objects to the Russellian notion of the subject or mind as uniting a number of terms with one another and with itself by the polyadic relation of believing, or by some other mental relation, e.g. believing in cohabitation as obtaining between Desdemona and Cassio, in which case there is only a belief which connects Desdemona, Cassio and cohabitation, and not also a dyadic relation of cohabitation between the guilty pair, which would make the belief true. He objected further that making the mind able to cement anything believingly with anything else would make it possible to believe syntactical and semantic absurdities, e.g. believing a pen-holder of the virtue of chastity (§5.5422). It is, however, arguable that the bringing in of a Subject improves the intelligibility of Wittgenstein's theory of conscious reference. For, as we have seen, the whole notion of a symbolic complex as putting forth correlating 'feelers' to the objective items in some factual complex, solely in virtue of having the same syntactical form as that complex, is a piece of magical fantasy. The notion of reaching out, or putting forth 'feelers', with a projective relation to the elements of fact, has all the properties of the ordinary conception of mental reference or intentionality, and certainly involves a subjective focus. It is after all only *we* who can put propositions together and assert them. The asserting or entertaining person, and not merely the 'names', external or psychic, that he logically combines in one form or another is essential to the assertion and entertainment. The picking out of one factual possibility rather than another is also essentially the act of a person, a point which seems to be realized in §5.5423. And there seems to be a freedom on the part of the speaker to devise propositional forms that may or may not correspond to the form of any objective complex in the world, e.g. to conceive of a 27-termed relationship, which Wittgenstein simply rejects as legitimate (§§5.541–5.542). And if a person is really unable to believe a pen-holder of the virtue chastity, it must be because such a freedom would violate the very structure of intentionality, which can only fit predicates and relationships on to instances, and not fit instances predicatively on to predicates.

In §5.5563 Wittgenstein then makes the celebrated remark that all the propositions of ordinary language are, just as they are, perfectly in order, an assertion which is thought to contravert Russell's view that the language talked of in the *Tractatus* must be an ideal and not an actual language. But propositions about, for example, infinitely many objects certainly occur in ordinary language, and would not be in order, on Wittgenstein's view, if there were only a finite number of ultimate Objects and names in the world.

In §§5.6–5.641 Wittgenstein speaks strongly for Solipsism, while also saying that one cannot speak of it. He holds that I, the speaker – any speaker or just Wittgenstein? – am limited in my speech-references to Objects, Facts and Possibilities that I find or can find in *my* world. I cannot go beyond these, nor conceive of Objects, Facts and Possibilities in some other world, e.g. a world involving other Objects, or a world for someone else who is not myself. I move among my own intentional Objects and their intended relations, and this is the only world I can speak of, and speak of in the only language that I can understand (§5.62). But he then goes on to say in §§5.631–5.634 that there is no central co-ordinating I to be discovered and mentioned among the Objects, Facts and Possibilities that I encounter in my world: it is a metaphysical limit to the whole field of what I can discover and talk about. Wittgenstein also compares the I to an extensionless point which has the whole of discoverable, mentionable, mundane reality in face before it, so that the I, at first perhaps looked for in connection with the body, vanishes, and leaves only the world that is co-ordinated with it: strict solipsism therefore comes to coincide with absolute realism. Obviously, we may say, if there are no objects nor foreign subjects independent of my conscious approaches, reference to myself, except as having a curious bodily centrality, will lose meaning from lack of contrast. Unless I am one among others, even merely possible others, and some of those others sensitive and responsive to the things in a world common to them and myself, I am really nobody. But despite this fading out of the subject if it is made unique and solitary, §5.641 says that there really *is* a sense in which a metaphysical subject must be admitted to exist, not as a human being, or a human body, or a human soul, but only as an extremity, a limit, not a part of the world.

It may, however, be argued that the world in which I speak and function is only to that extent *my* world that I take positiv account of it, recognize facts concerning it, have various correct or mistaken pictures of it, and have in addition all those forms of interest and volitional engagement with it on which Wittgenstein lays such stress. He himself says in the *Notebooks* 74e: 'The world is given me, i.e. my will enters into the world completely from outside as into something that is already there' and in 89e he even says 'All experience is world, and does not need the Subject.' The world, therefore, that I find around me, and which is to that extent taken to be mine, is also taken to be *not* mine in so far as I take it to have been there before I entered into a nexus with it, and it is also a basic presumption of common thought and speech, infinitely stressed in Wittgenstein's later writings, that it is a world for other sensitive, responsive subjects as much as for myself, who can confirm and correct my impressions of it, and who are also parts of the world to the extent that this is mine, just as I too am a part of the world to the extent that it is theirs. There is, however, in Wittgenstein's introduction of the metaphysical subject in these crucial *Tractatus* passages, no hint of a plurality of such subjects, who would be in some manner the limiting presupposition of all mundane communication and linguistic interchange. It seems clear, therefore, that Wittgenstein in these passages is harking back to some construction and projection of the whole world on the part of a solitary, single subject, such as he might have received from a reading of Schopenhauer or perhaps even Kant. Certainly he is also talking in and about a language which is the only one that this single, solitary subject understands, and which is therefore a language private to himself, however much it may be spoken and responded to by the many other *fleshly* speakers and auditors that he finds in his world.

Obviously, however, we may say in criticism of these difficult positions a subjectivity which is significant must stand in necessary contrast to an objectivity which is in large measure independent of it, which could be given in subjective, empirical encounters but which is not necessarily so given, and which is, moreover, capable of being given to many subjects and not to one alone. And the subjects themselves must be capable of being found in their common world by one another, at least in some of their aspects, and whatever other aspects of them are not so found, must at least be constructible with some reliability from their found aspects. All this is quite independent of philosophica difficulties which may attend hypothetical constructions going beyond immediately found aspects: these unfound, constructec aspects are, however, as much parts of the world as it is for each of us, as are its immediately found aspects. Wittgenstein is no loth to work with the notion of 'hypotheses', as involvec throughout in our dealing with our world, hypotheses sometime: confirmed and sometimes falsified by more immediately founc aspects. It is plain, therefore, that an emptily limiting, all embracing, metaphysical subjectivity, as set forth in these crucia passages in the *Tractatus*, is as void of sense as Wittgenstein ir some of his statements implies that it is, for subjectivity can only be significant in relation to an objectivity which may or may no confirm and fulfil it, or in relation to other subjectivities which may or may not agree or disagree with it. And not only doe: subjectivity of any sort fall a casualty to a complete lack o contrast, but objectivity becomes a similar casualty. The world a: we find it ceases to be a world if it cannot be contrasted with th( world as it subjectively seems to be or is taken to be, and if i cannot be contrasted as it seems to be to others or is taken to b( by them. A language, therefore, which professes to refer t( objects and facts, and to be understood by subjects, must plainl' be open both to confirmation and to refutation by findings a different times and by different persons. A language, according ly, which professes to refer to objects and facts, and to b( understood by subjects, must plainly be open either to confirma tion or to refutation of its statements by findings which onl' follow later, or are made by other persons, and a would-b( language which tried to evade both of these conditions could no strictly count as a language at all.

One difficult question remains. Did Wittgenstein in his defenc( in the *Tractatus* of a single, ultimate, metaphysical subjectivity mean to speak paradigmatically for *everyone*, much as Descarte did in his formulation of the *Cogito*, or did he only mean to spea) for himself, whatever this last possibility may mean? On th( former interpretation, he was saying that *everyone* must remai) the centre of his own unique world of reference, and that othe persons can only figure in it in so far as *he* endows their bodie with projections of his own attitudes, much as he said we did i) his Notebook entries for 17.10 and 20.10 of 1916. Such a positio) would, however, involve a rising above the limits of his own found world, which he would not be able to take as meaningful. But the alternative is that he accepted his own subjectivity as being uniquely central for all objectivity, and for all projected subjectivity, and it is not absurd, in view of his own deeply egocentric temperament, to hold that this was actually the case. We are, of course, saying for him, in our own crude realistic diction, what, on either interpretation of his views, he could not have said for himself. But, on either interpretation, his solipsism involved a remarkable dissolution or mitigation of the many problems of transcendent reference. His world became straight-forwardly accessible throughout, with no parallax of conflicting appearances or personal viewpoints to be considered. To many philosophers such a dissolution would mean a welcome liberation from all the problems of consciousness and the 'mirror of knowledge', but to others it would represent only a shallowing, not a deepening, of true insight.

## XIV

In §6 Wittgenstein provides us with the general form of a truth-function: starting with the total set $p$ of elementary propositions, it is what we arrive at by making any arbitrary selection among such propositions, and subjecting all selected to a comprehensive negation. This leads on to Wittgenstein's account of the operations which generate the natural numbers, which are simply those connected with the series of *powers* of any logical operation. An operation performed on a certain starting-point, which counts as zero, is thus *one times* that operation, a like operation performed on the original operation is *two times* that operation, a like operation performed on such a double operation is *thrice* the original operation, and so on. The conception of number thus developed is ordinal rather than cardinal, and it has nothing to do with the notion of a class which Russell made so central (see §6.02). In §6.21 Wittgenstein apes *Principia Mathematica* in proving that twice-twiceness is four-timesness. Wittgenstein is here developing a higher generality than Russell's: he is making numbers emerge in any case where we repeatedly re-apply a function or relation, e.g. fatherhood, next but one, to its own cases, and not merely to the special case where we augment a set by adding a new member to it (§6.031).

In §§6.1–6.13 Wittgenstein puts together a number of note-worthy aphorisms on the nature of logical tautologies. All theories that take logical tautologies to be making significant assertions about the world are false, e.g. the proposition 'All propositions are either true or false', which only *appears* to be like the significant proposition 'All roses are either yellow or red' (§6.111, a remembrance of a famous statement of Russell's). He goes on to say that it is a peculiar mark of logical tautologies that their truth can be recognized from the symbol alone (§6.113), a statement which, while it is true for theorems of the propositional calculus, does not hold for general propositions, since we at least cannot establish their truth by considering all the elementary cases to which they apply. §6.1203 provides an intuitive method for establishing the tautological character of a proposition: most readers of the *Tractatus*, including this one, will have found it hard to understand. §6.122 makes the claim that mere inspection, granted a suitable notation, will establish the tautological character of a proposition: this claim is, however, empty in the case of general propositions. Wittgenstein points out that, even when a proposition has complete formal generality, it may yet not be tautological, and cites Russell's Axiom of Reducibility as a case in point, the axiom invented to circumvent complications caused by type-restrictions, that there must, for example, be some lowest-order property corresponding to the higher-order property of having some lowest-order property of, for example this book. As I myself have never fully grasped the full import of the Axiom of Reducibility, I shall not join the discussion. Wittgenstein goes on to deal with the use of *proofs* to establish logical theorems, and holds such proofs to be merely expedient facilitating the recognition of tautology. This procedure would not be necessary if we could recognize tautology in complicated cases as we do in simple ones: the mere 'self-evidence' of logical axiom or rule of inference is, however, only psychological (§6.1271). Mathematics is then said to be as tautological as logic except that it expresses itself in equations instead of in tautological propositions (§6.22). These views of logical and mathematical proof were of course modified in the language-game era which opened for Wittgenstein in the 1930s.

In §§6.3–6.3751 Wittgenstein expounds a theory of inductive generalization. He refuses altogether to regard it as an *a priori* logical truth that every happening has a cause from which it follows according to a law. Such a proposition, if true, could only be true in virtue of the ultimate matters of fact in the world, and could not be logically necessary (§6.31). What corresponds to induction is not an *a priori* logical truth but a *procedure*, what will afterwards be called a language-game: we accept as true the simplest law that can be reconciled with all our experience (§6.363). There is no logical justification for such a procedure, no logical ground for believing that the simplest continuation of an experience will in fact happen (§6.3631). The procedure has only a psychological, not a logical foundation: it is how we actually think, and how psychologically we cannot but think. We cannot describe to ourselves what it would mean for the principle of causality not to hold (§6.362). That is, our whole attempt to forecast the unknown would be disorganized, and there would be no way to replace it. (Why not by arbitrary guessing or clairvoyant intimation, alternatives examined, and rationally rejected by Reichenbach?) We entertain general laws as hypotheses, and go on doing so as long as the facts of experience do not refute them. Wittgenstein emphasizes that there are countless such hypotheses, among which we merely select the simplest. Thus the facts described by Newtonian physics could be described, as they were in antiquity, by laws of circular motion, the need for a perpetual reinforcement if motion is not to cease, etc., and a complicated theory of celestial motions was thus devised for which Newton substituted a simpler one. Wittgenstein uses the analogy of a diagrammatic mesh (§§6.341–2) to explain how one way of mapping the facts may be simpler than another, but he altogether rejects the view that simpler laws of nature better *explain* the phenomena they cover (§§6.371–2). This rejection probably rests on Wittgenstein's physicist-engineer's desire for nothing less than an explanatory *mechanism*. A law is not a structured machine which can force an outcome. Obviously also to bring in issues of simplicity is to bring in issues of intelligibility, which is only a *value*, and values have obviously no place in a physicist-engineer's factual world. He says, however, that it *is* a fact about the world that it can be successfully mapped in Newtonian and other simple terms. Wittgenstein also makes some interesting remarks about Time (§6.3611), and about the asymmetry of Space, which are rather hard to interpret. §6.3737 deals with the problem of the incompatibility of colours. On the best interpretation, Wittgenstein is here suggesting that it is somehow possible so to analyse colour-propositions that it would be logically contradictory to attribute two different colours to the same location. It is not clear how he could think so, except in a naive physicists's manner and after 1930, with his paper on logical form, Wittgenstein opted for the position that propositions can exclude one another even in cases where they are not formally incompatible. There is, in short, a contentful logics, or a set of contentful logics, in addition to the one basic one that is purely formal.

## XV

In §6.1373 the world has been said to be independent of my will: I cannot make it be what I want by any sort of necessitation, and if it is, or is not, as I want it to be, I can have nothing logically to do with this. The values which guide my will are, accordingly, nothing that has any place in the world, but must lie wholly outside of what happens, and is the case (§6.41). They can transform the whole world with a touch of the good or of the bad, but must do this as it were from outside, and can make no difference to anything *in* the world, which remains merely factual. The good will chooses the good, and becomes blessed, but its blessedness is not any matter of fact in the world (§6.43). In some manner, also, the will which chooses the good takes a person out of time. The fact that he will have ceased to exist within a short time is irrelevant: his own demise is nothing that he will ever experience (§§6.431–6.4312). It is not a part of *his* world, which will vanish with him, and there is therefore an eternal blessedness outside of time gained by identifying our will with what is Absolutely Good. Presumably this means being wholly indifferent to whatever is the case, and so becoming invulnerable to it. This message seems also to be conveyed by the next aphorism (§6.432), that the world is indifferent to God, who does not reveal Himself in it. None the less, the next aphorism (§§6.4321, 6.44–5) seem to suggest that the world, while in n sense a creation of the Absolutely Good, is, however, capable of being used by the Absolutely Good as a test, or a task: it can be used for the purposes of the Absolutely Good, and for rising to a sense of the absolute invulnerability and independence of the latter. This sense of axiological invulnerability is described by Wittgenstein as the mystical feeling: it dismisses the world as a nothing which exists only to be thus dismissed. It absolutely does not matter, and exists only to make us by contrast aware of another Kingdom which *does* matter, and which is not of this world. There is then, Wittgenstein suggests, no real problem as to *why* the world of contingent fact exists, since the Why lies outside of the world, and has its own self-explanatory, self-justifying reality, which cannot be uttered or elucidated, except in mystical tautologies devoid of all factual content.

The final aphorisms of the *Tractatus* expose the senselessness of the whole previous discussion: the senselessness of the talk about ultimate facts, about the tautological character of logic, and now about mystical self-explanatoriness and invulnerability. The only significant talk left is the talk of natural science and ordinary life: in all other talk the bounds of sense are exceeded, or an attempt is made to exceed them. What can now be done is to preserve silence on all that is supremely important and spiritually precious, but which cannot be significantly uttered. The final illuminations of the *Tractatus* have considerable affinity with certain Buddhist utterances – the elimination of the ladder parallels the abandonment of the boat which has conveyed the pilgrim to the farther shore – but it has perhaps even more affinity with the doctrine of the Upanishads touching the Atman or Absolute Self, which can disassociate itself from everything in the world of finite, illusory being, and so enjoy complete inner blessedness and freedom. But while the Upanishadic mystic identifies his self with the self of all beings, there would appear to be no such embracing identification in the case of Wittgenstein. Other persons exist merely as structures in his world, and he himself, in so far as he can be significantly talked about, is merely one of these structures. The He or I for Whom all this is, and who both embraces, and yet also infinitely transcends all finite Ies and Is, remains unmentioned and unmentionable.

## XVI

We may wind up this chapter by a few final comments on Wittgenstein's *Tractatus*, and his whole earlier philosophy. The *Tractatus* may be seen as resting on a small number of basic insights which pervade its structure systematically, and which, by their profound mutual coherence, make it a metaphysical masterpiece, These insights are all, however, questionable, and must, on our view, all be ultimately rejected. They are, however, to a large extent complementary and interdependent, and the whole theory must accordingly collapse. We may set forth the axioms of the *Tractatus* in the following list, and comment on each briefly as we proceed.

(1)   All utterances concerning complex and many-sided empirical Objects, and their properties and relations, point ideally to utterances which permit of no analysis, and which accordingly concern objects devoid of parts or distinctions of aspect, and which are concatenated with one another in manners which are similarly unanalysable, and so wholly uniform. Presumably they are all wholly uniform, two-term relationships. Objection: no only are we unacquainted with such unanalysably simple objects but we also have the insight that they are not ontologically viable Whatever can be referred to, or can exist, must have qualitative contrasts with other objects of reference, and must have a internal structure of parts and aspects, and also must form part o a larger relational structure in which there are contrastingl different qualities and relations. It follows that no termination c analysis is conceivable or necessary for the sense of ou utterances. The Axiom of Ultimate Analysability is to b rejected.

(2)   All possibilities are limited to the elements of actu existence, and cannot go beyond these. It is significant to suppos that these elements might have been otherwise aligned an compounded, but not that any of them might not have existed, might have been augmented in number by others. This *limitatic to the actually existent* is to be rejected: it *is* significant to suppo that this thing that exists, or something that exists, might n have existed, or that other things which do not exist might ha existed, no matter how elementary any of them were. We can,

120

fact, have recourse to a Platonic scheme of diction, and say that certain universals might have had instances which they do not have, or not have had instances which they do have. Whether it is, or is not necessary that something or other should exist, or that there should be some single, unique existent, whose existence is absolutely necessary, and on which all non-necessary existences depend in one way or another for their existence, are, further, debatable questions, even if open to negative answers.

(3) All necessities are logical, formal necessities. This axiom is to be rejected. There are eidetic necessities which depend on the sense or content of certain universals (e.g. what is blue in a given place cannot be yellow in that place, what is purple is between red and blue in colour, what is higher in pitch than something else cannot also be lower in pitch than that thing, etc.). Wittgenstein's supposition that all such necessities can be so analysed as to reveal themselves as formal, logical necessities is unintelligible. There is a difference of inner quality among many properties and relations, which permits of no further analysis, and which is necessary to their being the properties and relations that they are, and which entails, further, the presence of relationships among them which cannot be varied. Wittgenstein admits all this in his later treatment of colours. In the same way interconnections among certain sorts of complex things, which impose simplicity and constancy upon them, are arguably necessary, not only for the intelligibility but also for the being of a world, and there could be no facts, elementary or non-elementary, without these. Possibly there are even peculiar laws or individuals. There are therefore other necessities than the purely formal or logical, whatever problems their presence may occasion.

(4) Axiom of Extensionality: the truth-value of all higher-order utterances is wholly determined by elementary facts about this world, and its existent objects, and has no sense which ranges beyond such facts and objects. This axiom is to be rejected. Since there is nothing necessary about many actual instantiations which obtain in this world, we can construct and understand propositions which might obtain in other possible worlds of existent objects. The sense of such propositions is not therefore determined by the things which exist in our world, and the universals instantiated in it. In general, the sense of higher-order

negations, disjunctions, implications and generalizations can remain constant while its existent implementation varies. An indeterministic theory regarding certain sectors of the world is, further, logically workable, e.g. concerning the future, and in this case higher-order utterances about what is thus indeterminate, e.g. that it will either be or not be the case, will be true, though this higher-order truth does not rest on the truth of more elementary propositions.

(5)   All logical necessities are tautological. Thus to say that, if $p$ and $q$ are both true, either not-$p$ or not-$q$ is not true, is a mere tautology which equates two utterances which have the same significant content. This axiom is to be rejected. Negations, conjunctions, disjunctions, hypotheticals, generalizations of a universal or existential sort, approach facts in the world in different ways, and can be held always to differ in sense. The logical truths which express their interchangeability, incompatibility, compatibility, etc., are significantly necessary even if they tell us nothing about the contingent structure of things. Logical necessity is perhaps a poor thing, but a case of significance and necessity none the less, since we can always violate it in thought.

(6)   Transcendental statements about logical forms, values, the world as a whole, ourselves as subjects, etc., are non-significant. Obviously they are significant, and essential in important forms of discourse, which are not concerned with the details of contingent fact and existence.

(7)   There is no intentionality, only isomorphism between symbolic complexes outward or interior, and facts in the world. Objection: our symbols have no 'feelers' which reach out to appropriate objects. We who use them must experience directions of awareness which bring appropriate things and connections before us. Intentional acts, however hard to analyse, and think of clearly, have to be acknowledged.

(8)   Solipsism: the world is *my* world and the language in which I speak of it is essentially *my* language. This solipsism is to be rejected. All reference to ourselves, whether ordinary or transcendental, implies a contrast with other selves and their conscious references, and the parallax which is involved in our inhabiting a common world, and seeing it perhaps differently. The world as I find it includes other persons, and the ways in which they find it, and, by contrast, the perhaps peculiar ways in

which I find it. Wittgenstein in his later teaching is resolutely intersubjective, but it is arguable that the old solipsism persists unexpressed in the later treatments.

# V

# THE *BLUE* AND *BROWN BOOKS*

In the present chapter we shall comment on the views o
language, mind and reality set forth in the two very importan
transitional works called respectively, from the colour of th
wrappers in which they were informally circulated, *The Blu
Book* and *The Brown Book*. These two books are really sets o
notes which Wittgenstein used for his classes in the early 1930s
after his return to Cambridge from Austria, and which h
distributed in the form of stencilled hand-outs. They were no
intended for publication, though much of their material wa
afterwards incorporated in the *Philosophical Investigations*. Bu
though Wittgenstein thought little of them, they are in man
ways fresher and more incisive, and at times more revealing, tha
the *Investigations*. The *Blue Book* further contains treatments o
solipsism and the problem of other minds which show how deepl
Wittgenstein continued to experience philosophical puzzlement i
that quarter, and also a view of philosophy as a quest for ne
fundamental notations which will bring out affinities an
analogies which are underemphasized in ordinary language
which underemphasis leads speakers to feel cramped in thei
ordinary speech, and to seek relief by revising such speec
fundamentally. The *Brown Book* likewise contains a much fulle
account of language-games than the *Investigations*, and a mor
revealing account of the ways in which Wittgenstein conceive
that his language-games were *taught*. All in all, both books ar

essential to the full understanding of his later views.

The main point which the *Blue Book* seeks to enforce is that the meanings of words and sentences are not transcendent objects to which our expressions correspond, nor are they to be understood in terms of remarkable occult activities taking place in the mysteriously conceived 'mind': they are more helpfully to be identified with the ways in which our words and expressions are *used*. This use is most clearly elucidated when we consider how it is actively taught or imparted to those who then are able to conform to such use, both in their speech and their responses to speech. When we see how people receive instruction in the use of words, and how they then proceed to build up an endlessly varied linguistic performance upon such instruction, a use which would be adjudged correct, or at least not incorrect, by others in the same speech-community, the temptation will vanish to connect the senses of words with something transcendentally objective or subjective: it will simply become something that we learn to *do*, and are publicly licensed to do in varying environmental, or personal, or interpersonal circumstances. It is, moreover, our use of a sign or expression *as* a sign or expression which makes it such, whether the sign be a set of marks written on paper, or a noise produced in the throat, or an 'inner sign' such as a mental picture, or a felt or unfelt muscular contraction, etc. Wittgenstein is not so absolute in his use-analysis of meaning in his later published works, but qualifies it in various ways, which will be later considered. Unknown to himself, his approach to meaning has many affinities with that of the 'existential psychology' of Titchener at Cornell in the early years of the century (see, for example, *Experimental Psychology of the Thought-processes*), who tried to banish meaning from the description of inner experiences. Meaning was not as such experienced, but showed itself in what people did with their outer or inner signs, and to introject meanings into the experiences themselves was to commit the 'stimulus error', the location of complex matters belonging to the environing world of things and persons into the inner life of the subject.

The *Blue Book* begins by commenting on the mental cramp produced by questions like 'What is meaning?' We do not investigate the various contexts in which the word 'meaning' is used, but try to conjure up a substance for a substantive, a single entity or thing which certainly cannot be readily indicated, and so passes as being wholly transcendental. This tendency to look for a substance for every substantive is said by Wittgenstein to be one of the great sources of philosophical bewilderment. We must elucidate 'meaning' by considering grammar, how the word can be combined with other expressions in sentences, and how its use in such sentences was imparted or taught. The teaching of a meaning is in some cases done by words, but Wittgenstein suggests that such explanation must ultimately depend on ostension: we must succeed in *showing* the person an actual thing, or situation, or matter of fact, which illustrates or embodies the meaning in question, of which we can say: 'This is a so-and-so' or 'This is such and such.' Wittgenstein makes the point that such ostensive teaching often fails of its purpose: the person instructed may think that the word 'pencil' means something long and yellow, not something that can write, etc.: he may interpret the act of ostension wrongly, not see it in the right light as illustrating what it is intended to illustrate. Wittgenstein then asks in what an interpretation or understanding of would-be imparted meaning can consist, and notes the temptation to conceive that it consists in the having of an interior image or images of some sort. He points out, however, that the understanding or misunderstanding of a meaning does not always involve having such an image, which need not in any case be interior or private, but could be an actual illustrative sample that one carried about with one. That we have correctly understood someone's imparted meaning is rather shown by what we *do*, e.g. pick out the right sort of object on several occasions, and not by anything interior, which may be quite absent, or be infinitely various on different occasions, and for different persons. Wittgenstein does not, however, consider that, while what it is to understand the meaning of an expression certainly covers a vast spectrum of cases, in some of which we merely apply that expression correctly without any salient experiences, that could be called a clear grasp of its sense, and certainly not with the use of any images that illustrate it, or of verbal images that symbolize it, there yet are cases in which there *are* such specific experiences which concentrate even a quite complex meaning as in a proverbial nutshell, and lead us to say that we fully know it, clearly grasp it, or enjoy it or even can savour it. The teaching of new meanings frequently involves the inducing of such specific experiences: a man's explanation, gestures, even simple use of an expression, leads us to see things in what seems the precise 'light' in which he is viewing them, and so to take over, temporarily or permanently, his use of that expression. It might be argued, therefore, that while saliently specific experiences of meaning do not normally accompany our use of expressions, they none the less occupy a paradigmatic place in our concepts of meaning and understanding, and quite properly so. They are paradigmatic for the understanding of meaning and understanding because in fact we do understand less clearly experienced, more unthinking cases of meaning and understanding, in terms of them, as more or less proceeding *as if* there were clearly experienced graspings of meaning behind them, and *as if* these determined what was actually done or said. They are further paradigmatic because they alone are truly explanatory of what is done or said: if a clear consciousness of meaning is a clear consciousness of what it is to be something of a certain sort, to be characterizable in a certain manner, etc., then it is clear why, granted the appropriate interests, it should lead us to apply expressions connected with such meanings to the sorts of things and situations that come into question. There is, we may note, an unavoidable circularity in explaining the use of words in words, but it is also a legitimate and illuminating circularity. Experiences of meaning and understanding may therefore play an important role in the meaningful use of expressions even if they are not always present when we use expressions meaningfully.

On p. 3 Wittgenstein comments on the general temptation to consider the use of expressions as having two sides, an inorganic side which consists in the handling of signs, and an inner, psychological side which consists in the understanding of those signs, the conferring of meaning upon them, the giving them a mysterious life which, as mere signs, they could not have. (Husserl in his *Logical Investigations* thus speaks of meaning-conferring, *bedeutungsverleihende*, mental acts, which enable the subject, *through* a sign, to intend or mean something objective.) Wittgenstein points out how mysterious this meaning-conferring activity is thought of as being: it can refer to something far away, or which has never existed at all. Certainly, we may admit, intentional references must seem magical, if we insist on picturing them as quasi-physical relationships among real entities, instead of, as in the analysis of Brentano, as relational properties which do not rest on genuine relations at all, since intentional references, unlike genuine relationships, are indifferent to the existence or non-existence of their targets, it being as possible to think of, or even perceive, a non-existent chair, while it is not possible to sit upon a non-existent chair. This difference in logical grammar, fully accepted in ordinary speech, will certainly generate a 'mystery' if forced into a language-form that does not fit it.

Rejecting the view, therefore, that there is a mind-given relatedness to objectivity, which is in no sense comparable to an ordinary relation among realities, Wittgenstein argues that the meaning-giving activity which imparts life to a sign is simply the way in which the sign is used (p. 4). It is not something that *accompanies* the occurrence of the sign in some occult sphere, but presumably consists in all the permissible combinations of the sign with other signs belonging to the same language, and the relation of such signs to actual and possible things and situations in the world, and to the responses of sign-using persons to such things and situations, and to one another, both in their sign-using and other capacities. Such an account of meaning need not, Wittgenstein suggests, be developed into a scientific theory which attempts to lay bare some hidden mechanism, whether mental or neural, which will explain why we use signs, as we do, but may simply remain a study of the actual use of signs, in which the use of the hand or larynx or other bodily organ is as important as the use of private imagery. Wittgenstein then goes on to consider the temptation to locate a mechanism of thought and meaning in the head or the brain. A meaning *could* be given to the location of certain interpretative activities in the brain if, for example, much more exact correlations between sensory and imaginal changes and neural excitations had been established. In default of these, the location in question has only a very indefinite sense, and the primary location of meaning is still in the things one does and says, which indicate how things have been understood. The location of acts of meaning in the brain illustrates, Wittgenstein says, a very common mistake, the use of expressions in new contexts, where they have as yet no definite use, under the impression that because they were significant in other contexts.

they will also be significant in this one. Wittgenstein compares such talk to that of water-diviners who say that they can feel water three feet under the ground. Such talk is completely senseless, unless, for example, they explain it to mean that, when they walk somewhere, the words 'three feet underground' come up in consciousness (p. 9). Only by fixing how an expression is to be used do we give it a meaning.

Wittgenstein ignores, in his account of the meaningful use of expressions, the fact that we can only specify this use or communicate it to others, by getting them to see situations from a particular angle or in a particular light, and from the same angle or in the same light as other users do, e.g. as an instrument to write with, as a case of unreasoning violence, as a potent source of danger, etc. The situations in regard to which it is correct to use certain expressions are not simple physical situations, but situations envisaged as being such and such and not as something else. It may, however, be argued that, whether or not we use words, to see things in a certain light is much the same as meaning it by way of words, the sort of consciousness which, whether expressed by words or not, is what could be expressed by appropriate locutions. Thus I can teach an infant the use of the past participle 'gone', by showing him things that are then concealed or made to disappear (Daddy here, Daddy *gone*, etc.). But we can only teach the appropriate locution if the pupil sees the situation in the right way, which arguably entails that he has in some sense to have an organized language of meanings written into the phenomena before him, if he is to succeed in attaching meanings to words. The belief in anything like a language before language is infinitely objectionable to Wittgenstein, but is arguably essential if there is to be ostensive teaching of meaning at all.

II

In pp. 10–20 Wittgenstein stresses the variety of procedures that might lead to an apparently simple judgement as to the distance, height, colour or other perceptual feature of some object, and the consequent difference in the meaning of the judgement as uttered by different people. Different people might, for example, have quite different techniques for estimating the height of a building, and one of these might simply be saying that it seems to be of such and such a height. It is quite delusive to posit a uniform inner process of judging or estimating, which takes place in all such cases, or a uniform process involving the use of images or pictures. Sometimes, in fact, we merely say the right thing ('That's yellow') without consciously following any rule or procedure: sometimes we do follow such a rule, and even formulate it verbally. Thus we can go on squaring a series of numbers, or finding rhymes to a series of words, without consciously following a rule or procedure or formulating it verbally, but sometimes we do consciously follow a rule, and perhaps formulate it verbally, or have before us, visually or in imagination, a chart or diagram or set of illustrative samples which makes the rule-following easier. In the case where we consciously follow a rule in what we do, we tend to use a language of *reasons* – we say we have a reason for our utterance or action – whereas, when we simply react appropriately, we rather say that our reaction was *caused* by the situation, or by our previous training.

Our whole interpretation of the use of signs is, however, warped, according to Wittgenstein, by a tendency, very strong among philosophers, which he calls the craving for generality. We like to think that in *all* cases where words and signs are used significantly, there must be one, uniform process which occurs unfailingly, and since there is no readily observable act which occurs in all such cases, we readily assume that there must be an unobservable, private act which prompts them all. When someone, meaning it, says that *p*, he must privately think or judge that *p*, whether in his 'mind' or his 'head', and it is this private act of thinking which gives sense to the saying or understanding of the utterance. Wittgenstein repudiates the view that there are any such uniform processes of interpretation or meaning, and that they are interior or private. He says that if we consider certain very simple uses of symbols, e.g. the use of cardinals in counting objects, we shall lose the temptation to think that elaborate, mysterious inner acts underlie them. One simply utters the expressions 1,2,3, etc. in series, as one runs through a stock of items, and then cites the last of them as the number of the items when this stock is exhausted, and does so without having accompanying images or formulated rules. By reducing all speech to such unmysterious rule-followings, we remove the temptation to introject correlated accompaniments into a mysterious inner thought-world. It is arguable, however, that the mystery is here all in Wittgenstein's imagination. To say that a man is nearly six feet tall, and to recognize that one is taking him to be such, is arguably not to pass into another mysterious dimension, but simply to bring out two inseparable sides of one situation, that something is the case in the world, and that it is also the case *for us*. It is irrelevant that this can be brought out in various ways and with differing emphases.

Wittgenstein says some other things about this baneful craving for generality, the typical Socratic disease, which invents one invariant inner grasping of a sense or meaning to underlie all, or nearly all, of the cases in which we use an expression. This craving makes us blind to the fact that our expressions do not each correspond to some single, perfectly uniform, common feature, present like an ingredient in all the cases to which the expression is applied, but that they rather cover a wide range of overlapping affinities, like the varied resemblances of nose, eye, gait, build, etc. which are characteristic of the members of a *family*, and which link them all into one group, without offering us anything that is uniformly present in them all. In failing to realize the loosely overlapping, family-resemblance sense of many of our common nouns, and our descriptive verbs and adjectives, philosophers are misled by the procedures of science, which always aim at discovering some invariant explanatory factor, e.g. gravitation, which lies at the root of a wide range of apparently disparate phenomena. True philosophy, Wittgenstein thinks, should rather try to describe all the different sorts of cases in which we might want to apply a word, and should not presume that they all involve some single, uniformly experienced sense, or act of thinking, or whatever. Intentional acts, inwardly experienced meanings, are accordingly a sort of science-fiction: they are confused and bad explanations of what we do or say. There is, in fact, no common element in all the cases in which a given expression or sign is used, and no uniformly present thought-content present in, or behind, them all.

Wittgenstein is, of course, right in bringing out the complex and shifting character of the meanings which inform almost all ordinarily used expressions, and their coverage of vague families or regions of cases, or stretches of difference, all bound together by varied, overlapping affinities, rather than by the presence of anything strictly uniform and exactly demarcated. In so arguing, however, he is not really denying that there are any exactly demarcated, strictly uniform points of likeness or affinity which link the cases we talk of with one another: he is rather saying that there are a *very great number* of these which underlie and overlap in the meaning and use of most of our expressions: he is not nullifying the universal meanings of traditional philosophy, but is rather multiplying and pulverizing them. Nor is he saying that, since philosophy is not science, it may not, for some of its purposes, legitimately aspire to a more precisely fixed, demarcated use of expressions, or a much more widely ranging, shifting one, than is common in ordinary discourse. Geometers certainly find it illuminating to use the words 'circle' and 'round' in a vastly more precise manner than we do in ordinary life, thereby creating ideal paradigms to which ordinary cases of circularity only approximate, and there is no reason why philosophers should not similarly paradigmatize the meaning of a term like 'belief', thereby achieving a better grasp of the whole range of cases of belief and judgement by seeing them all as approximating to a paradigm in some features, while falling short of it in others. Thus it is, for example, paradigmatically normal for people to *act* on their beliefs, but there remain some cases that we should not wish to exclude from belief, that are weak in this characteristic. In the same way philosophers sometimes like to follow the family-procedures of ordinary language so devoutly as to use certain common terms such as being, truth, object, negation, fact, etc. so widely and so variously that they not merely preside over a family, but rather over a race or a mob. Such a practice can certainly be legitimate in some cases, and is certainly not absent from the aphorisms of Wittgenstein.

It must further be emphasized that there is nothing in Wittgenstein's semantics of family-relations which implies that it is *we*, the users of language, who are the sole arbiters as to which cases will consort with which others, in a family-relation of universals. The overlapping affinities which are built into the meanings of many general terms are genuine affinities which are present in things as we find them, and which determine the range of application of our words: they are not created, only selected, by our use of words. Wittgenstein does not, for example, suggest that a word like 'belief' is arbitrarily tailored to suit us as jargon-loving precisians: it is adjusted to fit a genuinely distinct segment of human speech and behaviour, and of the world as given to men who speak and behave. It may in a manner be said to relieve *itself* from the general phenomenological background of human behaviour, and to call for a special locution to cope with it, and to communicate our responses to it. In the same way Wittgenstein a little later will say that philosophers verge on idealism or realism or solipsism because there are genuine analogies and disanalogies among the materials of discourse which ordinary speech tends to ignore, and which these eccentric forms of philosophical diction seek to emphasize. These analogies and disanalogies are not *put* into these materials by ourselves as speakers: they are already present in those materials, and are merely recognized by such new forms of diction. There are passages in Wittgenstein's later work, particularly on logic and mathematics, where the objectivity of the affinities which determine usage are underemphasized, and the suggestion seems to be made that we can shape our rules of diction by arbitrary personal decisions. It is important to be clear that this sort of anarchic linguistic libertarianism is not generally characteristic of the teaching of Wittgenstein, except in a few ill-considered suggestions made here and there.

## III

Wittgenstein on pp. 20–1 considers the vast variety of performances covered by such a phrase as 'expecting someone to come to one's rooms for tea'. One may give expression to one's expectation by fussing around with tea-things, putting out cigarettes, etc., looking at the clock, perhaps, but not necessarily, having feelings of tension, picturing the guest's arrival, etc. There is no single, entirely internal state called 'expectation' which is what we mean when we make use of the word, and it is not in some uniquely mysterious manner directed to a particular expected individual. Similarly with wishing and desiring: they sometimes involve specific feelings and sensations, sometimes particular mental images, sometimes little beyond a readiness to say 'I want *X* ', and sometimes leaving it quite unclear what we want, and whether we actually want anything definite. In the latter class of cases it is largely a matter of choice whether we say that we have a wish with an unknown object, or that we have a wish with no object at all. Wittgenstein comments on the use of the phrase 'unconscious thought', 'unconscious desires', etc. by certain psychologists: these phrases can be all right, provided we *give* them a definite sense, and do not surrender to vague pictures. Even an unconscious toothache can be given a sense if we want to give it one. In all cases where we bring in talk of a consciousness or knowledge of something or its negation, we must get clear as to how we establish the existence of the conscious or unconscious state in question, what are the *criteria* that establish its existence, and what the subordinate *symptoms* that merely make it likely that such a state exists. Wittgenstein says that there is not always a clear line to be drawn between criteria and symptoms. The effect of what he says is to suggest that giving meaning to expressions depends wholly on connecting them with such criteria and symptoms, and that these together are exhaustive of meaning. This is, of course, the verificationist theory of meaning adopted by the Logical Positivists, and read into many utterances of Wittgenstein. By universal consent this theory is now seen as one of the most deplorable errors in the history of philosophy, and Wittgenstein, in later times, explicitly repudiated it. It is deplorable, because, while certain forms of drooping behaviour are the best criteria *you* can have for establishing the fact that *I* feel sad, feeling sad yourself arguably affords the best illustration of what you *mean* when you attribute sadness to me. Wittgenstein, however, in the treatment of this issue, is highly ambiguous and ambidexterous, and will have to be considered by us again and again in many contexts. He never, we may dogmatically say, had the courage to rend in twain the umbilical cord which ties significant content, on the one hand, to the criteria which establish truth, on the other: they are arguably as absolutely distinct as they also have necessarily to work *in tandem*. To hold otherwise is certainly to go against what we ordinarily say, and how we ordinarily proceed, which is above all what Wittgenstein wishes us to respect.

Wittgenstein further points out that we are readily tempted to treat criteria and symptoms as more definite than they really are. We try to turn ordinary language into an exact calculus. He instances Augustine's worries regarding the measurement of time. How can time be measured? The past cannot be measured, having passed away, and the future cannot be measured, since it has not yet arrived, while the present cannot be measured since it has no duration at all. The difficulty, Wittgenstein says, arises because we think that length of time should be measured as length in space is measured, by applying a standard measure again and again to a restfully extended line or surface. Time, however, is measured by motions and positions of hands on clocks, by the states of hour-glasses, by the place of the sun, by our sensations of weariness, by our tendency to say 'That lasted about five minutes', etc. When all this is seen, puzzles regarding the measurement of time will disappear – as I, too, consistently thought when in 1936 I wrote an early Wittgensteinian article entitled 'Time: a Treatment of some Puzzles'.

Just as philosophers think that 'measurement' has a single uniform meaning, so they think the same in regard to 'knowledge', 'number', 'goodness', or any other of the rubrics central in philosophy. Instead of studying the varied uses of such terms, they look for one sense, generally interior and psychological, or otherwise transcending observation, to do duty for them all. Philosophy, as Wittgenstein understands it, must fight against the fascination of forms of expression, the suggestion that, because they are uniform, they must have one clear, definite use or sense. It is not even a legitimate ideal to strive towards absolutely fixed, clear linguistic uses except in special-purpose calculi: ordinary language, with its openness and its shifts, is all right as it is.

Wittgenstein, we may hold, is obviously right in pointing to the shifting, open-textured character of much meaning, but tends to exaggerate it. He complicates our use of 'expectation' with peripheral symptoms, e.g. what we may do when we expect someone, and ignores the fact that, over a fair length of time, a fairly definite state of affairs, in a fairly definite future modality, hovers before us intermittently, with variable fulfilment in imagery, whether verbal or non-verbal, and with variable bodily responses, which have an internally felt as well as a physically evident side, and with many lapses into the merely dispositional, which yet seem to carry, in some concentrated fashion, an unfulfilled sense of the confrontations and acts that would fulfil them. To say that over a certain period the impending arrival of someone for tea is more or less continuously *there* for an expectant person, and that its *presence* to consciousness, differently nuanced and emphasized from moment to moment, in some manner *colours* all his proceedings, is what we do tend to say when we try to describe our experience, and which we have no reason to try to replace by an account which atomizes such experience into a set of grossly palpable data, while ignoring the impalpable continuous medium in which they are bathed, and which carries them along. Accurate retrospective description of just past experiences is a difficult art, and requires a wide use of analogy. Some such analogies, however, recommend themselves readily to *all* who retrospect, and are thus inter-introspective rather than merely introspective. The use of such standard analogies, e.g. those that describe images, are, in Wittgenstein's sense, the *criteria* for the having of certain sorts of experiences, and it is nonsense to suggest that they should be described in some non-analogical manner, or in some quite differently, supposedly scientific style of diction. It is because Wittgenstein fails adequately to realize that the world as I find it points to highly specific manners of finding it on my side, that he tends to lose the light of conscious intentionality in the matters that it illuminates. Yet it can be studied for itself, and will reveal much when we do so.


IV


In pp. 30–40 of the *Blue Book* Wittgenstein considers, as a typical case of being misled by a form of expression, the philosophical puzzlement as to how it is possible to think of what is not the case. I can certainly think that King's College is on fire when it isn't, and this raises difficulty, since in other cases I can't do something to something which isn't there: I cannot, for example, shoot a non-existent man. The temptation then arises to hold that the object I am concerned with is other than the non-factual or non-existent object I seem to be concerned with, that I am really only thinking of the elements of this spurious fact, i.e. King's College, fire, etc., which certainly exist, though not in the combination in question, or that I am thinking of something quite different from the supposed actual situation, some sort of shadow or picture of a fact. This sort of solution does not, however, alleviate our puzzlement. For then we have to ask: what makes this shadow, this sense, this picture be one *of*, relevant to, what it is the shadow or sense or picture of? The answer to this question readily is: it is the mental *intention* of someone that makes it be a shadow, a sense, a picture of something else. What, however, is this intention? Wittgenstein does not believe in an interpretative act as something which underlies the use of an expression, and which gives it its objective direction. Sometimes we do translate expressions into other more immediately intelligible expressions, e.g. German expressions into English ones, a cipher into plain words, etc., but, when this process of interpretation ends, there is nothing beyond the expression that we finally use, and the use made of it in our language-game. The notion of a shadow, a sense behind the expression, arises because we are in quest of a final expression which is *self*-interpretative, so that nothing further can be asked for. Wittgenstein holds that we can never arrive at such a final, self-interpretative expression of possible fact, whether outside of us or within us: the sign-combinations we use, whether written on blackboards, or inscribed in our 'souls', always permit of further interpretation. Our explanatory words go as far in articulating our meanings as anything could go: nothing is gained by running to what is 'interior', which is merely another style of expression. When we treat meaning or thinking as a mental activity, we are merely using the word 'mental' to mystify, to indicate that we don't know *how* the trick is done. Wittgenstein ends this section (p. 39) by pointing to our erroneous belief that 'images' and experiences of all sorts, which are in a sense closely connected with one another, must be present in our mind at the same time. We tend to imagine them as if they were a string of pearls in a box, so that by pulling out one pearl I pull out the one following it. This, says Wittgenstein, is confusing a mental event with a hypothetical mechanism that would explain it. All the things that, as David Hume says, 'crowd in on us when one has a significant thought' are not, Wittgenstein holds, really there at all, but only emerge in subsequent performance, interior or exterior.

It may, however, be objected that Wittgenstein has simply

rejected, as due to a confusion, what is a categorial feature of conscious experience: that it always involves *in its actuality*, and not merely in disposition, what can only be unpacked in a variety of sense-encounters or images or acts of speech and behaviour. I orient myself to King's College as on fire without imagining all that this might involve, either for the building or for myself, but I also live through this orientation as having a perfectly specific objective direction whose fulfilment in acts, images and sense-confrontations is nothing less than astonishing, and which could not be other than it is. And actually *seeing* King's College on fire is not merely a dumb sense-confrontation, it is living through an experience which actually *fits* or *fulfils* my unfulfilled thought, and is, if anything deserves the description, only a fully realized form of the *same* thought. The mind, as Aristotle said (following Plato, according to Philoponus), is the place of forms, i.e. of pure meanings, not of dumb symbols of these, and nothing can be less mysterious than its harbouring them, and its ability to recognize them in their fulfilments. Only Wittgenstein's pictures of strings of pearls drawn out of boxes, and his physicists's recourse to 'mechanisms', creates a puzzle where none need be present: our whole interior life can be held to be nothing but an enjoyment of sense, whose intended objects, whether interior or exterior, only enter into this life in so far as they might instantiate or illustrate, or in some remote manner 'fit', or be 'covered' by such sense. It may further be objected that the temptation to turn remote or non-existent objects of reference into shadowy entities actually existing in a subjective or objective Neverland, is one that can be resisted, without denying that we cannot expunge remote or non-existent intentional objects from the characterization of mental attitudes that intend them: they are not constituent *parts* of those attitudes, nor perhaps of anything else whatever. There are other ways of playing a part in the world, than that of being a literal part of it.

Intentionality is, grammatically speaking, a relational property which does not involve a relation in the sense in which relations only subsist when their terms all actually exist. The grammatical ineptitude of the Greek Sophists and of Parmenides, who argued that thought or speech about what does not exist cannot be thought or speech about anything, may have rendered the point obscure, but there is no reason why we should not follow ordinary speech on the matter. But to follow ordinary speech means to recognize that intentional objects, even if remote or non-existent, must enter in the analytic characterization of mental attitudes and perhaps also of possibilities and impossibilities and absences, if such abstract entities are admitted, without thereby acquiring an unbracketed status anywhere. No ordinary speaker argues that because I believe in some mythic divinity, or even have a vision of him, that there must therefore in some sense *be* such a divinity. The possibility or impossibility or absence of some object is also infinitely far from entailing that there *is* such an object, except in some specially tailored, wholly *ad hoc* sense. It is simply part of the grammar of thought, and, dare we say it, of the world as given and present to thought, that its description involves a reference to many entities of which it cannot in any ordinary sense be correct to say that there *are* such entities.

## V

In the *Blue Book*, pp. 40–50, Wittgenstein considers the perplexities which arise in connection with such phrases as 'analysing an idea that we have in our mind', 'giving full expression to some idea we have in our mind', etc. He says that such phrases suggest that what we have in our mind is already expressed, but in some other interior or mind-language (mentalese) – actually a similar concept of thought as a universal interior language was held by Duns Scotus – and that all we have to do is to translate that thought into English, Danish, etc. Wittgenstein, however, says that we should avoid the temptation of conceiving that there *must* be an interior process of thinking, wishing, etc. independent of our verbal expression of such attitudes. We imagine that all that develops when we elaborate a thought verbally must have been there before, which is by no means the case. Plainly Wittgenstein is right to the extent that we often only have a certain thought as and while we are expressing it verbally, which does not, of course, mean that having the thought consists solely in the verbal expression, though it may at times amount to little more, being called a thought only in virtue of its affinity with a more fully developed paradigm. Wittgenstein asks us to think something without expressing it in any way, and presumes that we shall find it impossible to do this. We can say and mean the sentence 'It will probably rain tomorrow', and we can utter it more or less without meaning it, but we cannot, he thinks, cease to utter it (even in inner speech) and still mean it. Wittgenstein is not here rejecting the possibility that one might express one's meaning in an image-symbolism instead of a verbal one, or hang it on to what is before us in sense-perception: he is only saying that some sort of expression is necessary, and that the seriously meant expression only differs in context and consequences from the merely automatic one, and that verbal expression is as good a way of doing one's thinking as any other, better in fact than most others. He argues further that 'meaning' is one of those words which do not do one job, but countless jobs in our language. What they connote varies vastly from context to context.

The experiment appealed to by Wittgenstein is not, however, a good one. For when a thought has just been induced in me by words, it is not easy at once to disinvest it of words and entertain it wordlessly. On the other hand, without any effort on our part, the thought expressed by the words 'It will probably rain tomorrow' may linger on, in depressing wordlessness, *after* we have formulated it in words. And not only the thought, but even the sound of the words may linger on with it, quite wordlessly and soundlessly even to the inner ear, for it is not necessary that one should even imagine a sound in order to experience its inner after-effect. (If this were not the case, we could not apprehend a musical phrase without imagining all its tones cacophonously sounding together.) And countless thoughts occur, in which a complex meaning crosses the mind, sometimes top-heavily carried by an inadequate sensation or image, and only *afterwards* receives expression in a verbal protocol. Thus the seeing of the numeral 67 on a car's licence-plate may prompt the quite wordless thought that this is a prime number, a thought that I may then jestingly clothe in words for the benefit of a travelling-companion. There is indeed reason to hold that a preponderant amount of our thought is conducted in mentalese, i.e. the naked apprehension of meanings without relevant phantasmata, even of spoken or imaged words. Particularly in dreams, we move among situations where an incredible amount of meaning-content attaches precariously to mental images so exiguous that we find it hard to describe them: we encounter nameable persons harbouring definite attitudes towards ourselves to which we respond with highly complex attitudes of our own, such as, e.g. shame or horror, and at every turn we have in our experience a wealth of organized detail that it would take a very long report to formulate fully. We can also distinguish the cases in which we say what are rated as highly intelligent things without inwardly grasping their meaning, from the cases in which their point is inwardly clear to us. And a great deal of our thinking involves paradoxically a quite wordless use of words: though we do not even inwardly sound or utter the word 'innocent' when we look at a certain face, its semantic atmosphere may enter into the phenomenology of what we perceive as much as does the physiognomic character of the face, and this is why it comes so easy to describe the face as innocent. It was merely an accident of Aristotle's psyche that he required very definitely formed sensuous phantasmata to hang his thoughts upon, and perhaps this explains the whole character of his thinking, as it does that of many other great psychologists and philosophers.

Wittgenstein then goes on to consider all the problems that arise in connection with the term 'personal experience'. He says that when we start talking in terms of this expression, we seem to lose our grip on the world around us. Everything becomes foggy and transient, and is moreover seen as spread among different individuals. The solid world of everyday things seems to vanish in a mist of sensations, associational links, etc., much as it also seems to vanish when the physicists say it consists of electrons with big spaces between them. Wittgenstein says that these problems of 'inner experience' are really problems of language: we do not know where to classify certain personal experience reports in the ordered scheme of our utterances, we do not see where they fit in. When they are properly placed, like books in a well-classified library, all these problems will disappear. Wittgenstein in all this recognizes some of the problems and difficulties of inter-introspective diction: we have to learn to use expressions analogically – e.g. William James's 'slow dead heave of the will' – to convey the phenomenological character of certain inner states, and to secure the agreement of others that such analogical language fits in with what they too are inclined to say. Such agreements can be extraordinarily complete, quite on a level with the results of applying foot-rules in measurements. Above all, we have to avoid an inner-life language borrowed from physics, with . a stress on mechanisms and interacting elements, as in the mythology of the Wundtian psychological laboratory. Our inner life is best talked of in a manner which respects the articulated forms of our speech – predication, quantification, etc. – and does not seek elementary processes underlying these, and which also respects the analogies by means of which we describe our inner states to one another, and successfully communicate their character, with a readiness at times to modify and combine such analogies, or to venture on phrasing suggestive of interpenetration and iridescence and reversible perspective that would be inadmissible in the description of physical things. It is doubtful whether even the simple phenomena of binocular vision can be talked of in a language resembling that of physics, and Berkeley's *Theory of Vision* convincingly shows that it cannot, but not that visual depth-perception should be explained or analysed away. Similar objections apply to the Berkeleyan rejection of general ideas, where logic rather than physics is the culprit: the demands of his logic would imply that even a stomach-ache should have a definite size and shape. There is indeed a grammar of inner experience which licenses much that the language of logic and science would not tolerate, but with an analogical 'as if' or 'as it were' all becomes permissible: the densely packed emptiness of certain thoughts often resembles that used to describe certain mystical experiences. The language of the inner life of the mind is and ought to be *queer* from the standpoint of the physicist or the formal logician, but can, none the less, be given its proper place in the well-classified library of forms of speech, though it includes forms that a logical or scientific purist would not sanction. This is a well-known matter, and regretfully accepted by many who value their inner life and are not ashamed to talk of it, as Wittgenstein himself, despite some pronouncements, very often did.

Wittgenstein then goes on to discuss the temptation towards solipsism, which was, of course, his own, towards saying that only one's own personal experiences are real, and that one cannot even form a significant idea of anyone else's experiences, since there is no possibility of one's actually having them. We can know that *we* see, hear, feel pain, etc., but not that anyone else does. Other people can at best behave as if they were feeling the sort of pains, etc. that we feel, so that to say that they are in pain is to give such an expression either no sense at all, or a different sense from what it has in our own case. Wittgenstein here divagates on our tendency to picture inner experience as something gaseous and ethereal, quite different from anything solidly material or performed by what is solidly material. It seems nonsense to attribute such a gaseous side to a machine, and we are at times thrown into strange doubts as to whether such gaseous processes circulate in our friends and neighbours as they do in ourselves. If, however, we become fully clear as to how we actually talk about seeing, hearing, pain, etc., we shall lose the sense of mystery and perplexity which surrounds such talk, and shall drop the demand that we should be able to establish that someone else is feeling pain in precisely the same way as we establish it in our own case. We can, in fact, correctly say, since this is what we do, in fact, say, that pain, etc. have the same meaning in their case as in our own, since it is quite correct to associate the same words with somewhat different criteria in the two cases. Meaning, it would appear at this point, is not identical with any *one* of its criteria, nor yet with their totality, and is thus very much an all-job word. The demand that we should know of another's pain just as we know of our own is, moreover, an unfulfillable demand. We can certainly imagine that we might feel a pain, and yet locate it at a spot in someone else's body, but such an imagination, if fully realized, would still leave it *our* pain felt in *their* bodies, and not really be *their* pain at all.

Wittgenstein perceptively suggests that it is a grammatical abhorrence which makes it impossible for us to say, even in such imagined cases, that we are actually having or feeling someone else's pain, and that this grammatical abhorrence is delusively felt as an ontological barrier. We should like to be able to have or feel someone else's pain. But, if the barrier is merely grammatical, and not at all ontological, there are conceivable situations in which it might reasonably break down. For one good reason why we refuse to identify someone else's experiences, however well divined, or empathetically constructed by ourselves, with the actual experiences in question, is that such constructions often fail to be confirmed by other behavioural and divinatory tests: we find from what people do and say, or from other efforts at divination, that their inner state is not what we imagined it as being. If, however, there were privileged states in which such critical revisions were seldom needed, and confirmation rather than discrepancy were the order of the day, we might well say, not that we were imagining other people's states, but actually having them. The notion of the having of an experience can arguably be taken to involve no more than a certain profound togetherness of an experience with a whole system of experiences which are all together with one another. There would then be no reason why we should not concede the possibility of certain experiences which had as it were a double allegiance, and which were together with each member of two distinct systems of mutually together experiences, without bringing the *other* members of the two systems into togetherness with one another. All that would be necessary would be a refusal to make mental togetherness in all cases a transitive relation: there might then be experiences so similar in the two systems as to count as the very same, and yet not to unify the two systems into a single one. Perhaps certain cases of telepathic clairvoyance would fall into this cadre. If we then went further, and refused to make mental togetherness invariably symmetrical, we might have an experience which was together with another experience, while the second was not together with the first. All these possibilities might be held to have actual instances in the cases of co-consciousness and multiple personality written up long ago by Janet and Morton Prince. Leonie I, it would appear, could embrace in her consciousness all the doings of Leonie II, whereas Leonie II could not embrace in her consciousness the doings of Leonie I. Go a little further, and we readily arrive at the experience of a God, to whom all hearts are open and from whom no secrets are hid, who in a sense effectively *has* all the experiences of creatures, while supplementing them with many other higher, divine experiences that they do not in any manner share. The notion of a God's-eye view of the total cosmos or world is arguably a transcendental presupposition of our references to all the objects in that world: the world of science is the world as a God would see it. But the world as a God would see it must arguably also be the world as a God might feel himself into it, entering into all the experiences of his creatures, while also transcending them and subjecting them to his judgements. It is at all events clear that we so reconstruct the notation and grammar in which we speak of inner experiences as not to involve the least declension towards an unacceptable physicalism or behaviourism or solipsism, which all stem from a like state of conceptual or notational narrowness and rigour.

## VI

In pp. 50–60 of the *Blue Book* Wittgenstein continues his consideration of imagined cases in which one might say that one experienced pains in someone else's body: if, for example, the tactual, kinaesthetic and pain sensations usually characteristic of touching a decayed tooth and neighbouring parts of one's face, were correlated with the visual experiences of seeing one's hand touch the tooth and parts of the face of another person. We should then undoubtedly want to say that we were experiencing a toothache in someone else's tooth. But we should probably refuse to say that we were experiencing *his* toothache – I myself should *not* refuse – thus evincing an insuperable grammatical abhorrence to a departure from a linguistic rule – I myself would *not* experience this abhorrence – which forbids us to say that we are experiencing someone else's experience. Wittgenstein admits that we do, in fact, often do something which we call imagining how someone else feels, but denies that this counts as more than a picture, whose true sense only comes out when we bring in its 'mode of projection', consider how we decide whether it agrees with reality. (Again an identification of meaning with a mode of verification.) This decision is made by way of bodily behaviour, and we feel confusedly that there is something inadequate and defective in this, and that we can only *conjecture* that the man is feeling pain, and not know it. But, in saying this, we are, Wittgenstein says, misunderstanding our own language, and are imagining it as aiming at a goal which is not a part of such a language-use at all. We have, in fact, no use for the expression becoming another person, and feeling his pain as he does.' (Such an expression is, however, often used to describe acts of deep sympathy or the goal to which these aspire.) In all this, Wittgenstein says, we are treating a grammatical rule which forbids us to say something as if it stated an empirical fact, and that something hinders us from having the same experiences as another person. There is a similar grammatical rule which makes some people unwilling to speak of unconscious experiences, while others experience no such unwillingness. And it is a similar rule which makes us unwilling to attribute both red and green to the same location. In this case, however, the writer of the present study experiences no unwillingness to speak of and imagine a state in which personal separateness and non-togetherness will be in some manner and measure overcome. Discourse in the Life to Come may well take a form in which one may want to say that one is for a time actually *having* one's interlocutor's experiences, instead of merely imagining them, as one has to in this life. One hopes that, in such a state, it may be both grammatically and ontologically proper to transcend the earthly grammar of Wittgenstein.

Wittgenstein now makes the very important point (p. 58) that if we introduce a usage for an expression which differs in some sense from the ordinary, it does not follow that we must be *using* our expression in a different sense. For whether we are using an expression in the same or a different sense is itself a matter of linguistic usage. Wittgenstein elucidates this by considering the uses of a hammer which may, if we like, be rated as the same, but which can equally well be rated as different. Thus we might say we were using a hammer in a different way if we drove a nail into wood with it or drove a peg into a hole, or if we smashed something with it, or made it do duty as a paper-weight. There is, Wittgenstein suggests, no clear line to be drawn between using an expression in the *same* way or sense, and using it in a *different* way or sense. If we therefore elect to say that, though one set of test is used to determine when we are having toothache, and another set when we determine that someone else is having toothache, we can, if we like, treat these differences as irrelevant, and say that we are using our expression in the *same* way in the two cases. The same would apply if we elected to say, in certain contexts, that we could experience someone else's pain, or that red and green could both be present in the same place (e.g. in cases of iridescence). It is hard to see more than very clever sophistry in what Wittgenstein is here maintaining. For plainly, as we said in regard to the notion of 'family relation'

Wittgenstein does not maintain that there are no genuine likenesses or affinities among cases which are *not* fixed by our decision to say this or that, and that the closeness and remoteness of such affinities is not fixed by such decisions, but rather helps to fix them. He is being sophistical, therefore, in suggesting that, because it is legitimate in our speech to neglect minor differences among cases, and because there is no absolutely clear line to be drawn between a negligible and a non-negligible difference, that we therefore have *carte blanche*, whatever the differences among cases, to apply the same expressions to them, and to say that we are using these expressions in the same sense. Obviously, to exaggerate, one could, on this reckoning, say that difference simply was identity, and that men had given these two terms precisely the same sense. Because human conventions fix the sense of terms, it is not therefore proper to hold that human conventions can determine whether these senses, once fixed, are the same or different, and we may exaggerate a little further, and say that to maintain that they are, is not only false, but a little wicked. For it corrupts the honesty of human speech at its source, than which no form of pollution or adulteration could be more vicious. If we cannot, then, condemn Wittgenstein's contentions on logical grounds, we can do so on axiological ones. We may note, further, that Wittgenstein is here abandoning his own close connection of meaning with criteria. For, if we can have identity of meaning despite total difference of criteria, criteria must be irrelevant to meaning.

Wittgenstein now returns (p. 58) to the consideration of solipsism. He points out that the solipsist who insists that only his own experiences are real, cannot be answered in any common-sense way. We cannot, for example, retort: 'Why do you tell me that only you have real experiences if you think that I cannot understand you?' The perplexities of philosophy are not really perplexities about empirical matters or our responses to such: they are difficulties regarding *fundamental notations* (p. 59). Our ordinary language, which pervades the whole of our life, sometimes holds us rigidly in one position or posture, and so engenders a sort of notational cramp from which we experience a need to escape. Sometimes the need is for a notation which recognizes a *difference* more strongly – the difference, for example, between the *a priori* assertion that $2 + 2 = 4$, and the

147

*inductive* assertion that the sun will rise tomorrow: we then call the former knowledge, and the latter mere conjecture – and sometimes the need is for a notation that will recognize an *affinity* more strongly – all so-called knowledge is merely probable conjecture. The solipsist is not a merely eccentric speaker: he is a speaker who experiences a deep need: he wants to use language to bring out the very different way in which we are sure that *we* are having certain sorts of experience, from the way in which we establish that other people are having certain sorts of experience, and he does so by saying that only his own experiences are real. This use of 'reality' is highly misleading, for it suggests that we suppose that all others are merely pretending to have certain feelings and other experiences, while we alone genuinely have them. In reality we are merely substituting the use of the adjectives 'real' and 'unreal' for locutions involving the use of personal and possessive pronouns. Instead of saying 'I am having toothache' or 'He is having toothache' we elect to say 'Here is a case of real toothache' or 'There is a case of unreal toothache.' Nothing is really gained by such a notational substitution, since we shall still have to distinguish 'unreal' toothaches that are simulated, from those that are unfeigned. Wittgenstein compares such a notational change to one in which we have a special notation for mere objects of thought, and proceed to say 'I wish that this paper were pink', to indicate the unreal character of merely wished-for redness, instead of saying, as we ordinarily should, 'I wish that this paper were red.' Such a usage is 'all right', but it can obviously lead to grave misunderstanding if not fully explained and followed.

We may here acknowledge that Wittgenstein's explanation of philosophical controversies as being really the expression of a need for a new fundamental notation, which will bring out underemphasized analogies and differences, is very illuminating, and one of the most important in the history of philosophy. Very arguably, philosophical controversies do not, for the most part, involve genuine differences in regard to the actual things in the world, and the matters of fact which concern them, nor in regard to the persons in the world, and what they can, in an ordinary sense, know, understand and experience, but rather differences in regard to certain very pervasive conceptual slants in the light of which we view them and speak of them all. These conceptual slants are, strangely enough, the seat of many conflicting tendencies, so that there is always an interest in following one of these to the limit, and sacrificing others to it. Thus Spinozism, as a young Wittgensteinian called Bosanquet was to argue shortly after Wittgenstein's death, talks of the world and its contents in a manner which stresses its pervasive interconnection and close continuity, whereas other systems lay stress on its disjointed disconnection and random multiplicity. Solipsism, in the same way, sees everything in relation to the single conscious person rather than to his society, or his objects, while Platonism sees everything in relation to generic meanings, rather than in relation to their multiple, multiform instances, and so on. That we may shape our talk and our thought so as to make certain aspects of the world and of experience 'fundamental', and others merely derivative from, or 'parasitic' upon them, and that we may thus derive a greatly enhanced understanding of the world and experience by speaking of it thus variously is undoubtedly the case, and Wittgenstein, in recognizing it, has uncharacteristically provided us with a fine justification for revisionary metaphysics and traditional speculative thought, which is not by him seen as a mere excursion into the unmeaning, but as a valuable cultivation of alternative ways of articulating the world as it comes before us, and deciding in what fundamental terms and manners we may best speak of it. Philosophy as the science or art of basic linguistic recommendations and proprieties is still philosophy, and the problems and answers of ontology, epistemology, axiology, etc. do not wholly change when we regard them as considering the best ways of speaking about being, knowledge, value, etc. rather than as investigating transcendently objective structures.

## VII

In pp. 61–7 of the *Blue Book* Wittgenstein is led to consider the role of the pronoun 'I' in the metaphysical statement 'Only I can really see.' He points out that we cannot substitute the name of a particular person, e.g. 'Ludwig Wittgenstein' for 'I', since a person who refers to himself as 'I' is not talking about the particular person that he is, with such and such a description, e.g. the man in the funny Bohemian clothes with the piercing blue eyes. For he does not need to refer to himself by any description, and can have no problem in identifying himself. We may add to this that he may without absurdity imagine himself to be someone other than the actual historical individual that he is: 'If I had been one of Socrates's interlocutors, I should have answered . . . '. He points out, further, that all our talk about persons other than ourselves depends on conventions which in their turn depend on factual uniformities that might have been quite different. A world is conceivable in which the same bodily person so varied his psychological traits on different occasions that we were inclined to talk of him as several persons, and we might ourselves talk only of our present selves as 'I', and other variants as he. Some disassociated psychological subjects, such as Janet's various Leonies and Prince's Miss Beauchamp, in fact did so, and so did St Paul in certain remorseful passages. Wittgenstein rightly says that we must try to see the actual role of the first person pronoun in our language, and see how differently it functions from a proper name or a personal description, and how it is nonsensical to use it in contexts where all contrast of subjects is eliminated as in 'Only I really see.' Nonsense or no nonsense, Wittgenstein continues to see the merits of a solipsistic notation, and it is arguable that he never ceased to see it even when he later wrote about the impossibility of a private language.

On pp. 67–74 Wittgenstein now sets forth his famous analogy of different sorts of expression with the different tools of a carpenter. There is no single, standard use, or sort of use, of a hammer, a chisel, a square, a glue-pot or its glue. In the same way, we must not try to assimilate different language-performances, such as the giving and obeying of orders, the asking and answering of questions, the telling of jokes, the description of immediate experiences, the exhorting of our friends ethically, the telling of our dreams, etc. If one avoids assimilation, one will realize that a man who says 'I' is not using his pronoun to point to himself, nor to describe himself, at least not in the normal case: he is simply showing who he is by being himself the speaker, the one who moves a certain mouth, larynx, etc., and he might simply say, for example, 'Feel tired', without prefacing it with a redundant reference to himself. The word 'I' no more means the actual speaker than a groan means the actual sufferer: it merely shows who is the speaker or the sufferer. This is why many languages do not need the first personal pronoun except for special emphasis (*cogito*). But the fact that the word 'I' is not an ordinary proper name, nor a description, suggests to philosophers that it names something mysterious and transcendental. Wittgenstein compares this with what happens when we start brooding on the way, as we say, things *look* to us, and then imagine that we are describing a queer set of entities, sense-data, with properties quite different from those of physical things. If a penny *looks* elliptical, we say that we are seeing a sense-datum that *is* elliptical, and that it is a real existent distinct from the seer and the seen penny, and that it in some way mediates between them. But sense-data are merely an eccentric device for describing the way that things look to us, that thereby creates the false impression that we have discovered a new sort of entity. (G.A. Paul, of course, worked out these basic Wittgensteinian points more elaborately.) In the same way we are impressed by the non-descriptive character of the pronoun 'I', and think it must refer to something quite out of the ordinary. There is, further, a first-person use of language in which we talk only of what appears to us as speakers: in that use what appears to others, whether in perception or thought, counts for nothing, and is not a relevant case of seeing. Solipsist language is like a clock whose dial rotates with a clock-hand, so that it registers only a single position of that hand. But our normal language does not merely aim at registering the speaker's own experiences and observations, and hence has no temptation to say 'Only I really see.' This could at best be said by a man with normal vision to a group of blind men who were using visual language to deceive him. 'The kernel of the proposition that that which has pains or sees or thinks is of a mental nature is only that the word "I" in "I have pains" does not denote a particular body, for we can't substitute for "I" a description of body.'

Wittgenstein may be adjudged correct in saying that the use of the pronoun 'I' to show who is the speaker, cannot be equated with that of a name or description that could be used by anyone. Only the speaker can bring out who he is by employing the pronoun 'I', and the word's prime function is to bring out just this. Wittgenstein does not, however, comment on a very important use of the pronoun to put ourselves into other people's shoes', or into the *personae* of animals, in imagining, for example, that *we* are Cleopatra, or a Mexican peon, or a hunted stag, as we often do in moral assessments. Here, very arguably, the word is used to bring out a trait that Hegel calls the 'absolute negativity' of the thinking subject, its ability not merely to ignore and bypass, but to transcend personal difference. In putting ourselves into everyone's shoes, our 'I' becomes, as Hegel says, a universal 'We'. It is this expanded 'I' or 'We' that, in the truly compassionate, suffers, and even sins, in and with everyone. Leaving such compassionate transcendence aside, we may say that some transcendence of the merely personal, solipsistic standpoint is involved in all language, and Wittgenstein is correct in emphasizing it. Significance is always shareable, and *my* world is always part of *the* world, and of *our* world. I am always one among others, and must accord myself a place in a genus which has an infinite, open membership. But what is wrong with Wittgenstein is that he does not sufficiently stress the fact that there is no clear *division* between the comprehensively public world, and the section of it that is personal to each of us. There is not and can be no such division. My experience can correctly be said to overlap in content with the experience of others, in the general experience of 'people' or 'men' or 'living things', perhaps terminating in the all-inclusive experience of an ideal experient, of whose postulated presence science, morality, and above all, semantics would seem to be in some need.

## VIII

Turning to the *Brown Book*, we begin with a reference to a passage from Augustine's *Confessions*, which is more fully discussed in the opening sections of the *Philosophical Investigations*. Augustine, he says, conceives the learning of language as a learning of the names of things, of such names as, for example 'man', 'sugar', 'table', etc. He does not consider the learning of the meaning of such non-substantial words as 'today', 'not', 'but' and 'perhaps', and Wittgenstein likens this account to an account of the game of chess which leaves out the role of the pawns. There might, however, have been a very simple language-game which would correspond more closely to the Augustinian description: in this a child would merely be trained to utter the

names 'brick', 'cube', 'slab', 'column', etc. when his teacher
pointed to an appropriate object, and this game could be made
part of a more elaborate game in which the pupil had to *bring* an
object of the sort named when the teacher uttered the name in
question. *We*, in fact, when the trainer said 'Brick', would wish to
translate his utterance into the sentence 'Bring me a brick', so as
to make plain that it was meant as an *order* to bring something.
Wittgenstein, however, deprecates the notion that such a
translation is obligatory, or that it represents more fully what the
trainer had in mind. Wittgenstein does not deny at this point that
there are all sorts of inner experiences, images, feelings,
beginnings of responses, etc., which coexist with the use of words
like 'Brick', 'Bring me a brick', etc., and which can be said to
have definite connections with what we have in mind, or how we
have it in mind. He denies, however, that there is anything
uniform about these experiences from occasion to occasion, or
person to person, or that they can therefore have anything
importantly relevant to the significant use of the expressions in
question. It may, however, be argued that a significant use of
expressions is best understood in terms of certain salient
paradigms to which many common cases only inadequately
approximate, and that it is in the light of such a paradigm that we
say that the well-trained pupil understands the single word 'brick'
as being an order to bring a brick to his teacher. Wittgenstein
does not deny that our language-games are complexly structured,
both in respect to our performances and to things and situations
they perform with and upon. It is not, therefore, clear why he
should deny the superiority of linguistic expressions which bring
out more of this structuring over forms of expression that leave
this largely inexplicit.

In §§2–11 Wittgenstein considers various elaborations of the
simple language-game of ordering, and fulfilling orders, to bring
specimens of a few sorts of generically named objects. The pupil
has been taught the cardinal numerals from 1 to 10, and when
given the order 'Five so-and-sos' he goes to where the so-and-sos
are kept, picks up a so-and-so while he utters each numeral up to
5, and then brings the lot to the trainer. One must not imagine
that, in performing in this way, the pupil does more than respond
appropriately to the spoken words 'Five so-and-sos.' He is not,
till his language-training is more complete, responding to the

153

brick as being of a certain shape or size, and the numeral as meaning a number. One might, however, prefer to see the pupil's performance as a move in the direction of a paradigmatically comprehensive sortal and numerical performance and understanding than in the artificial arrest sketched by Wittgenstein. From games with configurational names and numerals, Wittgenstein proceeds to games that involve proper names (§3), and to games involving the use of indexical expressions such as 'this', 'that', 'here', 'there', 'now', etc. (§4). In the case of these last Wittgenstein comments unfavourably on Russell's view that these are the real proper names that point to particulars as such, without pinning them down descriptively. Russell, we may agree, was obviously very wrong on this point, since not only are indexical expressions not devoid of a very general descriptive content – thisness, hereness, nowness and myselfness involve, as Hegel showed, the most emptily universal of contents, that of the sheerly immediate – but their reference is not directly to individuals, but only by way of their immediate context.

From proper names and indexical expressions Wittgenstein proceeds to naming in general. Names are the category of expressions that each provide an answer to the question: 'What is this?' It is the fact that we ask this question in the case of very different types of expression that leads us to say that colours and directions are 'objects' quite as much as tables and tea-cups are. We can quite as easily, in a given case, ask what they are, and can answer the question by giving the name of the 'objects' in question. (What colour is that? It is magenta.) Wittgenstein then constructs an interesting fantasy in which men walk about with pictorial charts in which pictures of objects are correlated with expressions that name them, and make use of such charts to bring the right objects to their co-ordinator. There can also be names for parts of speech which appear in a chart in correlation with definite expressions – e.g. What is clever? An adjective, – including those complete expressions which we call 'sentences' or 'propositions' (§§7, 8). All this leads to new language-games in which trainees present their trainers with cases which fit the names which their trainers utter. 'Green circle' effects the bringing of a green circle: 'Sentence predicating green of a circle' effects the utterance 'This circle is green.' All this training leads on to a case in which the trainee's task is to bring the traine something which more or less exactly *matches* a paradigmatic *sample* of the word's sense or meaning. Thus the trainer may give the trainee a sample of a sort of coloured material, in order that the latter may pick out and bring him a piece of material that matches that sample. This use of a sample is not significantly altered if the trainee is merely *shown* the sample, and has to pick out the material that matches it *from memory*. Such matching from memory *may* involve having a memory-image as a sort of internal sample, but it may equally consist merely in saying 'That matches the sample', with perhaps a drop of tension, and a feeling of 'rightness.'

Wittgenstein here remarks on our temptation to say that this cannot be all that comparison consists in, and that it must involve a specific experience of comparing and recognizing. He holds, however, that there is no uniform experience or process of comparison which occurs when we match a sample from memory, or from a sample before our eyes.

> We hold pieces whose colours we want to compare, together or near each other for a longer or shorter period, look at them alternately or simultaneously, place them under different lights, say different things while we do so, have memory images, feelings of tension and relaxation, satisfaction and dissatisfaction, the various feelings of strain in and around our eyes accompanying prolonged gazing on the same object, and all combinations of these and many other experiences. The more such cases we observe and the closer we look at them, the more doubtful we feel about finding one particular mental experience characteristic of comparing (p. 86).

Wittgenstein says that what connects cases of comparing is a vast number of overlapping resemblances, and that, once we see this, we shall no longer feel disposed to say that there must be one feature common to them all. He admits further that there is an ideal case of comparing in which we have a clear memory-image or real sample before us, and a specific feeling which justifies us in identifying the shade of the image or sample with that of the material chosen, but goes on to ask what connects such a paradigmatic case with the many actual comparisons we perform, which are by no means so perspicuous. Must the connection be thought to depend on some hypothetical physiological or psychological mechanism which explains why we choose the material we choose? And are we really any better if we assert the existence of a wholly specific experience of recognition, for are there not countless such experiences, many of which lead to wrong choices of material, which are not found to match the samples whose characters we seemed to recognize in them? Wittgenstein has here rightly shown that comparison and recognition point to a paradigm of experience of which we very often fall gravely short, and seldom indubitably achieve, but he has not shown that we can proceed otherwise than by presuming the normal realization of more or less close approximations to such a paradigm. There may, of course, be 'mechanisms', unconceived by anyone but the psychologist of the unconscious, or the speculative neurologist, which help to explain such paradigmatic experiences, but what we have of the latter must be used to justify such speculations rather than the other way round. Universal characters are the one case of identity that can at times be quite plain to us, and on these all identifications of individuals, forces, etc. are wholly dependent, so that, if we cannot compare and recognize universal characters, we can recognize nothing whatever. Certainly there are specific experiences in which we confront the same or highly similar characters in a paradigmatically clear and distinct manner, and everything in the whole structure of our knowledge presupposes this, and rests upon it. The infinitely varied non-paradigmatic ways of being assured of identity and difference have no relevance to such an absolute certainty. As Moore might say, we at times *know* that certain specimens match one another in character, and we know this far more certainly than we have reason to believe in any subtle set of arguments which seek to undermine this conviction.

In §§18–21 Wittgenstein generalizes the use of tables to connect names with objects: in all such tables there will have to be correlations between names on the left, and pictures or samples on the right, or some other arrangement. It is in some such manner that the endless series of cardinal numerals is introduced, though obviously we cannot produce more than a finite number of illustrative samples of such a series, and those only the lesser ones. How then do we introduce an open infinity of pieces into a language-game, as we do in the case of the cardinal numerals? The difference between a finite and an infinite game does not lie in the pieces or instruments with which the game is played: we are inclined to say that infinity cannot be illustrated in terms of these pieces, and that we can only conceive it in our thoughts. Wittgenstein, however, prefers to say that the difference is one of the *spirit* in which the infinite game is played (§§21–32). It has, presumably, a boundless *openness* to the introduction of new pieces which is foreign to the finite game. It seems clear that Wittgenstein has seen how simple and straight-forward a thought is that of the infinite: even children catch on to the infinity of certain re-entrant rhymes or stories, and shout out 'It goes on forever.' But to Wittgenstein, with his love of the small-scale and clear-cut, the infinite amounts to no more than a rather nebulous spirit in which an always finite numeral game is played: instead of stopping short at, say, 159, as §31 suggests that a certain tribe might have done, we obey rules which permit us to construct new numerals indefinitely. We can here only lament the limitations of the spirit in which Wittgenstein regularly philos-ophizes. Confronted by a concept of the utmost perspicuity, which involves no more than a reference to *all* the members of an openly constructed series, he has yet to construe the notion in terms of a mere procedure which remains obdurately within the limits of the finite. If there remain stale empiricist problems regarding the fulfilment of references to the transfinite, it is arguable that we can and do think in terms of fulfilment to which counting procedures in succession will never be adequate. Abolish counting procedures which involve counting one term *after* another in time, and intuit *all* finite numbers at once, as we certainly intuit them at once in the case of rather small numbers, and we can readily imagine the Lord of Hosts taking the transfinite tally of his angels, solely by being aware, at a single glance and at one go, of all the finite cardinals as exemplified in some selection of the hosts before him, and so aware of a transfinite number in the whole aggregate of those hosts. All of our thought arguably works towards a God's-eye view of all things, which cannot be other than non-successive and transfinite, however little we may like to admit such a view into our ontology or our cosmology.

## IX

Wittgenstein next moves on in §33 to consider the nature of rules, which was later to become one of his abiding preoccupations. Such rules govern our use of language, and can be applied repeatedly to their own applications and to an indefinite range of instances. They may be set forth verbally or diagrammatically, or they may be simply followed without such aids. This leads Wittgenstein on to consider what may be involved in the sense of the auxiliary verb 'can', the ability to operate in a certain regular manner (§§43–4). He considers cases where we say that an ability is being actualized, and cases where it remains unactualized, also cases where we say it is present, *because* it was actualized in the past: a man, we say, *can* swim a certain distance because he *did* swim it on a past occasion. He asks whether the sentences 'He has done so-and-so' and 'He can do so-and-so' have the same or a different meaning, and argues that, if we use the truth of the former as a criterion for the truth of the latter, they must have the same meaning. But, if the circumstances in which an expression is used help to constitute its meaning, then the meanings will have to be different. We may here, however, go further than Wittgenstein and hold that '*A* can do so-and-so' never can mean the same as '*A* has done so-and-so', since it registers a universality which is not present in the latter case. And it is hard to hold otherwise than that the sense of such an inductively based universality, covering unexperienced future cases as well as experienced past and present ones, merits to be regarded as an *a priori* sense or conceptual slant, in terms of which all speaking, and also all non-speaking, animals see all happenings that they encounter in the world. It is not because we have been taught to use the auxiliary verb 'can' that we have come to have the concept of ability, but it is because ability based on past actualities is part of the phenomenology of the life-world of speaking animals, and, dare we say it, of non-speaking animals also, that the former can be taught the use of the auxiliary verb 'can'. Even Locke recognized the manner in which we always 'collect' a power to fit in with every performance, and to make its possibility general.

From the use of 'can', and other verbs of ability, Wittgenstein passes on to consider how a child could be trained in the game of narrating past events. He has been taught to name a dozen toys, and they are now taken away from him, and he is trained to say that he *had* a ball, that there *were* a stick and a rattle, etc. Wittgenstein says that here there is a queer misunderstanding that the child has already been using the past tense in an interior thought-language, and that he is now only being taught to translate this interior past tense into the past tense of spoken language. He has, in other words, already referred his ball, stick and rattle to the past, and has only been taught to use a linguistic past tense to express this reference. Actually, however, the theory informs us, we do not learn the meaning of the linguistic past tense by connecting it with the thought of the past, but only acquire the ability to refer to the past in thought, by acquiring the past tense. Wittgenstein's contention here is most perversely unacceptable. For, if one could not acquaint the child with passage, as the actual phenomenon of the vanishing of something palpable and showable into what is neither of these things, he could not learn the meaning of all the phrases that express memory and a former state of things. The vanishing of objects and states of affairs from the present scene, is one of the most poignant and pervasive of human experiences, and it is nonsense to suppose that a teacher's mere transposition of a verb into the past tense would be sufficient to make us have it. That the past tense could be given a sense without any experience of matters vanishing into the past, is plainly absurd: here is a case where the articulation of words must be preceded by the articulation of phenomena. Wittgenstein does not, in fact, deny this experienced lapse into the past, for he incorporates the *taking away* of the child's toys in the circumstances of the teaching. He speaks further (§§51–3) of the manner in which the child is taught to associate certain daily activities with certain positions of the sun and the clock, and so to locate these remembered activities at definite 'times', and to measure the time-lapse between them by definite criteria, some amounting to little more than a felt readiness to say 'about five minutes ago', etc. All this is good empirical common-sense, but it does not eliminate the need for pre-linguistic experiences of coming to pass and passing away, difficult as it has proved to give good phenomenological descriptions of such basic experiences. William James and

Edmund Husserl have, however, done marvellous work in this field, and Wittgenstein has not surpassed their efforts, nor rendered them superfluous.

From the past we proceed to the future, and here the Wittgenstein instructor trains a child in the use of the future tense by pointing to a regularly changing set of traffic lights, and then teaching him to forecast their colours, red, yellow and green, before they arrive. Plainly this will provide a successful way to teach the use of the future tense, but only because experience is already articulated in a manner which includes an open place for the future, which is then filled by a definite content, just as it also always has a place for the past. The primitive protention and retention which has places for what has been, and for what will be, is indeed a sort of proto-language that makes tense-language possible. Wittgenstein further condemns as falsely mystifying (§56), philosophical ways of speaking which treat all events, whether past, present or future, as in some fashion coexistent, and coexistent in a medium which somehow carries them all along, one after another, like logs by a river. He rightly points out that the grammar of our temporal talk is not symmetrical, with a mere change of sign, in regard to the past and the future. The dialectical puzzles of time are not, however, gone into here by Wittgenstein, nor is this the place for us to go into them. Husserl in his *Phenomenology of the Internal Time-Consciousness* has probably illuminated them more profoundly than any other philosopher. The need to develop a complete logic of tenses, and to put it into accord with a logic dealing with matters that transcend time and tense, remains highly urgent, but Wittgenstein has not contributed importantly to it.

# X

From the talk about the future, and a brief consideration of proto-bets and wagers (§§62–71), Wittgenstein returns to talking about what one *can* do. He develops the notion of a rule-governed sequence of numbers, e.g. 1, 5, 11, 19, 29, etc., in whose case, once the rule has been grasped, one readily remarks 'Now I can go on.' Wittgenstein says that the rule-follower may guide himself by a verbal formulation of the rule in question, or may simply be glancing back at what he has just written, or may simply be uttering what seems the appropriate next thing. Following a rule is simply doing one thing or other out of a long list of such performances. But there is a feeling that such an account is inadequate, and that there must be something more, on a higher plane, as it were, an activity, a process, a state, or whatever, which really constitutes the power to continue the series in question, and that glancing at a formula, saying what seems appropriate, etc., are the mere symptoms of this higher factor. It is, however, hard to lay hold of the factor in question, or to find any evidence of its presence, except that one somehow *does* go on in a manner that is deemed satisfactory. The experience of following a rule, and doing so with smooth ease and a feeling of 'rightness', is evidently not the factor in question, for we sometimes have this when we are not, in fact, able to go on in the proper manner, or in a manner deemed correct by ourselves and others. Plainly, Wittgenstein suggests, the factor in question can be no conscious experience, but must rather be a purely hypothetical mechanism, a mind-model meant to explain conscious phenomena, not unlike the perforated roll inserted into a pianola to control the hammers which strike on the piano-chords. Similar mechanisms can be invoked to explain what happens when a man reads from a script before him, following a set of rules which establish regular connections between visual shapes and oral and laryngeal movements. But, we may object, such hypothetical mechanisms themselves have to be explained in terms of rules, and if rule-following is intelligible in the case of such mechanisms, why not in the case of our inner experiences? The traditional laws of association at least attest that there are rules connecting experiences of one character with experiences of another character, and certainly also that differences in intentional direction, however analysed, are in a regular fashion interconnected, whether in terms of affinity or some other close interweaving. Why explain these cases of rule-following, already sufficiently mechanized, in terms of other mechanisms in the unconscious brain? And if rule-following is an all-pervasive feature of experience and the world, why should there not be specific experiences in which rule-following is emphatic, and luminously cognized and referred to? If general connections among senses and meanings are not matters of which there can be a perspicuous grasp, not limited to the particular cases which embody such general connections, and which have a graspable content only in and through the regular connections they embody, then discourse and practice would be alike impossible, and it would certainly be impossible to give general accounts of language-games and of forms of life, as Wittgenstein regularly does. However much structured out of overlapping alternative senses we hold the senses of our main expressions to be, they are still structured out of what is generic, and are themselves generic. And even our indexical expressions are universal in having relevance to the unique immediacy of whatever situation is thus uniquely immediate.

Wittgenstein goes on to argue that rules, if symbolized or diagrammatized, always permit of an infinity of alternative interpretations, and that we can therefore never correctly maintain that someone is not, on *some* interpretation, following a given rule. The fact is, however, that this statement itself states a negative rule, and is therefore inherently self-refuting. The sense embodied in a rule cannot be wholly bound up with the use of a particular expression or diagram, and our grasp of that sense is likewise not bound up with a particular expression or diagram, but points to a certain paradigmatic experience which we do not, indeed, invariably have when we perform correctly, and which we sometimes think we have when we do not have it, but which we at times certainly *do* have, and which is the sole criterion of the presence of certain universal connections, and of their strict identity in different cases, and their possible difference in one and the same case. We know that there are infinite possibilities of confusion and misidentification in the realm of interconnected concepts and meanings, but we can also be sure, with Descartes and Moore, that there are, and must be, certain limiting coincidences between the general connections which actually hold and those that are understood, and that this is far more certain than is any cleverly argued theory that maintains the contrary.

There is a second part to the *Brown Book* which contains many illuminating *aperçus*. The points raised in these are, however, for the most part taken up in the *Philosophical Investigations*, and will be best dealt with when we consider that work in the final chapter of this one.

162

# VI

# WITTGENSTEIN'S LATER PHILOSOPHY OF MATHEMATICS AND LOGIC

## I

The present chapter will attempt to deal with a tantalizingly slippery, highly controversial and very influential side of Wittgenstein's later teaching: his conventionalistic, anthropologistic theory of such basic logico-mathematical procedures as definitory sense- or concept-fixing, selection of primitive or indefinable expressions, categorization of types of expression, and distinction of the formal from the non-formal ones, listing of the ways in which expressions can be combined into propositional unities, and distinction of formal from other sorts of truth and falsehood, enumeration of rules that will enable us to transform propositions or sets of propositions into other propositions, and prove the latter from the former, selection of certain propositions whose assertion requires no proof, and can be taken as primitive and axiomatic, and so on. Wittgenstein does not go into any very detailed consideration of all these logico-mathematical procedures, but presupposes their systematic elaboration in the work of Frege, Russell and others, including himself as author of the *Tractatus*. His task in his later studies of logico-mathematical foundations is not to carry elaborate foundation-laying any further, but rather to question it fundamentally. Being inveterately opposed to any 'transcendental' elucidation of the governing expressions and usages of logic and mathematics, whether this be in terms of Platonic entities and their timeless interrelations, or in terms of mysterious private acts in men's heads or minds,

163

which give life to their uses of expressions and perhaps introduce them to the Platonic entities just mentioned, Wittgenstein is concerned to elucidate the fundamental logico-mathematical usages and procedures in terms of the basic needs of men, which all involve the success of communication with their fellows, and the successful and agreed application of their words to things and situations in their common world. The foundations of logic and mathematics, if they can be said to have foundations, lie in the nature of men as physical, physiological, psychological and social creatures, and in the constraints of their environing world. This anthropologism of Wittgenstein's later teaching involves strong criticisms of the notion of a rule. For a rule, as transcendentally conceived, is a linkage among Platonic universals, or among inwardly savoured generalities of meaning-intention, or object-constitution, or whatever, and in either case the transcendental linkage in question is taken as somehow compelling, or at least prompting men's use of expressions, in which they are guided by or obey a rule. Wittgenstein, however, questions the mythology of rule-guidance and rule-following, whether as individuals or as a community. It is we who, by our applications of terms and by other actions, not only apply rules to cases, but also invent or create and modify such rules, and have the further power, not only to obey or disobey them, but also to determine their identity or difference, so that performances which in our estimation violate a given rule, and introduce another, can be transformed into fulfilments of one and the same rule, a performance which transcends the omnipotence usually imputed to a God. The appeal of all these demythologizing contentions, has been great, and perhaps in some respects vulgar: Wittgenstein's arguments for these contentions are, however, anything but vulgar, and it is by no means easy to refute them. The ingenuity of a Platonic Socrates, pitted against an infinitely evasive Protagoras or Cratylus, would be necessary. Wittgenstein's contentions are also so often full of aphoristic charm as to make their refutation a disagreeable duty. A duty, however, it remains, since significant discourse is destroyed if there are not identities and differences of sense which are unaffected by what men elect to say, and which preside over wide spans of diversity, regardless of men's preferences, and if there are also no acts of synthetic understanding which subordinate whatever is thus multiple and multiform to such bound-setting unity. There are many writings, whether informally circulated in manuscript or posthumously published, in which Wittgenstein's later views on logico-mathematical foundations are set forth, among which we may mention a very interesting set of lectures given in 1939, and preserved in the notes of four auditors, and later edited by Cora Diamond. We shall, however, confine ourselves to exposition and criticism of the revised edition (1978) of the *Remarks on the Foundations of Mathematics*, first published in German in 1956, but later translated into English by Miss Anscombe. The revised edition divides the *Remarks* into Seven Parts, roughly concerned with (1) rule-following in general; (2) the special problems of irrational, transfinite and 'real' numbers; (3) the Russellian attempt to derive all mathematics from logic; (4) the differences between logico-mathematical and experimental discovery; (5) the meaning of existence-proofs in the case of mathematical entities; (6) further problems of rule-following and agreement among calculators; (7) general contention that a 'good angel' will always be necessary to ensure agreed, successful rule-following among many speakers and calculators.

## II

The first part of the revised edition of the *Bemerkungen*, dating from 1937–8, deals with the nature of the determination by a rule of the successive steps that are taken in 'obeying' it. The rule followed can often be expressed by a verbal formula, e.g. 'Add three at each step', which would determine such a series as 0, 3, 6, 9, etc. Such a rule may either precisely determine the next step at each point, or may leave it more or less indefinite, e.g. 'add some multiple of 3', etc. Wittgenstein holds that however exactly we may seek to determine the next step by a formulated rule, this must still be open to a variety of interpretations, and at each stage of obedience to the rule. Thus 'Add three at each step' might be taken to be obeyed if one added three units at each stage *till* one reached 100, then three couples for the second hundred, then three triads for the third hundred, and so on: one could also vary the length of each successive step in what purported to be a regular manner. Obviously there would be an infinity of different ways in which even such a pellucid formula as we have cited might be applied by a sufficiently casuistical subordinate, though it is hard to believe that he would not get a cuff for his pains. In what, however, Wittgenstein asks on p. 37, does the peculiar inexorability of mathematical rules consist, the rules, for example, that govern the successive citing of the cardinal numerals as we add one item after another in an enumeration? The answer we receive is that counting objects, as we have been trained to count them, with all the endless practice and merciless exactitude involved in such training, is an all-important part of our daily life's activities, whose disruption would disrupt those activities, and occasion countless mishaps. Our counting procedures have no *truth* to the objects counted by their means, but they are *useful* and, above all, actually *used*. This answer is illuminated by conceiving that we might find it useful, on occasion, to vary our measuring procedures by using foot-rules that expanded or contracted – we might wish, for example, to discriminate among our customers – and obviously we could, for similar reasons, vary our counting procedures, and perhaps omit or repeat numerals at certain junctures, or fail to count certain items at all. Such things, it is plain, are sometimes found advantageous by unscrupulous salesmen and purchasers. Whatever we did, we could plainly say that we were following rules, and were following the very same rules covered by a certain formula, and interpreted in the usual sense. If decision determines sense and use, then the sense and use of the words 'same', 'usual', etc., are subject to them also. Obviously with sufficient audacity and lack of scruple we could maintain this in all cases, and vary our usage to suit the emergency. The disruption of communication could become for us its furtherance, its disadvantages its advantages, and so on. At this rate even the damned in hell could put an end to their penance simply by declaring their state to be paradisal, and their use of this term to be altogether regular and ordinary. Similar devices have at times been used by Stoics, Vedantins and Christian Scientists, without thereby achieving respectability: plainly one can only change the uses and senses of expressions, as Wittgenstein says we can, if they *have* perfectly definite uses and senses to start with that can now be replaced by others, and which have their own absolute identities and differences which are not determined by those of the expressions connected with them. The question as to *how* the senses of expressions, or the rules governing their use, can inexorably fix their application from case to case, is plainly idle and silly: they would not be senses or rules if they could not do so. There is no obstacle to the understanding of this mere tautology except the baseless notion that there is some obscurity in generality of meaning, and that its explanation is to be sought in the detailed particularity of application. Whereas the particularity of application only makes sense as embodying or, on occasion, failing to embody, generalities of meaning, and there is consequently no problem in saying why such a logical rule as that whatever is true of all *x*'s is true of this *x*: it absolutely holds because such holding is just what it absolutely *is*, no matter how much this may mystify certain people. Perhaps, however, this is all that Wittgenstein means to emphasize. It is, in fact, simply a principle which underlies every field of discourse or practice, that nothing can be understood or known or spoken about or responded to practically, including the field of our own understanding, knowledge and practice, if it is not governed by rules that limit its variety in certain directions, and that it is simply nonsensical to ask *how* this is done, since, if it were not done, nothing whatever could be done, or be, or be conceived, or spoken of at all. The irregular certainly has its place in every field, but only as an exception parasitic upon some rule or other. If this is not so, nothing whatever is so, and, if our argument is not a good argument, then there are no good arguments anywhere. The discussion of this point would, however, take us far beyond any commentary on Wittgenstein.

The rest of Part I explores the construction of pictures which after a fashion illustrate, and so make it easier to grasp, the manner in which rules govern their instances. We can, for example, make pictures of two organized patterns of items or pieces, and can then draw lines connecting each item or piece in one pattern with one item or piece in the other pattern, and so prove the equality of the two sets of items, since there are plainly no items in one pattern correlated with either no items, or with more than one item in the other pattern. The pictorial proof *compels* assent simply because I *persist* in the one–one correlative procedure, and refuse to be diverted from it: if anyone tries to modify it, I simply accuse him of misunderstanding it, which is not unfortunately an argument at all (§38). We can also, in such pictures, surround sets of items with an *enclosing* line, which as it were gives us a picture of their cardinal number, since a line enclosing five items, say, looks different from a line enclosing only three items, say (§41). By the use of such pictures, we can illustrate addition, subtraction, multiplication and devision among cardinals. Wittgenstein, like Plato, finds multiplication especially fascinating: two-dimensional figures with four rows and five columns of items yield palpable proof, if conventional counting procedures are followed, that $4 \times 5 = 20$, and will yield such proof to anyone who counts up the items conventionally. There is no mysterious action at a distance in the way in which our picture influences what we say: its seeming action on us is merely the way in which we, as members of a community of speakers, have learned to react to our common pictures or diagrams. But these paradigmatic pictures, given currency by our common use of them, are readily transformed into ethereal structures, having a sublimed sort of existence, and supposedly put together by a God in an act 'out of time'. The conventions which regulate the use of such pictures are then turned into the 'essences' of these sublimed entities: it is of the essence, we say, of the paradigmatic five to be the sum of the paradigmatic three and the paradigmatic two, and to yield one of these by the subtraction of the other. Wittgenstein stresses that we can manipulate our paradigmatic images much as we manipulate a lump of clay (§80); we thereby enfold the role which each cardinal plays in our system of calculation. Though the paradigms we manipulate are vanishing particulars, their essences or internal properties seem unassailable and timelessly interrelated (§§102–3). We cannot even say that we believe in the internal relations thus revealed, for belief can be correct or incorrect, true or false, whereas the kind of insight we enjoy in regard to the internal properties of our paradigms only can arise when we have calculated correctly, and according to the rules which the paradigms embody (§112). Wittgenstein admits that we *say* that our paradigms compel us to construct them and to analyse them in certain ways, and to go on inferentially from one of them to another: the laws of inference certainly seem to compel us as railway lines compel the locomotives moving along them. None the less, Wittgenstein holds that the seeming compulsion of such paradigmatic images is really a compulsion exerted by a speaking society, and springs from the punishments, differing in seriousness according to the infraction, that it will mete out to us if we use language unconventionally. We form the picture of the uniquely hard logical mesh (§121), far harder than anything in kinematics, and imagine that, just as kinematic mechanisms predetermine certain dynamic possibilities, so the logical *must* covers all rule-guided speech in advance, and we are for that reason able to grasp the whole use of a word in a flash (§123), and see what it will involve in a given case. Wittgenstein holds, however, that all these postulated mechanisms are mythic, and their anticipatory insights likewise mythic, and that they are no more really present than the whole game of chess, in all its complexity of alternative moves, can be present to us when we start on a game of chess, and can direct every move that we make. What compels us to go on with certain calculative or inferential procedures simply springs from the natural history of men as social, speaking animals in a world common to them all, and though it is not by any ordinary sort of experimentation that they determine what has to be said in a given case, yet it is guided throughout by goals of unequivocality and reliability of mutual response which certainly shape what men say in different cases, and make them more and more uniform. In all these passages Wittgenstein may be said to have given an anthropological explanation of the Platonism which he repudiates as a theory: the paradigmatic pictures which seem to explain why we feel impelled to use certain expressions certainly imitate Platonic forms in their transcendental invariance. They are not, however, the true agencies which underlie linguistic usages: these agencies are matters to be explored by the anthropologist or the neurologist or the physicist and not by the transcendentalist. It is, however, arguable, as against Wittgenstein, that entities of reason are as reasonably to be postulated in the explanation of our more reasonable procedures as are obscure physical and neural mechanisms in the explanation of our more mechanical ones.

Part I is followed by three Appendices written in 1933–4 which deal somewhat airily with very important issues. The first (pp. 102–10) deals with two different senses or uses of negation, one in which a double negative cancels out negation altogether, and one in which it merely reinforces it. 'It is not not raining' may mean the same as 'It is raining', or it may merely say that it is not raining with added emphasis and force. Plainly there are a whole family of senses of negation, as has been long recognized, the contrary and the contradictory, the negations of properties and the negations of classes, etc., let alone those negations which live comfortably with affirmations, as when Cusanus makes opposites coincide in God, or as when G.E. Moore defends the use of 'It is and it isn't' when one attempts to say whether it is raining in a Scotch mist, or when one attempts to say whether a certain man is or is not bald. Wittgenstein compares these contrasting 'nots' with the two contrasting 'ises' of copulation and identity (§17). What Wittgenstein, however, deplores is the superstition that there is some inner thing, or hidden mechanism, which underlies 'not' or 'is' in these differing cases, and explains why they function differently (§16). Any multiplication of things or mechanisms in the senses they have for physicists is, of course, deplorable – there are, we may say, far too many of them as things are – but it is not clear why we should not here recognize a limiting constraint on our speech and action which neither we, nor society, nor physical things, can make or unmake, and which we may describe, if we so desire, as the force of consistency, or the pressure of truth.

Appendix 2 stresses that a mathematician is not a discoverer, but an inventor, even if he at times comes to conclusions that astonish himself and others. Each step in an inference, or in any other operation, involves a new semantic decision on his part, even if it comes quite readily and immediately, and even if it seems to spring from something already present. It is not, however, clear, why Wittgenstein prefers the innovative connotations of 'invention' to the more receptive connotations of 'discovery'. Perhaps, indeed, we cannot but think of all realities, and all possibilities and impossibilities, as timelessly present to some all-grasping Intelligence, with which we stand in some sort of remote rapport. The notion of an all-conceiving God has its regulative uses, and there are more foolish philosophical moves than that of Malebranche who holds that we see all things in God, or with the assistance of a God. Certainly such a transcendental Idea would greatly ease the many problems of reference and inference and generalization, and do so better than the Idea of any pre-existent total world, whether natural or non-natural.

Appendix 3 (pp. 116–23) deals with the question of sentences that can be formulated within a language, but which cannot, without contradiction, be proved or disproved in that language, and which are accordingly, 'undecidable' in that language. Such sentences may, none the less, be demonstrable or refutable, but not with the resources of the language in which they are formulated. A sentence of this undecidable sort was constructed by Kurt Gödel in a famous article entitled *Unentscheidbare Sätze im System von Principia Mathematica und verwandten Systemen* and published in *Monatschefte für Mathematik und Physik* vol. 33, in 1931. It is this problem of undecidable sentences with which Appendix 3 is concerned. Gödel's sentence was one that said of itself that it was indemonstrable, but it referred to itself, not directly, but by way of a propositional function containing a variable, for which, if the propositional function in question was substituted, we should obtain a sentence which simply *was* the original sentence. Gödel's sentence, put into ordinary English (as I myself restated it in my article on 'Gödelian Sentences' published in *Mind*, 1942, pp. 269–65*) ran as follows: We cannot prove the sentence formed by substituting for the variable in the statement-form "We cannot prove the sentence formed by substituting for the variable in the statement-form X the name of the statement-form in question" the name of the statement-form in question.' It is obvious that, if we carry out the substitution prescribed in the original statement, we obtain this original statement itself, which accordingly says of itself that it is un-provable. The paradox of the formula extends further, however, than the mere possibility of proving its own unprovability, which would merely put it on a level with the paradox of the Liar, for the expressions in terms of which it is stated can all be 'arithmetized' in a regular manner, and then multiplied with one another to yield an arithmetical product, thereby yielding what corresponds to an arithmetized proof that a certain number has a certain numerical property which entails, when it is de-arithmetized, that it does not have that property. That undecidability should have penetrated the sacred edifice of logic was sufficiently serious, that it should have penetrated into the even more sacred edifice of arithmetic was more serious. We shall not consider how the problems of

*This article is my sole venture into this highly technical field.

undecidability were later dealt with by proving or disproving in a meta-language what was undecidable in an object-language that it merely talks about: Wittgenstein's treatment in this Appendix is much less tortuous. He says simply (§11) that, if we have proved that $p$ is not provable in Russell's system, we have by our proof proved $p$, since this is what $p$ states. and that, *if* this proof is in Russell's system, we have proved at once that $p$ belongs, and that it does not belong, to Russell's system. This is indeed a contradiction. But so what? Does it do any harm here? We have merely carried out a profitless performance, of which no use can be made, not even the use of proving that we can never succeed in proving such an unprovability (§14). The meaning of 'proof' has, in fact, been altered by the Gödelian argument, and we have now to decide whether we have a new sort of proof or non-proof before us, or refuse simply to make any decision. There is something appealing about Wittgenstein's simple refusal to liquidate a logical paradox on some sort of general principle. What he suggests perhaps is that we should, when faced by a paradoxical situation, simply turn our backs on it in an *ad hoc* fashion. The logico-mathematical terrain is like a skating-rink on which there are many well-known hazards and regions of thin ice. These must simply be sign-posted and avoided, without constructing a general theory that excludes them. If we sometimes elect merely to mumble and say nothing, as we in fact often do when asked an inadmissible question, Gödelian and other paradoxes will certainly do us no harm. They will merely mark the points at which silence should replace speech.

## III

In Part 2 of the *Remarks* (pp. 125–42) Wittgenstein deals with the problems raised by the transfinite and the real numbers, i.e. the numbers which seem to confront us with an infinite task. The unending, open series of the cardinals yields us the lowest of the transfinite numbers, $\aleph^0$ on which, by processes that Wittgenstein does not go into, and that we also shall not go into, Cantor raised higher and higher orders of transfinitude, equality and inequality being here determined by the same procedure of one–one correlation that determines it in the case of finite assemblages

The real numbers arise when one considers the infinitely many fractions, vulgar or decimal, that are *less* than a given cardinal number, and sums them all up in a single total aggregate. In this way one obtains a seemingly definite equivalent for the endlessly long decimal or other expansions that tend indefinitely towards a limiting outcome that they never can reach, e.g. being the ratio of a circle's circumference to its radius, or being a precise square root of some other number. These so-called 'real numbers' have, however, the unattractive property that there is no regular way of ordering their component fractions in a series which progresses uniformly from lesser to greater, and leaves nothing out. This is impossible, since new fractions always make their appearance between any given pair of fractions, and since there are no fractions which are *next* to any others. We can order the real numbers in relations to ordinary cardinals and fractions, which serve as their upper limits, but intrinsically they remain non-denumerable. Wittgenstein responds to all these mysterious conceptions by uttering a general warning: we should not form pictures which lead us to conceive that there really *are* queer numerical aggregates which transcend denumerability and ordinary one–one correlation procedures, and that we can ask the same questions about them, e.g. regarding their equality or inequality, that we can raise in the case of the orthodoxly constituted numbers. There is no paradise of the transfinite, or of the compactly or otherwise continuous, to which Cantor or Dedekind have given us the key: they have merely introduced us to high-sounding forms of diction for which we have no proper use, but which fascinate us by their queerness, as in the parallel case of raising questions regarding the 'direction' of time (p. 141, §56). 'Ought the word "infinite" to be avoided in mathematics?' 'Yes', answers Wittgenstein, 'where it appears to confer a meaning upon a calculus, instead of getting one from it' (§58). We, on the contrary, might argue that infinity only raises problems for enumerative procedures that take place in successive stages in time. Even we, however, to some extent transcend succession when we directly recognize, without successive counting, that we have two pairs of apples before us, and consequently four pieces of fruit, and we have no difficulty in extending this conception to that of an intuition and intelligence able to perceive *any* cardinal number intuitively in some assemblage before it, and so to judge that *all* cardinal numbers are exemplified in such an assemblage, and so also the transfinite number which is the number of *all* the ordinary cardinals, though not, of course, one *of* them. Kant in his *Dissertation* tells us how an intuitive intelligence might grasp an infinite assemblage *uno obtutu*, at a single glance, and both Neoplatonic and Christian theology operate with similar conceptions. The fact that we here enjoy a concept of the uttermost simplicity and perspicuity, though our human glances can be baffled by quite inconsiderable degrees of multiplicity, could be brought in to defend Cantor and Dedekind against Wittgenstein's anthropocentricism. The God's-eye view, with its non-successive grasp of an infinite totality, is arguably a necessary regulative idea for mathematics, logic, semantics and the theory of knowledge. And the accounts which it engenders have an illuminating use which compensates for their lack of a pedestrian use in direct application. In any case we have, in the so-called specious present, a limited transcendence of succession, which makes its unlimited transcendence perfectly graspable.


IV


In Part III of the *Remarks* (pp. 143–221) Wittgenstein considers Russell's attempt to base mathematics completely on logic, in the sense that every mathematical assertion involving numbers, numerical variables and numerical relations, permits of a complete translation into statements involving at first only classes and class-members and the identity and diversity of the latter, and also the relations which correlate the members of one class, one for one, with those of another class, but which then permit of a further translation into talk involving only propositions and propositional functions and their varied compoundings, and also variables with the quantifications which give them reference to cases or instances, and so on. $3 + 2 = 5$ is in such a programme given lucidity by being translated into some such statement, expressed in special symbols and not in ordinary words, that if one has something and something else and yet something else of a certain sort, and yet again something else and something else of the same or another sort, then one will certainly have something and something else, and something else, and something else, and something else, of some sort. (It is not suggested that this crude verbalization is even remotely adequate to the fine symbolism of *Principia Mathematica*, or that it is in the power of a mere philosopher to achieve such adequacy.) The question then arises whether such a translation of succinct number-talk into intolerably prolix, repetitive talk, which is ultimately only about the identity or diversity of the instances of various concepts, or, what is the same, the members of various classes, and about their consequent capacity to be exhaustively correlated with instances of other concepts or members of other classes, in such a way that, if there is a correlation between anything and anything belonging to distinct classes or concepts, there is not a parallel correlation between either of such terms with any other, the question arises, we may ask, whether such elaborate, prolix talk really represents an illumination of ordinary number-talk, a rendering perspicuous of what is obscure. The view of Wittgenstein is that it isn't an illumination, but rather an obscuration, a rendering of language-performances that involve some obscurities into what is most complexly obscure.

Part III begins by stressing that a mathematical proof must be perspicuous. We must be able to see it as an identifiable configuration which can be exactly reproduced on another occasion: it must not merely leave us with a vague sense of having seen something. If it involves a diagrammatic picture, as Wittgenstein's proofs by preference do, this need not be wholly precise in its manner of depiction, but must bring out whatever is *relevant* to the picturing. Wittgenstein says that, if one has a proof-pattern that cannot be readily taken in, and a change of notation or representation suddenly makes the whole matter perspicuous, then one has a proof where one previously had none. If, for example, a two-dimensional figure consists of three horizontal rows each of five items, or, what is the same, of five vertical columns each consisting of three items, and this figure is used to illustrate in a pregnant fashion the multiplication of three by five which is also the multiplication of five by three, then, if the sum total of items is counted in the usual manner, we shall achieve a perspicuous proof that $3 \times 5 = 15$ (§2), which can be readily repeated on other occasions. The trouble about a multiplication of 234 by 537, or a sum of 7034174 and 6954321, in the language of Russell is, however, that it never can be perspicuous: we cannot even remember all its lengthy intricacies so as to be able to see it and reproduce it reliably (§3). And if one was coping with a Russellian formula a mile long, and having variously bracketed its contents and counted whatever was in each bracket, we could never be sure that we were keeping all such contents in mind, and that it was not from time to time being magically altered. Wittgenstein is here almost neurotic in thinking that we can never be sure that we have gone through certain contents completely, and identified all its items properly, and are now remembering the outcome rightly. And he lays quite undue emphasis (§15) on the empirical fact that different methods of counting practically always lead to the same result. Obviously if the outcome of a count depended wholly on variable conventions and decisions, and not also on something else which, granted such conventions and decisions, still determines what is their consistent continuation in the given circumstances, there would be no reason to expect uniformity of results of counting, nor to attach great importance to it. It would represent at best an anthropological or social quirk, and no more. Obviously it is only if there is something commonly called an identity or unity of sense, something previously appealed to and used by Wittgenstein himself in his conception of a tautology, which ensures that there is some sort of deep identity between what our linguistic conventions approach in a variety of ways, and therefore that, when such an identity becomes perspicuous, we shall tend to connect these linguistic approaches in a uniform manner, and extend such connection from the past and present to the future. Wittgenstein has, in fact, recognized such a unity of sense in his insistence on the perspicuous character of a proof, that we can take it in *as a whole*, and see it as a procedure which can be a model for countless cases, but he has gone astray in holding that the mere assurance of *having* taken such a whole in, perhaps by a procedure perspicuous at each stage, but involving too many stages to be perspicuous as a whole, must also count as a case of the perspicuous. Descartes recognized that our confidence might be validated by plainly remembered, as well as by actual insight, and Wittgenstein is here very much in a Cartesian bind. He even brings in a Cartesian demon who can deceive us by adding signs, or causing them to disappear (p. 158), and who cannot, it seems, be exorcised by the magic slogan of 'Meaning is use'. The

176

Cartesian God, who is the guarantor of all the rational enterprises, seems to be a better exorcist than this down-to-earth slogan.

Wittgenstein goes on to argue that, what a proof really does is to enable us to win through to a decision, and to place this decision in a system of decisions (p. 163): the proposition proved serves as a rule, a paradigm that we thereafter go by, that defines a correct procedure (p. 161). Every proof really introduces us to a new paradigmatic concept: it changes the grammar of our language. It may seem to point to a reality outside of itself, but is really only the acceptance of a new measure of reality (p. 162). The unshakeable certainty of a logico-mathematical rule, e.g. $(x).fx. \supset fa$, rests on its purely grammatical character (p. 170): it is a model for all future statement and argument. But such a status is only achieved when genuine surveyability (*Übersehbarkeit*) attaches to a proof – we may add the Cartesian codicil 'or certainly *has* attached to it'. Wittgenstein goes on to say that the introduction of a new notation in logic or mathematics, e.g. $a^n$ for exponentiation, may well be said to introduce a new concept, or to find a new aspect (pp. 180–1). It is plain that Wittgenstein is not willing to talk in terms of surveying procedures, and of entities surveyed, when this happens to suit his purpose: the use-slogan is not always in evidence. Wittgenstein goes on to consider the implications of the fact that the theorems of logic and mathematics can be said to be established by many, even by infinitely many proofs. In a sense, he says, each proof constitutes a different logico-mathematical entity, but, in another sense, always the same one (pp. 191–2). And all logico-mathematical propositions can be regarded as predictions of the result that men trained to follow certain rules will inevitably reach: if they are in a sense anthropological, they are generically so, and do not set forth results that only *one* man could reach, and only *once* in his life (p. 193, §67). This is perhaps an early anticipation of Wittgenstein's later critique of private language conceptions. Calculations are in a sense experiments, and the consensus that results from them is an empirical as well as a calculable result. A correct multiplication is the way we all proceed when we are wound up to perform the task (§69, p. 195). The danger in all these cases, Wittgenstein says, is our attempt to justify our procedure where there is no such thing as a justification possible, and where we ought simply to say 'That's how we do it' (p. 199, §74). It is not, however, clear at this point to what extent Wittgenstein's empiricistic anthropologism really differs from a psychologistic appeal to self-evidence, or an ontological appeal to Platonic structures, appeals which all rightly put an end to the indefinite raising of further questions. Wittgenstein also rightly says that men who demand a proof of consistency, to make sure that they are not miscalculating at each step, are like small children that have to be lulled asleep: if their previous reasonings could be inconsistent, what can guarantee a consistency-proof in regard to them (p. 204, §78)? If deceptive demons are really about, our best resource is to turn our backs on their possible presence, and not to worry about them, the same policy Wittgenstein has counselled us to adopt in the case of the logical paradoxes. Contradiction, Wittgenstein says, is harmless provided it can be sealed off; this is the policy of the thin ice notice that we previously commented upon. We need not assume that our calculi are infected by a pervasive, secret sickness merely because they fail to work properly at certain points (p. 209). It might even be possible to find a use for contradictions: we might wish to show that everything in the world is uncertain (p. 211). We might also, as said previously, wish, with G.E. Moore, to bring out the borderline vagueness of certain expressions (e.g. in 'He is and he isn't bald'), or the absolute limits to certain forms of discourse (e.g. 'God is and isn't a person'). Russell's Theory of Types is an elaborate device to avoid certain contradictions, but Wittgenstein asks whether it is not perhaps an artificially restrictive, mutilating device for which much better devices could be substituted (p. 217). The fences we build round contradictions are not super-fences, and we might prefer other fences, or wholly unfenced avoidances (§86).

## V

Part IV deals with the self-evidence which attends our survey of certain verbal or pictorial patterns, the picture, for example, that seems to show the truth of the axiom of parallels, in that lines which diverge from an obvious parallel seem to move towards, or away from, a given line (p. 223). It is not relevant, Wittgenstein says, that we find a proposition self-evidently true, but that we place that self-evident proposition among the rules and theorems that we accept (p. 224). Axioms, he says, receive a different sort of acceptance from empirical propositions, which does not, however, mean that some inner act of acknowledgement is psychologically different. In the case of mathematical axioms and theorems, we have no positive experience of their truth apart from their uniformly successful application: we rather have a *non*-experience of imagining anything different, which we, assuming an understanding of the variously used word 'possible', describe as the impossibility of so imagining. Mathematical propositions are thus over-determined, and stand upon several feet (pp. 226–7). Wittgenstein canvasses the suggestion that mathematical propositions might be given a wholly prescriptive meaning: they should not seem to tell us how things are, but only what we should do with our expressions. For people who took such a normative view of mathematics, there would be no mathematical, but only physical, discoveries, but they would not thereby miss anything (p. 233, §16). Wittgenstein also says that the real outcome of mathematical calculation is not a discovery but a concept: the limit of empiricism is concept-formation, in which we say, not 'It will be like this', but 'It must be like this', thereby setting up a new criterion of identity for something or other (p. 237, §29). The creation of this new concept or criterion is not compelled by our calculations, which rather only guide us towards it: we accept the proposition we have arrived at as self-evident, i.e. our way of seeing it is remodelled, it is released from all responsibility towards experience, despite its connections with the latter, and the possibility that experience should realize it is seen as the only possibility, and the exploration of others is abandoned (p. 239, §30). For Wittgenstein, accordingly, self-evidence is not a special mental phenomenon, but a phenomenon of human action. We elect to see things only on a certain pattern, and to make all our future seeings and predictions on the same pattern (pp. 240–2, §§32–3). The rigour of mathematical patterns lies in the rigour of our own decisions, and we henceforth turn our backs on such decisions, though we continue to *lean* on them in our further explorations and decisions (p. 243, §35). Wittgenstein comments on the often surprising, synthetic (in the sense of 'non-analytic') character of the results of calculations that we then transform into self-evident necessities: the most salient instance of this is the position and distribution of the prime numbers in the cardinal number series, for nothing in the concept of a prime number analytically entails that they will be distributed as they in fact are, and yet we call this distribution a necessary one. We thus have an indisputable case of the synthetic character of arithmetical propositions, for which Kant argued so impressively: that there are two primes between 11 and 19 is seen to admit of no possible alternative, yet illustrates no general numerical rule (pp. 246–7, §§43–4). We might almost call it an intuitively known empirical fact, an *a priori* truth that is also known *a posteriori*.

Part IV then returns to considering the effect of contradictions within a language. He emphasizes that there may be contexts in which contradictions play a valuable linguistic role. It might be desirable for some reason to produce the astonishment and indecision that normally goes with contradiction. The contradictions which Russell strives to eliminate could all be looked upon as something supra-propositional, that towers above all ordinary assertions and looks in two directions like a Janus-head: it might, in fact, be a Cusanan coincidence of opposites from which determinate things count as one-sided excerpts (p. 256, §59). Contradictions, Wittgenstein says, are only to be avoided in cases where they genuinely work havoc. We may in conclusion comment on the brilliant semantic and phenomenological treatment of the issues raised in this section of the *Remarks*. They illuminate the strange blend of empirical surprise and logical unsurprise that confronts us in the field of mathematical and logical calculation, and the decisions that force themselves on us by the way things prove to be, and yet are also the ways that we then freely decide to look on them. Plainly the commerce of thoughts, words and things is as rich in contrasts and connections as the structure of an Athanasian trinity.

## VI

Part V (pp. 257–302), dating from 1942 to 1944, is mainly concerned with the sense in which logico-mathematical entities or subject-matters, e.g. the 2000th digit in the expansion of $\pi$, ca be held to *exist* before any technique of calculation can establish that, and what they are. Wittgenstein begins by considering the nature of calculation, and holds that it involves no *inferences* regarding the subject-matters referred to in the propositional steps of the calculations, but solely to those steps themselves, and to whether their sequence conforms to certain Rules. Calculation, however, does involve the existence of subject-matters to which it is or can be *applied*, and which, if it is so applied, will be legitimated by and for the subject-matters in question. A calculating machine that determines the product 25 × 20 to be 500, can only be said to calculate because its results can be applied to countable objects and assemblages of objects, and can legitimate inferences regarding them. If no such application were in question, the term 'calculation' would not be applicable: mere dancing, however regular in its steps, would not amount to a process of calculation. The question then arises as to what extent calculation and application can or should be pursued independently. Would it be legitimate, for example, to devise and develop a system of calculation which employed the expression 'the square root of −1', which seems to refer to an imaginary number whose square is −1, and then to look around for a thinkable application for this system, as in fact happened in the historical development of the complex numbers, or should calculation always go hand in hand with application, and there be always a regular passage from the one to the other? Wittgenstein does not say how this practical question should be answered, but he does strongly deprecate carrying out rule-governed calculations without caring whether they ever receive a definite application, and then constructing the picture of a realm or kingdom that one is opening up or exploring, and populating it with objects styled 'ideal', to which one delights to attribute a number of queer properties that one's pattern of calculation seems to justify. The construction of such *ad hoc* 'ideal' applications resembles the hypostatizations which occur in various forms of mystical ceremonial (p. 265): the multiplication of mythic aeons by the Gnostics certainly has analogies with the multiplication of transdefinite and real numbers by Cantor and Dedekind. Wittgenstein is particularly severe on pictures which make calculators imagine that the unbounded expansions which their rule-bound calculations treat as possible, in some manner harbour definite *places* for existent terms which will fulfil certain conditions. Here the Law of Excluded Middle is invoked: we argue that $2^{\aleph^0}$ must either be greater or not greater than $\aleph^0$. and that since $2^n$ is the number of subclasses in a class of $n$ members, and, since it has elsewhere been proved that the subclasses in a class cannot be correlated one for one with the members of that class, but always exceed them, it is further argued that $2^{\aleph^0}$ must be greater than $\gamma^0$. In a similar manner Dedekindian analysis professes to cut the ascending series of rational fractions at an imaginary point so that one has, on one side, all the rational fractions whose square is less than 2, and on the other side all the rational fractions whose square exceeds 2, and so take ourselves to have found a place in the infinite series of rational fractions for what can be identified with the square root of 2. Wittgenstein thinks that these argumentations fail to establish the existence, even in the attenuated sense of a fulfilling semantic content, of anything to which our expressions can be applied: it is only *as if* our expressions could be applied to something, in some manner in which the that and the how of such application, are left wholly obscure. Without the ability to apply a propositional or other expression, we do not really understand it, though we may paint pictures which create in us the illusion of such an understanding (§29). Wittgenstein's restriction of understanding to what can be exhausted by a temporal process of counting, may, however, arguably be resisted. For, while we certainly cannot *imagine* infinitely increased or divided assemblages, we can perfectly see that it is only the *successive temporality* of counting procedures 'that stands in the way of apprehending them, and that, if we could apprehend *all* the finite cardinals, as we perfectly apprehend a few of their lesser members, without needing to count them, we might very well, as argued before, be intuitively confronted by an assemblage, selections from which instantiate any and every cardinal number, and so provided an intuitive illustration of the transfinite. The notions of a transfinite number of arbitrary correlations, which would establish equality or inequality, is likewise without a flaw. The God's-eye view, which takes in even the transfinite at a glance, is arguably the irremoveable background of all our references, whether pictorial or otherwise. There is also something to be said for the Neoplatonic view that there is a portion of ourselves which live absolutely out of time, to which therefore the prospect of envisaging a transfinite aggregate at one glance, by recognizing its transcendence of all the finite cardinals exemplified in selections from it, would be only a trivial exercise, not differing from seeing the sixness present when one has two rows of items before one of three items each. It is here interesting to see how deeply Kantian is Wittgenstein's whole approach to number-theory. Like Kant, he sees number in terms of the temporal process of successive counting, and so infects it with the perpetual incompleteness and supersessiveness of all temporal exercises. It is very proper to dwell on this pervasive side of our life and experience, but it is also proper to dwell on another side of that life and experience which, at least in principle, transcends time. Every case of the so-called 'specious present' in fact does just this. It lies within the scope of that side to entertain the possibility that 777 occurs *somewhere* in the infinite expansion of $\pi$ (§27) without being able to say where it does so, and without being sure that anyone will reach it within any span of human life, or within any definite span that one might care to specify. Only in some non-successive complete view is there some definite span, or perhaps no definite span, within which it *is* reached.

## VII

Part VI (pp. 302–353), dating from 1943–4, deals in further detail with the problems of rule-following and consensus among rule-followers. Proofs, he tells us, organize propositions and give them an order: a transformation-rule links one proposition with another, and the rule is grasped in and through the technique which leads us on from one to the other. The definiteness of the result, which can be arrived at along several routes, reflects back on the route that has led to it: the uniformity of the result authenticates the route or rule that has led to it, just as the rule authenticates the result to which it leads (pp. 304–5). The proof, in fact, shows us how and why a rule *can* be used in passing from one proposition to another, and in looking at the latter in the light of the former. It is as if it were an imaginative experiment without application to a definite case before us (pp. 316–17). Thus there is a definite technique for finding a prime number between $p$ and $p! + 1$, which by its generality proves that there always is a prime greater than any given prime, and hence an infinity of prime numbers (pp. 307–8). We have now acquired a new concept in whose light we see all prime numbers: each is seen as one of an infinite series, no matter if we know of no rule which gives each a definite place in that series. In the case of Fermat's last theorem, we know of no definite technique for proving it, and hence can only understand it to the extent that it bears likeness to theorems for which we have probative techniques, and that we can therefore try to construct in its case (§13). Wittgenstein goes on to maintain that there are a number of independent criteria which establish that we are proceeding according to a rule, a feeling of satisfaction, an intuition of rightness, and certain practical consequences: that we are proceeding according to a rule is, in fact, overdetermined by all these criteria, and this is not therefore, Wittgenstein says, an empirical proposition (p. 320, §16). This plurality of criteria does not mean that 'following a rule' is indefinable: countless definitions of it can be given, but they will not be illuminating or useful (p. 321, §18). It can, however, be said with firmness that 'following a rule' presupposes a *custom*, and that there cannot, therefore, be only one occasion in world history on which a given rule was followed. And it is further the case that disputes as to whether a rule is being followed or not will normally be rare – one seldom disputes, for example, whether 'red' is being rightly applied in most cases – if a rule is to *be* a rule. The agreement of people in calculations is, further, not an agreement in opinions or convictions, which might have differed: it implies a feeling that the rule is inexorable, that one can only do one thing and nothing else, if the rule is to be followed (§30). But the nature of a rule also has an element of the inexplicable about it: 'the difficulty here is not', Wittgenstein says, 'to dig down to the ground, but to recognize the ground that lies before us as the ground' (§31, p. 333). We must not, that is, try to penetrate to something deeper and more explanatory: only to the extent that one unhesitantly follows a rule, can one recognize that it *is* a rule. Being a rule further involves the participation of many persons over a considerable period of time: if a God were to create a phantasmal replica of England, with persons apparently doing sums just as we do them, but only for two minutes, could such

eople be said to be really following the same rules that we
ollow? Wittgenstein hesitates in his answer (§34), but plainly
ney could not in any ordinary sense be said to do so. And he
wells with emphasis on the blessed fact that all or most of us
gree in the application of certain expressions to certain objects,
or without this measure of agreement there could be no such
ing as language at all (§39). Granted that there is such a
easure of agreement, we can, if we like, treat a rule as a
etaphorical agent that guides us (§44), or say that we have an
tuition of such a rule. This last is only possible if such intuition
troduces some regularly recurrent element, and cannot be
retched to cover any and every variation (as, for example, in
e case of the monadic essences of Leibniz, which cover all that
monad will ever be or do). Wittgenstein ends the section by
enying that only one person could calculate according to a rule,
d says this is as impossible as that one man should engage in
ommerce (§45, p. 349). The argument is invalid, since
ommerce is *by definition* an interpersonal activity, whereas
alculation is not. We here come upon an early instance of
Vittgenstein's denial of the possibility of a private language,
hich is so much emphasized in the *Philosophical Investigations*,
d which will be commented on in our next chapter. Here we
all only say that, while the notion of an entirely private
nguage, or a necessarily private language, is an unprofitable
xercise in imaginative experiment, the notion of a language in
hich there are both interpersonal and personal segments is
terpersonally recognized – 'I know that so deeply inspired a
erson must mean something by what he says about his inner
xperiences, but what he means I cannot even begin to imagine.'
Ve admit, accordingly, that there may be rule-followings by
articular persons which will never become intelligible or
stomary beyond the person in question. There is, further, a
alogue within the bounds of the single subject which may go
rther, and would be more profitable, than dialogue among a
urality of subjects, and it is arguably wrong to regard talking to
neself as in all cases derivative from talking to others. Divine
scourse may, further, at its higher level, be entirely discourse to
d from self, proponent and respondent being no more than one
od.

## VIII

Part VII of the *Remarks* need not engage us for long, since it is more loosely organized than any of the previous parts, and since it often recurs to points previously treated, without discussing them differently or more deeply. There is a second discussion of Gödel's theorem (pp. 385–8) in which, as explained previously, a statement asserting the indemonstrability of the proposition resulting from the substitution for the variable in a certain propositional function the very propositional function in question, can be shown to assert indemonstrability of itself, and so to be provably unprovable. Worse still, if we translate this unprovably provable statement into a regularly arithmetized equivalent, we are able to prove that certain propositions concerning the *numbers* which correspond to the expressions in this statement, are quite undecidable as regards truth or falsehood. Wittgenstein's reaction to the possibility of such undecidability in a system of discourse or calculation seems simply to be the 'thin ice' policy previously canvassed: one should not eliminate the undecidable statement, but should not attempt to make use of it inferentially. Heterologicality might similarly be accorded the logical property of *not* being heterological if it is taken to be heterological, and of being heterological if it is taken *not* to be heterological, and so having an undecidable status, which means simply that we can make no use of it in any context. We can, if we like, follow Russell, and say that the heterologicality and the non-heterologicality of heterologicality are alike 'non-significant', but this characterization need carry no stigma, and can, moreover, be applied also to all the logical tautologies. That heterologicality has no use in regard to itself does not, however prevent it from having a use in other cases, and we need no elaborate type-restrictions to keep it out of our language (pp 395–8, §§28–30). The God's-eye view which establishes whether 777 occurs or does not occur in the expansion of $\pi$ is dealt with on pp. 407–8, §41. It is, however, said not to be a harmless picture, since it conceals weighty problems. For while God could know whether or not calculators will reach a 777 by the end of the *world*, this being a contingent matter of fact, his omniscience cannot decide whether they *would* have reached it *after* the end f the world, i.e. if time had continued further. For even God an determine something mathematical only by mathematics (p. 08, §41). It is not, however, clear why God cannot calculate the whole infinite expansion of $\pi$ at a single *go*, and not in successive tages. In that non-successive vision not only the presence of 777, ut the places this will occupy in the total expansion, or its total bsence from any place in that expansion, will be perfectly ccessible to the accomplished vision of Divinity, and we resumably can enjoy the vague inspiration which stems from uch an accomplished vision.

Wittgenstein further considers the kind of compulsion that a ule seems to exert upon us, and argues that, like a line, it only ompels the course of those who have decided to stick to it (p. 14). But the mere resolution to keep to the same course is only ffective according as the use of the word 'same' is connected with that of other words. Surely, however, there are closer or ooser analogies among the uses and applications of words, which e can neither make nor unmake, and surely it is part and parcel f the use of 'same' to apply better where the analogy is close han where it is loose and distant. (The failure to stress the istinction between close and distant analogies is the fault in rofessor Goodman's 'grue' and 'bleen', which can hardly be said ) designate properties at all, and evince this defect by the mpossibility of using them inductively.) Wittgenstein, however, not able to distinguish the following of a rule from obedience ) a kind of inspiration. A voice within him says 'This way' (p. 17, §53): its only distinction lies in the fact that one is trained in ule-obedience, but not in inspiration. Listening for the inner oice, and being ready to obey it, might, however, require a ertain sort of training also. Wittgenstein repudiates the view that here are differences of deep affinity among the cases of rules which justify us, in different degrees, in recognizing them as rules t all: all regularities, it would seem, are on a level. Despite these uggestions of the oracular, Wittgenstein still insists that the utcome of rule-following in the conduct of calculation is to cquire a new concept of the cases under consideration, or to rrive at a new norm of diction (pp. 430–3, §§67–70). Mathemat-:s is in fact a network of norms, of regulative, calculative rocedures which are to be obeyed or followed, and whose utcome is a proved proposition, one that expresses an internal relation, which should and must ensure conviction (pp. 434–5, §72). All this is very far from giving a clear sense to the concepts and norms that he speaks of: his norms are as vague as the boy-scout adjuration simply to 'follow the gleam'.

As we reach the end of Wittgenstein's *Remarks on the Foundations of Mathematics* we experience difficulty in achieving an oversight and evaluation of them all. Certainly they have made us aware of deep puzzles in matters that we tended at first to see as quite straightforward, and they have at times also created in us a perhaps unwarranted sense of illumination. Certainly they have made plain to us, if it was not already sufficiently plain, the central role of human language in the economy of our human existence, that it is in and through language that our inmost reactions acquire a definite and seizable form, and that even our most wordless awarenesses often build on distinctions first articulated in words, and therefore readily lending themselves to translation into the latter. And all the categories of phenomenological psychology – the intentional act and the intentional object, the intuitively fulfilled and the merely thinking reference, the positing and non-positing reference, the focal, the marginal and the merely dispositional awareness, etc. are all arrived at by way of the study of language, which is likewise responsible for whatever distinctions are allowed in our ontology: the thing, the predicate, the relation, the state of affairs, the fact and the norm, the past, the present, the future, the possible, the probable and the necessary, etc. There can be little doubt that the world and its contents and its conscious inhabitants are there for us through a network of language from which it is impossible to separate them. None the less, it will not do to make this network a wholly independent object of consideration, internally structured but not tied by definite bonds to the infinitely varied nuances of our subjectivity, the varied ways in which objects become present to us and are responded to by us, nor to the infinitely varied nuances of real and imagined objectivity, which our attitudes of mind have the strange power to elicit. Traditional philosophy made human language a gateway to ontology and phenomenological psychology. Wittgenstein tries to make these only a gateway to language and its uses, and so only to themselves.

The conception of the use of an expression is, moreover

deprived of all sense when we make it creative, and not deferential to the way things are, or to the way in which we and others are oriented towards them. The use of an expression is not like the use of a hammer or a wheel or a wash-rag, characterizable in terms of some gross physical effect: it can only be characterized in terms of the orientation towards real or imagined things that it evokes or expresses, or in terms of the aspect of such experienced things that it particularly serves to bring out. In his very interesting examples Wittgenstein often recognizes these phenomenological and ontological attachments, but the general tendency of his talk is to liquidate such attachments, and to move towards a form of talk in which the use of expressions by a community of speakers is taken to be self-justifying and self-explanatory, and only through a misunderstanding to demand the recurrence to something underlying or deeper. That the attempt to use language to penetrate to what is beneath or beyond language, is a difficult exercise is very plain, but this will not exempt us from undertaking such a task. Language is in fact well-fitted to bring out the phenomenological and ontological structures that underlie it and are reflected in it, and the researches that went in this direction before the general invasion by the use-semantics achieved much that was very valuable. One can succeed in talking about what the ordinary use of language implies, rather than talks about. Particularly we would here dwell on the immense worth of the realistic, Platonic treatments of logico-mathematical entities and presuppositions by Frege and Russell, and also, if we dare mention it, the value of Husserl's intentionalistic *Philosophy of Arithmetic*. These works, whatever their mistakes, have truly cast light on the foundations of logic and mathematics, and the same is, of course, true of Wittgenstein's treatment of such issues in the *Tractatus*. The later writings of Wittgenstein on these basic themes are, however, almost without ultimate value. Like all his writings they are thought-provoking and abound in brilliant *aperçus*, but these all cancel one another out, and leave nothing whatever standing. Their final message is simply that the logico-mathematical game is played, and played by many, and played with success, but that it is misguided to try to understand *why* it is played with success. Not even the anthropological suggestions made by Wittgenstein at certain points yield anything like a firm purchase on these issues. They resemble the appeals to conventional standards and usages made by certain of the Greek Sophists. It is with Protagoras and Zeno that Wittgenstein, in this side of his Protean thought, must be ranked. He has led us all into a labyrinth from which only the guiding thread of the Ariadne of our own previous wisdom can enable us to escape.

# VII

# THE *PHILOSOPHICAL INVESTIGATIONS*

## I

In the present chapter we shall attempt to comment on a number of the main points raised in Wittgenstein's rambling, uneven masterpiece, the *Philosophical Investigations*: our comments will often take the form of suggesting quite other ways of conceiving certain matters, and in particular those concerned with the findings and language of introspection, on which Wittgenstein's views, strange for one brought up in Vienna, and perhaps acquainted with introspective psychologists such as Bühler, are oddly elementaristic and Wundtian. The Wittgenstein literature is, however, so largely given over to purely positive appreciation and wholly immanent criticism, that assessments in a more traditional, acts-of-mind notation may perhaps prove not unprofitable.

Wittgenstein begins the *Investigations* with a long quotation from Augustine's *Confessions*, which he has already made use of at the beginning of the *Brown Book*. Augustine in this passage is concerned with our calling *things* (*res*) this or that, and with the way in which we were first taught such appellations, the things called or named being mainly the sorts of things present in our neighbourhood that can be pointed to or shown. Bodily movements in appropriate directions made us see *what* things were being thus named, while other movements of the face, eyes and body were able to indicate, in an almost untaught, natural language, common to all men, the mental states of seeking and

191

laying hold of, or alternatively of rejecting and shunning objects. Augustine, Wittgenstein says, regards all sorts of words as being taught us in much the same manner as we learn the proper names of persons, or common names such as 'table', 'chair', or 'bread'. Actions and properties also count as 'things' that can be named and our elders moved their bodies in appropriate directions just as they did when they taught us that 'table' meant table, and that 'Cassius' named Cassius. It is a little doubtful whether Augustine in this passage really held any uniform conception of the *res*, the things or matters, named by words, or believed that they were all of the gross sort represented by tables or chairs or pieces of bread. The affections of the mind in seeking objects, or in steering clear of them, are obviously not things in this gross sense, and yet he says they are referred to in an untaught, natural language which is presupposed by the teaching of a conventional one. Wittgenstein is obviously only making use of Augustine as a stalking-horse for an attack on reification, the tendency to regard each word in a sentence as standing for a distinct thing or object and treating the sentence, which is composed of such names, as itself standing for and naming a complex object. Augustine, Wittgenstein says, does not recognize any radical differences in the roles of words: the difference, for example, between property- or action-names and thing-names. Even a connective like 'and' could at this rate be taken as standing for a something. As opposed to such a simplicistic conception, Wittgenstein then instances the following use of language: on a slip of paper someone inscribes 'Five red apples', and the receiver pulls out a drawer marked 'Apples', looks up the word 'red' in a table which has the right colour-sample correlated with the word, and then proceeds to intone the cardinal numbers up to five, and at each intoning withdraws an apple that matches the colour-sample. A man's understanding of the slip is shown by these ceremonial actions.

We may at this point raise the question whether the reification that Wittgenstein attributes to Augustine is always so wholly misguided as Wittgenstein suggests that it is. Plainly to treat expressions such as 'red' and 'five' and 'here' and 'not both' as naming things of the same order as chairs or tables or bits of bread would be a peculiarly gross error, which hardly anyone seems to have made. Is the function of reification not often rather an honorific one, a recognition that certain words have as important a function in bringing out the character of the world as it comes before us and impresses us, as do the names of common things such as 'table', 'chair' and 'bread'? To say, as Wittgenstein says at the beginning of the *Tractatus*, that the world is the totality of facts, not of things, is to make this plain: the world as we find it does not consist merely of tables, chairs and bits of bread and the like, but consists also of the communities of character which link such things, and of many other important relations between them, and of the past from which they all spring and the future towards which they all tend, and so on. To reify characters, relations, states of affairs, logical connectives, values, and what not, is precisely to recognize that reality is more than an assemblage of tables and chairs and suchlike, and requires many other subtler additions to be what it is: that the addition is totally different in each case need not be denied by such reification. The generic identity of chairs is plainly not at all like the individual identity of this chair. Reification of properties, kinds, states of affairs, etc. is also valuable in that it makes plain that the primacy of sensuous individuals in what may be called Being is by no means unquestionable: when we reflect, we find the characters, the types and the laws which govern ordinary things much more graspable than the mysterious individuals which are held to underlie them, and to be made manifest in them. Platonism, and also Aristotelianism, in fact suggest that we should put lucid things first, and that we should interpret particulars in terms of the universal senses that give them lucidity, rather than the other way round. Wittgenstein's troubles with rules rest on his refusal to accept any such principle. If this is correct, we must also be grateful to language for its introduction of terms which not only have a clear-cut meaning, but which can further be cut from their moorings by various forms of abstraction: this device may demote common-or-garden objects from their place of honour, but it will also acquaint us with what are objects in a much more interesting and illuminating sense. Natural language with its power to turn practically anything, even negation or conjunction, into the subject of a sentence, can illuminate the world in that unique manner which interests a philosopher, and need not make him think that what it illuminates is only another sort of table or chair, which can be subjected to the same questions as they are. And natural language is also well able to bring out the attitudes of mind in which objects come before us *as* this or *as* that, or as believed, asked, objected to, requested, approved or what not, and it need not lead us to picture these attitudes as being some sort of ectoplasmic ray which reaches out to objects. Reification should not therefore be allowed to become a philosophical *bête noire*: its function is precisely to highlight the part played in the world by its characterizing and connective features, and its higher order relevances, and to stress the superiority of this role to that of the common-or-garden things which merely instantiate the latter. Numbers have an interesting part to play in the language-games of Wittgenstein's imaginary village, but they can only play such a part if they play a more important part in the world as we find it – Frege said they were as objective as the North Sea – and also play a part in the manifold conscious lights in which that world is envisaged.

Wittgenstein goes on to maintain (§2) that philosophers fail to stress the variety of the ways in which words are used, and so invent simplicistic accounts of their meaning, as in Augustine's treatment just given. He says, however, that Augustine would be not so far wrong in the case of an artificially simple language in which an assistant was ordered to bring a builder a block, a pillar, a slab or a beam according to the name that the builder called out. The names 'block', etc. would in this language stand for the common-or-garden things the assistant was required to bring. There are, however, countless word-performances that do not conform to this simple pattern, and Augustinianism is like trying to assimilate the role of a punctuation-mark to that of a vowel or a consonant. Wittgenstein further says (§5) that the attempt to give a wholly general account of meaning surrounds language with a fog which is best dispelled by considering certain extremely simple, abstractly isolated word-games, in which the disparate use of expressions comes out most plainly. Thus we might train people (§6) to associate words with things by showing them the things when the words were uttered, and then demanding some reaction from them which might simply be repeating the word when the teacher points to the thing, or repeating the word after the teacher (§7). That the pupil should learn to form a mental image of the thing pointed to is not

194

normally the aim of the teaching, but it might become so in certain cases. In §8 Wittgenstein next supposes that the pupil has in addition learned to utter the numerals in series as objects are responded to, and to interpret the demonstratives 'this', 'that', 'here' and 'there' when the teacher points to objects and places. '*N* slabs there' then leads to his counting out *N* slabs, and taking them to the place indicated. A colour-sample can also be used to indicate the colour wanted, and to avoid anything so obscure as the use of a private image. The counting use of numerals, Wittgenstein argues, is quite different from the non-counting recognition of the numbers of sets of things, which are all taken in at a single glance: the latter is only possible in the case of the first few cardinals (§9). Wittgenstein then rightly suggests that the use of the numerals and the demonstratives is quite different from that of common names, to which many try to assimilate them in giving a general account of meaning. (This difference of use may be conceded, but to reify numbers and particular places may none the less be, in certain contexts, illuminating.) The disparate uses of different sorts of expressions are then compared by Wittgenstein with the disparate functions of the tools of a carpenter (§11) or of the handles in the cabin of a locomotive (§12). It is therefore quite senseless to say 'Every word means something', unless one wishes to contrast words with certain nonsense expressions, e.g. 'Abracadabra', which none the less have a place in language (§13). It is further, Wittgenstein holds, merely artificial to treat all words as if they were some sort of labels attached to things and to sorts of things, or to conceive of them all in the light of a single analogy (§§14–15). There are, further, things other than words, e.g. gestures, emphases and samples, which should also be counted as parts of language (§16), and to say merely that there are different classes of words, fails to recognize that there are different ways of classifying these (§17).

In §18 Wittgenstein goes on to say that we may be tempted to think that some of his language-games are incomplete, since they are less complex than our actual language is: the latter is, however, always growing in intricacy, and Wittgenstein memorably compares it to a mazy old city which is steadily being surrounded by new, rectilineal suburbs. Wittgenstein, we may note, shows no tendency here to prefer the crooked ways of ordinary speech to the straightened tracks of scientific and philosophical diction. He notes further that we are tempted to say that someone who orders a slab by simply uttering the word 'slab' must be speaking elliptically, and that he really means 'Bring me a slab.' But to say this is merely to treat *our* language as being more basic than his, and to suggest that everyone speaks our language in his soul. But that 'slab' is an order is merely shown by the response that is made to it, and not by anything soulful. It is likewise nonsense to suppose that a Russian who says 'Stone red', must be thinking a 'the' and an 'is' without uttering them.

Wittgenstein is obviously quite right in holding words to have disparate functions which should not be assimilated. Some, such as demonstratives, serve to pick out something in the immediate environment or in the context of recent consideration, without determining what object, or what sort of feature of an object or situation it is, some attempt to fix the character of something, others to bring out its relation to something else, yet others to give voice to confident or hesitant acceptance, or to induce these attitudes in others, yet others to express or induce such attitudes as approval, interest, sympathy, etc. Ordinary grammar, in fact, fully recognizes the disparate functions of different words, e.g. verbs, nouns, adverbs, conjunctions, plurals, tenses, etc., even if it has not always defined or described these functions in a satisfactory manner, and the advanced grammar of such as Chomsky is merely an invaluable extension and deepening of ordinary grammar. Philosophers have tried to arrive at linguistic functions of highest generality, e.g. referring, predicating, asserting, commanding, interjecting, etc. and such categorial distinctions are valuable even if there are more specialized distinctions that they do not cover. The prescriptive function is very different from the declarative one, whether or not we have special ways for expressing it. Wittgenstein's objections to our saying that we ought to regard 'Slab', in his simple order-game, as 'really meaning' 'Bring me a slab', ignores the fact this order-game fails to bring out the deep distinction between the merely referential and the prescriptive use of language, and that a language which fails to bring out such a significant difference, which is none the less really present, is less fully expressive than others. The all-important point is that affinities and disparities of usage (or of anything else) are objective matters which do not

depend on our notations, and that notations that bring them out
are better linguistically than others which do not. This is the true
sense which underlies the misleading assertion that the man who
says 'Slab' in the order-game really means 'Bring me a slab.'
Affinities and disparities may be irrelevant for many purposes,
but neither they, nor the closeness or distance of their likeness,
are anything that language can either make or unmake. To
espouse any more radical linguistic relativism would be to destroy
all discourse on language, or on anything else, and would
certainly make nonsense of Wittgenstein's own view that changes
in notation are valuable if they bring out analogies and
disanalogies which ordinary notations ignore. Obviously, too,
when we use expressions differently, the world, and our acts in it,
may come before us differently articulated and highlighted, but
equally, of course, a change in the articulation and highlighting of
the world and ourselves, may induce a change in our use of
expressions. The different roles of words are not therefore
merely what we *do* with them, but go with the whole
phenomenology which they either express or induce. Some
words, further, single out definite items or features in the
confronting world or the confronted subject, whereas others
merely help in the constitution or registration of the conscious
appearances, without singling out anything in particular.

## II

*(§§22–43)*

Wittgenstein here comments (§22) on Frege's idea that every
assertion involves *two* mental acts, one of simple entertainment
of a state of affairs, and one of believing it to be the case.
Wittgenstein says it is legitimate to introduce a notation in which
an assertion sign precedes an unasserted proposition, but there is
nothing mandatory about such a usage, and the supposed duality
of the acts behind it is quite mythic. We may say, however, that
while the experience involved in an assertion is certainly unitary,
and is not built up out of two distinct and incompatible mental
stances, of pure entertainment, on the one hand, and definite
belief, on the other, it may, none the less, when compared with

such attitudes, reveal an interior distinction of 'moments' or aspects which is certainly worth drawing. For something to seem a part of reality is certainly different from its merely seeming a significant possibility, and there is something more potently *present* to us in the former case, whether we call it a distinct mental act or not. Husserl and others have in any case made quite clear that 'mental acts' are a term for nuances or aspects of our intentionality, and do not necessarily connote activity or separability of direction. In the thought, for example, of the velocity of light there can be said to be many distinct constitutive *acts*, together with an added act of reference to reality, but such 'acts' are certainly not separable mental postures or active doings of any sort. One must be permitted to use expressions that enable one to stress different sides of a matter without being accused of some vicious sort of hypostatization.

In §23 Wittgenstein lists various ways in which sentences may be used, the different language-games that may be played with them, e.g. giving and receiving orders, asking questions, making jokes, etc., and in §24 he dwells on the difficulty of saying what language-game a man is playing when he asks a question. Is he, for example, declaring his ignorance and his need of information, or uttering an interjection expressive of uncertainty, etc.? Obviously such moments can be distinguished in questions, and will be variously emphatic in different contexts. In §25 he then points out how impossible it is to imagine animals doing anything such as we do in our various language-games, e.g. questioning, recounting, commanding, etc. One does not, however, need to be sentimental to think of cases in which there are analogues of such performances in animals, e.g. a dog 'pleading' to be taken out for a walk, or drawing one's attention to a remediable lack or defect, etc. §26 then points out the absurdity of treating all language-learning as a training in name-giving, e.g. the naming of men, of shapes, of colours, of pains, of numbers, etc. He also points out (§28) that teaching meaning ostensively, by pointing to what is meant, suffers from the difficulty that the pupil must interpret the ostensive gesture correctly, must see exactly in what light a thing is to be viewed when it is called an 'X' or a 'Y'. We can, of course, assist ostension by saying 'This colour, number, length, etc. is called *X*', but this presupposes training in the use of the words 'colour', 'number', 'length', etc. What emerges from this is that ostension only succeeds when the shown person collects the correct use of an expression from it, and himself goes on to practise it correctly. To be taught the use of a name by a single act of pointing presupposes familiarity with quite an elaborate game in which a pointing-gesture is to be fitted, e.g. pointing to a piece in chess, and saying it is the *King*. Only someone already proficient in a language-performance can ask the meaning of a name which occurs in it (§§30–1). People like Augustine (§32) conceive of us as foreigners, who already know how to perform in *some* language, but who have to be shown how to perform in *this* country's language. We may, however, hold Augustine to be in a certain sense right: it is only if matters come before us in certain appropriate lights that we can be taught to use words which express such lights correctly. There is, on this interpretation, such a phenomenon as that of a *danger* which comes before us in certain situations, the danger of a fall or a blow or some other untoward circumstance, and it is only if we can already see impending dangers in things that we can be taught the language of the dangerous. There is therefore what may be called a phenomenological language, a language of conscious lights or stresses, in which things primitively come before us, whether for notice or reaction, and learning the use of words presupposes this more primitive language. Only if one can see dangers in things, can one learn what the word 'danger' means. There can be little doubt that even animals see and respond to many things as dangerous, and can even learn the use of words which warn them off from such perils. Language, therefore, undoubtedly builds on conscious forms that are pre-linguistic, and the brilliant work of such a linguist as Chomsky, has merely emphasized and built upon this plain fact.

§33 then raises a very important point. Wittgenstein denies that there is any single, simple performance to be called 'attending to a certain feature of an object', e.g. its shape, its colour, its number of elements, etc. There are, perhaps, certain characteristic experiences that we tend to have when, as we say, we lay stress on colour, shape, number, etc., but there is no reason to suppose that these occur, or are uniform, in all people. And in any case the understanding that shape or colour or number is intended is shown by our agreed use in all cases, and not by the doubtful occurrence of characteristic or uncharacteristic experiences (§§34–5). It is the sheer difficulty of summing up all the ways in which a person may grasp and adopt a use that leads us to suppose that all such ways must spring from some single, occult, spiritual act (§36). Wittgenstein instances the view of naming as some queer occult rite of baptizing an object. This leads to his famous statement that philosophical problems arise when language goes on holiday. When we fail to consider the varied circumstances involved in a word's use, we stare at words uncomprehendingly, and locate mystic acts behind them. It was, for example, the false mystique of naming that led Russell to hold that only a non-descriptive, purely demonstrative word like 'this' can be a true name, or that led Wittgenstein himself to hold that true names can only be of absolute simples, since these latter alone are indestructible, all complex entities being liable to dismemberment, and in that case destroying the sense of a name. It is, however, quite wrong to identify the meaning of a name with its bearer: there are countless ways in which a name can continue to be used after its bearer has been dismembered (§§39–42). Wittgenstein asserts as a general thesis (here not extended to absolutely all cases as in the *Blue Book*) that the meaning of a word is its *use* in the language. (The restriction is probably meant to point to the treatment of 'aspects' in the concluding parts of the *Philosophical Investigations*.)

The most general point that merits criticism in §§22–43 is Wittgenstein's ignoring of the *angled* nature of *all* conscious experience, that objects always come before us in certain 'lights', as of a certain colour or shape, as dangerous, as being the same again, as growing larger and larger, etc., whether or not we dispose of words to express the light in which they appear to us. It is only because our experience is always of things in certain lights, that we can learn the words that express such lights. Such words in a sense fix the light in which something appears or is viewed, and can make it something to which we ourselves and others can *recur*: it can also lead to possible reification or abstraction, which is even more stabilizing. But if the world did not come before us, or we see it, from an angle, or in a specific light, we should never learn the sense of the interesting words which bring attributes or relations or kinds before us: we should truly be condemned to a language of mere names and demonstrative grunts, in which nothing could be described or characterized. Such a 'language' is, in fact, merely the unthinkable limit to speech. It is not, as Wittgenstein often insinuates, that we learn to see things *as* such and such because we have learned to use certain words in relation to them, though words vastly consolidate and expand our seeing of things: some seeing of them as such and such, is in fundamental respects necessarily prior. Wittgenstein, of course, fully admits the existence of what we have called angled seeing in his doctrine of 'seeing as', or 'aspectual seeing', in the final parts of the *Investigations*, and we shall, in due course, consider what he has to say on the matter. But he regards seeing *as* this, or *as* that, as a somewhat singular development of normal perception, connected with ambiguous puzzle-pictures and the like, and not as something characteristic of *all* conscious experience, of any sort whatsoever. Even the consciousness of something as an undetermined something or other, which we frequently have, is a consciousness of it from an angle, in a certain light: indeterminateness is, from the standpoint of intentional objectivity, a species of determination, sometimes a highly sophisticated one. But to see something as bright pink, is simply different from seeing it as a bath-mat, or as very soft underfoot, no matter how much the object may be, even for us, all these distinct things. Such a difference is then best expressed by metaphors of lighting or salience, or by the well-established talk of noticing and attention. We can only say that the object stands out remarkably, impresses us specifically and in given respects, etc. There need not be anything that one specially *does* or *feels*, apart from what these metaphors of highlighting and angles cover. And there is plainly something *invariant* in the cases, present or possible, that are thus covered, however much they may be enriched by overtones which vary from occasion to occasion, and from person to person. Everyone understands the standard metaphors and analogies in terms of which one speaks of highlighting or noticing special aspects of objects, and uses his own experiences as a paradigm for others, and only an obsessive solipsism can conceive of something inaccessibly private in such proceedings.

Wittgenstein further fails to see that seeing how a man is using an expression as much involves seeing his performance in a certain interpretative light, as seeing an object or situation in such a light. To see how someone uses an expression is as much seeing things from an angle as seeing anything else from an angle, and so cannot throw light on seeing things from an angle at all. The use of an expression to express the seeing of something in a certain light is, moreover, not like the use of a bat to hit a ball. To point to a use is as clear or obscure as pointing to a colour or a shape, and cannot illuminate the latter. Wittgenstein's use of the term 'experience' is, further, much too dramatic. He thinks one should only speak of an experience where there are noticeable sensations, images or feelings or contractions of one's musculature. He does not follow ordinary usage in recognizing that for the street, for people in the street, and for cars in the street, etc. to be quietly *there* for us, will rate as an experience quite without specially recognized sensations, mental pictures, kinetic innervations, etc. It is simply a myth that one's eye must follow the outline of an object, or perform some other cunning manoeuvre, for one to be aware of its shape: it may merely *look* elliptical or cubical, and no more. In the only sense in which an experience is semantically interesting, a man *does* have the same sort of experience whenever something appears, or is seen as being of a certain shape, size, colour, etc., and such experiences are in their essential aspects adequately expressed by the words he uses, but could exist without them, and could in their essential aspects also be shared by others. In fact, we only understand how a man is using certain expressions when, as we say, we see the world and himself in it through his eyes, making use of our experiences as paradigms for his or for anyone's, a proceeding which requires no justification, since it is *the* proceeding which governs what we say and think in this area. Behaviour is therefore semantically senseless without introspection or appresentation, to use Husserl's word. Our use of expressions reflects the way in which the world comes before us, and to describe the world as we find it is, if a few enrichments are added, to describe our experience of it. For the rest, Wittgenstein's stress on the very different ways in which words are used is most valuable, but all these differences also reflect differences in the world and the people in it, as these come before us, and it is not necessary to erect each and all of them into separate psychic performances. They are themselves rather aspects of a single phenomenological total which is the world as we all find it, and think of it. It is further clear that, while some of the angled awarenesses that we have could *not* be shared by dumb animals, e.g. the awareness that this is Tuesday, or that a number is prime, others could be so shared, e.g. the awareness that something is edible or that sabbatical quiet portends a dog's compulsory bath. And countless other uses of words can only be taught because we already see things in appropriate lights, e.g. as having happened or as having a definite capacity, etc. In general, the slogan is true: one must be able to mean things non-verbally if one is to be taught to mean them verbally. The two forms of meaning may, however, arise concomitantly: thus I may be taught the meaning of 'punishment' by an actual punishment inflicted on me by someone for some misdemeanour.

## III

*(§§44–63)*

After discussing some uses of names like 'Nothung' or 'Excalibur' which name nothing actual, and of demonstratives such as 'this' which are restricted to what is contextual, Wittgenstein returns to the consideration of the *Tractatus* doctrine that true names ought to signify *simples*, and quotes Plato's *Theaetetus* as holding that no definition can be given of the names of the primary, simple elements of things, and no question raised as to their existence or non-existence (§46). If they are nameable, they must exist, and, if they do not exist, they can have no names. Wittgenstein, however, points out how vague and indefinite the concept of simplicity really is (§47). Are the simples of which a chair is composed pieces of wood, or molecules or atoms? Can they be colours or lines? Can they be such things as the squares which make up a chessboard? Can our simples be properties, and, if so, which? A pictorial instance is then given of a design to which different types of composition can be assigned, according as we resolve it into colours or coloured configurations. An expression, moreover, that is a simple name in one context, since it ignores the elements that compose something, may amount to a propositional complex in another context, if it stands for the way those elements are compounded to form the thing in question (§49). He also criticizes the view that it is improper to ascribe being or non-being to last elements, only to complexes which can be put together out of elements, and taken apart into them (§50). This view, if correct, would mean that it would not make sense to ascribe non-existence, and hence also existence, to something one had named – a name of a non-existent simple would be a name of nothing – any more than it would make sense to ascribe the length of a metre to the standard metre in Paris. (The standard metre imparts its length to all other objects without setting a standard for itself, and just so, simple objects make the existence and non-existence of complex objects possible, without themselves having either possibility significantly.)

Wittgenstein also comments in §51 on the obscurity of saying that colour-names correspond to *simple* properties: how does one pick out such properties, and what is the nature of the correspondence? Does it consist in a resemblance of mental images to external objects, which is, of course, absurd? §52 then makes the point that one must not have recourse to mystical acts and properties without considering the detail of what actually happens: otherwise one is like a person explaining the presence of something by an absurd form of spontaneous generation. (We may, however, suggest that 'what actually happens' in one's inner state may require strange analogies to describe it, and these, though perfectly geared to what is actual, may seem mystical to those trained to notice only the crassly sensuous.) §53 shows how a use of samples or charts carried in one's hand or pocket might do all the work commonly credited to images or ideas carried in one's mind or head: these images or ideas are merely another sort of samples or charts.

Wittgenstein also dwells (§54) on the many senses in which a man might be said to learn to play a game according to a rule. He might be *told* the rule and be practised in it, or he might simply pick it up by joining in the game. There are, he argues, non-verbal ways of indicating when a move is countenanced or discounted. All this is unquestionable, even if it fails to illuminate what it is to understand and follow a rule. §55 comments on the silliness of saying the simple senses of our basic names must be indestructible: it amounts merely to saying that as long as we do mean something, we do mean something. We must not in discourse cut off the branch on which we are sitting. But, Wittgenstein says, we can cease to remember even a simple sense, or lose the sample that fixes it, or be unable to determine whether this sample has or has not undergone a change, etc., and in this sense even a simple sense can be destructible (§56). It makes no sense, of course, to suppose that the meaning of 'red' has been torn apart or pulverized, but it may have passed out of circulation none the less (§57). The existence of redness can only mean that 'red' has a meaning, and is a true existence as long as it has a meaning (§58), and to talk of absolute elements of reality which cannot be destroyed when a complex thing is disassembled, is merely to think in picures (§59). (Indeed in pictures, we may say, but not in the glorious analogical pictures of Platonism.) §60 contains a good criticism of the *Tractatus* view that we ought to translate talk about complex objects into talk about their ultimate, simple components. Would it be sensible to translate talk about brooms into talk about broom-handles and brushes, and the way that they are fitted together? The two ways of talking can be said to amount to the same, but only when they are parts of the same language-game. For some purposes brooms are treatable as simples (§§61–2). It is quite wrong to think that a highly analytic way of speaking of something is in some way more fundamental than an unanalysed way (§63).

Wittgenstein's critique of his own previous prepossessions in favour of simples is trenchant and amusing, but also somewhat tedious to those who see little merit in his original atomism. Obviously there are unities of different kinds, and a unity is not less genuine because it consists of less comprehensive unities related in various intimate ways. A bit of space is as unitary as any of the parts that can be distinguished in it. One does not get down to anything more absolutely fundamental by descending to less and less comprehensive unities: in some cases one is only getting down to something falsely isolated, and lacking in self-sufficiency, though this may indeed be valuable for certain purposes. And one may reject Wittgenstein's view that a wholly simple thing, if such there were, might not simply pass out of existence, and yet be remembered as having existed: there was, we say, something named by this name, but now there is nothing. And, as Moore pointed out, we can always say of anything before us, and nameable as 'this', that it might not have existed. Existence and simplicity are unconnected.

## IV

*(§§64–87)*

In these sections Wittgenstein is mainly concerned to emphasize the undefined and shifting manner in which we use language in different contexts, and the great mistake of trying to substitute something clearly defined and invariant for what is thus blurred and shifting. Wittgenstein talks in terms of a variety of language-games, and it is objected that he has not explained in general terms what a language-game is (§65), or what is common to all the games he is considering. He replies (§66) by pointing to the vast range of ordinary performances that we call 'games', an array of kinds of case bound together by overlapping affinities, and not by any single, invariant property, or set of properties, uniformly present in them all. In a human family, similarly, some members have similar noses, some similar smiles, some a similar gait or way of speaking, and so on: there is not some definite set of traits characteristic of them all. Wittgenstein points out that, although for certain purposes we may wish to use words that are clearly defined, and that cover a perfectly definite region of cases, there are very many other contexts in which this is not advantageous, and in which we are perfectly satisfied to use a word which has only a family sense, and which slightly varies in meaning from case to case. Inexact, shifting, regional meanings are, in fact, the normal meanings of discourse. Wholly exact meanings would in ordinary circumstances be an embarrassment rather than a convenience: we should not know when to apply them, and should have no good use for them. As Wittgenstein observes in §70 we understand what is meant by saying 'The ground was quite covered by plants', without having to have an exact definition of a plant, or of the force of the adverb 'quite'. In fact, we say what we do not mean when we try to give an exact definition of some term that we employ inexactly and shiftingly (§77). Thus we all understand what is covered by the sentence 'Moses did not exist', and this understanding is not invalidated by the fact that each of us would describe Moses to ourselves in a different manner, nor by the fact that it is not clear what are the true facts about Moses (§79). Obviously there is no such thing as a perfectly definite, uniform manner in which Moses might be described, even to himself by himself, as by anyone else, and it is quite wrong to think that each person who speaks of Moses has the same definite description of him in mind. (Modern causal theories of reference are not here considered.) What characteristics a man connects with Moses will come out if he is asked questions, or if he goes on to say other things about Moses: they are not determined by what he explicitly has in mind at the time. Because logical calculi demand that symbols should have uniform senses, and be manipulated according to strict rules, we must not assume that ordinary forms of speech must do this too (§81). In the ordinary use of symbols, the rules are always being stretched or modified to fit new cases: sometimes the game we are playing may be said to have rules that we make up as we go along (§83). And even when we do follow rules, their interpretation may be inexact, which does not affect the fact that it may be clear enough for a great number of purposes, and does not give rise to hesitation or to question.

Wittgenstein's view of the inexact, open-textured character of most ordinary meanings is unquestionably correct. As is also his view that some meanings cover variable affinities that shift from one sort of case to another. It is only in certain contexts, and for certain purposes, that exactly delimited meanings become desirable, and Wittgenstein does not question this desirability. Nor does his family approach attempt to replace universal meanings as ordinarily conceived, by some totally different view: he admits the objectivity of semantic affinities and disparities, but argues that most words involve a *multitude* of such affinities and disparities, from which speakers make different selections in different cases: universals remain what they are, but words cover many alternative sets of them. The world of universals is, moreover, a continuum, as Plato showed in the *Phaedrus*, and our words select different ranges within that continuum in different cases, with varying limits. Consider, for example, the sense of 'brightly coloured', 'very noisy', 'many telephone calls', etc. Neither does what Wittgenstein says affect any theory of understanding as having a genuine intentional direction, which only comes out in the use of words. For in many thought-references to objects there is genuinely a nutshell summing-up of a range of characters which distinguish the object. These are not severally discriminated, but given together in a single thought-

207

package, in which some characters are much more central than others, while on the outer margin it is far from clear where the package ends. (Is it part of the package which describes Moses that he had a sister called Miriam?) What one does and says brings out the content of a thought-package, and is necessary to bring it out, but it is quite wrong to say that what use unpacks was not there before, and did not determine and condition use. To deny the existence of such thought-packages, with their peculiar phenomenological make-up, describable only by way of analogies, or to reduce them to mere 'dispositions', which are not actually experienced at all, is to ignore the most important of all mental properties, which Kant recognized in his doctrine of synthesis, and which Wittgenstein himself recognizes in his stress on *Übersichtlichkeit* or surveyability. Structured wholes, sometimes of great complexity, can be apprehended *as* wholes without a detailed spelling out of their structures, and all mental mastery rests on this possibility, without which our apprehension would become hopelessly fragmented. It may be a metaphor or an analogy to speak of grasping a whole series of musical notes, or words in a sentence, or designs in a picture, or items in a description, in a single comprehensive survey, but it certainly describes a fact of living, actually lived-through experience, and by far the most preciously significant fact in our confusedly piecemeal universe. A thought-package may further embrace matters that are clearly articulated, though not actually spelled out, and other matters that are quite obscure and penumbral, and requiring further articulation. This penumbral character of much of our consciousness is fundamental: it is neither luminously structured, nor lacking in structure. It is something which *has* structure, though this requires to be brought out point by point in order to be talked about. When we thus bring out what is penumbral, we must forget neither that what is thus brought out *was* only penumbral before, nor that it also embodied the form that we now clearly articulate. The general notion of 'dispositions' does not cover the variety of stages that we recognize in our analogical account of such a bringing out, which accounts have ultimate authority in a field which cannot be otherwise spoken of.

## V

*§§88–133)*

In these sections Wittgenstein reproves all those who try to 'sublime' our ordinary language, to analyse the sense of its expressions into wholly clear elements, and to make language obey rules of complete rigidity. He points out that the whole ideal of the 'exact' is confused: what is exact for one purpose ('He came exactly at two') is inexact for another. And what is inexact does not mean what is unusable (§88). He points out, further, that it is only through an illusion that we imagine that the exactitudes of formal logic underlie the inexact reasonings and assertions of ordinary life (§89). This tendency towards sublimation also leads us to enquire into such things as the nature of propositions as such, and to treat this nature as something queer and remarkable, which lies *behind*, and is not to be found *in*, our actual sentences (§§95–7). People thus start operating with super-concepts, e.g. language, experience, fact, world, etc., rather than with ordinary concepts such as those of table and lamp and door. We imagine that our language is always striving towards an ideal, whereas it is evident that it is perfectly adjusted to its purposes, and that, if it came closer to such an 'ideal', it would become like slippery ice on which we could no longer walk (§§98–107). Wittgenstein says that we ought not to look for linguistic *ideals*, nor try to *explain* our linguistic utterances, but ought simply to take language as it is, and try to describe it faithfully. We must merely arrange what we have always known, and resist the lure of fascinating novelties, which will lead on to misinterpretations of our ordinary, inconstant, inexact speech. 'Philosophy is a battle against the bewilderment of our intelligence by means of our language' (§109). 'The problems arising through a misinterpretation of our forms of language have the character of *depth*. They are deep disquietudes; their roots are as deep in us as the forms of our language, and their significance is as great as the importance of our language' (§111). (In these last utterances, as in the interpretation of basic changes in notation in the *Blue Book*, Wittgenstein is conceding that deep puzzlements are endemic to linguistic forms, and are not merely the result of philosophical misunderstanding and abuse of the latter.) Wittgenstein further holds that, by resisting such transcendental or metaphysical misinterpretations, we shall gain, or regain, a true comprehension of language and the world: we must bring back words from their metaphysical to their ordinary use, and faithfully describe the latter (§116). In this faithful description, wide-ranging oversight (*Übersichtlichkeit*) is above all necessary (§122). We must not consider any single, special case of usage, but must let our gaze range over a wide variety of cases, in all of which we shall find differences that will preclude one-sided interpretation. The aspects of things that are most important for philosophy remain hidden on account of their simplicity and uniformity: we must learn to be truly superficial, and to avoid false depth (§129). Wittgenstein further says (§130) that his clear and simple language-games are not to be taken as idealizations of ordinary language, but only as *objects of comparison* that will enable us to envisage the more complex games of ordinary diction with a similar clarity of vision. We shall see them as the same sort of imprecise shifting performances, only a little more tidied up, and elaborate.

Wittgenstein's criticisms of those who seek to rigidify and logicize all our thought are important. There are, in fact, few ordinary concepts of such clarity and uniformity as to make the logical Laws of Contradiction and Excluded Middle strictly applicable. The continuum of cases is often such that there is no clear line to be drawn between $p$ and not-$p$, in which case 'It is and it isn't' may be illuminating, and an inexact logic, which does not seek to eliminate all borderline vagueness, may not only be more convenient, but truer to our thought and experience. This does not, however, affect the value of rigorous logical treatment for determinate purposes, and on suitable material. On the other hand, it seems wrong to deny that ordinary language does involve inherent tendencies which pull in opposing directions, and readily give rise to conflicts: the tendency towards absolute exactness which gives rise to the notions of points and instants is a case in point, and the quarreling tendency to think in terms of wider and wider, and in the end infinite, stretches which opposes it. Our ordinary speech fails, similarly, to draw a clear line between what is subjective, and what is objectively real, and hence philosophers are tempted to draw such a line at different points, and hence to develop comprehensive realisms or subjectivisms which only exist in germ in ordinary language. Wittgenstein is not correct in describing philosophers as misguided persons who stare at words, and who lose sight of their normal working: their fault, if it is a fault, and not a profitable exploration, is to carry tendencies present in ordinary language much further than they are normally carried, and to make them daringly systematic and exclusive of contrary tendencies. Wittgenstein in the *Blue Book* has himself pointed to the deep craving for alternative notations which will bring out neglected analogies and disanalogies, and which will cure the linguistic cramps that we experience when such revisions are excluded. And he used these deep cravings to justify his own leanings towards solipsism, plainly an extreme deviation from ordinary language.

All this being so, we can further say that Wittgenstein's determined superficiality, and passion for diversified specificity, is as much a departure from ordinary speech as are the philosophical deviations that he criticizes. His attempts to describe types of experience in terms of largely irrelevant imagery, muscular postures and not very definite feelings, take him far from what ordinary speakers would say of their states of mind, and he never hesitates to throw out any introspective account as falsely mystical or metaphysical if it fails to conform to the sort of trivialization and fragmentation in the inner life that he, as a philosopher, prefers. Wittgenstein's language-games, further, take their place with the simple objects of the *Tractatus* and the simple ideas of Locke, as explanatory models which go far beyond the ordinary, and are of questionable value even for comparison. It is not clear that we understand numbers better by studying the counting game as practised in Wittgenstein's imaginary village shop, than by immersing ourselves in the symbolism of Frege and Russell. They are equally far from the ordinary.

VI

*(§§134–55)*

Wittgenstein is concerned in these sections to illuminate the concept of understanding a general meaning or rule. People tend to talk as if this can be done in a single mysterious act, whereas, on Wittgenstein's view, they only manifest understanding if they go on correctly, using the word or words which carry the meaning in what passes for the correct way. He first examines what it is to be a proposition: this seems to be captured by some such formula as 'A proposition tells us how things are' or 'A proposition is whatever can be true or false' (§§134–6). But these definitions make no sense unless we know the statement-game, and its use to inform us about situations. The notions of 'words fitting the facts', or fitting some merely experienced flash of insight, really explain nothing, and are a mere case of picture-thought. What do we do when we understand what is meant by a 'cube'? Only by identifying cubes as cubes when we see them (§139). A misunderstanding of meaning similarly comes out in use, not in our entertainment of a wrong picture (§140). If we try to make someone understand what a 'cube' means by employing a certain method of projection, such a method of projection is just as hard to impart as to recognize a cube as a cube. Any anticipatory picture is inadequate to meaning, which only comes out in the way a picture is applied. §142 then makes the important point that it is only in *normal* cases that the application of a word is clearly prescribed. If the circumstances are abnormal as in many thought-experiments, it is not clear what should be said. Wittgenstein further implies that it is not how a man privately envisages the circumstances that decides whether he understands something correctly, but rather what the circumstances are: to establish understanding one need not delve into inner interpretations.

In §143 Wittgenstein begins his very long treatment of grasping a rule, and being able to go on speaking and acting in accordance with it. Such accordance with a rule is embodied in what a man does, and not in any inward flash of understanding (§146). The ordinary system of decimal counting embodies one such rule, a series in which each member is five more than its predecessor embodies another rule, a series in which each member differs by two more from its predecessor than its predecessor differs from *its* predecessor, embodies yet another rule, and so on. If a man understands a rule he shows this by, and in, his performance, though we have to except cases where he makes a slip and has to correct himself (a proceeding clear to an observer): such slips

iffer from cases where he goes on, confidently but wrongly, and
as therefore *mis*understood. What Wittgenstein rejects is the
onfusion of the true sense of understanding, which is disposi-
ional, and means that we *will* perform in a certain way when
ircumstances are such and such, with a picture-sense in which we
magine some machine or apparatus in the mind or brain whose
onstitution and mode of operation explains this ability. In the
ense in which there are processes characteristic of understand-
ng, he says, understanding is not a mental (i.e. an experiential or
nterior) process. Wittgenstein then expresses his allegiance to
he most abject sensualism in the realm of inner experience: 'A
ain's growing more or less, the hearing of a tune or a sentence,
hese are mental processes.' And mental processes they indeed
re, but at the very lowest level of mentality: to understand the
erspicuous sense of the universal quantifiers 'all' or 'some',
erhaps the most important symbols we ever use, can plainly be
n experience, too, an act of rational inwardness, and in an
nfinitely more paradigmatic sense than our experience of a pain's
rowing more or less. Those, further, who would confess to an
xperience of the sense of the words 'all' and 'some', at least in
ome cases where they are used with poignant emphasis, would
ot try to explain such an experience by pictures of explanatory
nechanisms in the mind or the brain, which are certainly nothing
hat we have any need to postulate.

These passages are followed by a long excursus on reading
§§155–78) which we need not comment on in detail: it rests its
ase on an unquestioning acceptance of the Humean view that
causation is surely something we establish by experiments, by
bserving a regular concomitance of events for example' (§169).
rom this it is made to follow that we cannot be said to have an
xperience or feeling of causality, and not, in particular, of being
*aused* to pronounce or imagine certain sounds by the printed
ext that we see before us. Whereas it may be held, *pace* Hume,
hat the difference between activity and passivity, is something
vith which we can at times be so undividedly *one* that we cannot
lo otherwise than say that we are living through it, directly
xperiencing it, or whatever other analogical phrase we may use
o express intimate identification and undistanced interiority.
This does not mean that such a difference is always experienced
vherever we assert causal connection, and that Humean accounts

have not their legitimate place in experience and knowledge. It only means that they rather refer us back to our experiences of activity and passivity, than that the latter merely point to the former. It is important to realize that the dogmas of philosophical empiricism can be at work in a thinker even when he purports merely to be reporting experiences in a philosophically unbiased manner. This is particularly so in the case of a reporter like Hume, whose whole temperament tended towards wholly passive, observer's attitudes. All this being allowed, it may be held that we simply do feel a larger measure of passivity in reading from a strange text before us than in pronouncing or writing a piece of discourse that we ourselves improvise, and that there is an experienced causation connected with the text in the former case, which is absent or reversed in the latter case.

After his treatment of reading Wittgenstein returns to the issue of being able to go on conformably to some rule, and continues thus to §242, dwelling greatly on pictures of inner mental mechanisms that are supposed to explain the steps that we successively take. But obviously the only mental mechanism involved (if the notion of a mechanism can be applied at all) is simply the sense of the word 'all' together with the set of characters that it generalizes. That these should generate an endless series of performances or expectations or whatever, requires no explanation by mechanisms: if we want to do or expect something of a certain sort in *all* cases that may arise, no mechanism is required to explain how or why we go on to do it, or at least try to do it. It is only the baleful idea that generalities have neither meaning nor causal relevance apart from the particular cases of their application, that causes our problem, whereas it is equally correct to say that particular cases only have meaning or influence in virtue of the generalities that they exemplify, and which determine what they can and must do or be in given circumstances. The generalities that we call the natures of things certainly restrict what they will do in given circumstances, and all reference to things in the world must embrace such restrictive generalities, if they are to concern anything at all. And we ourselves, forming practical projects as to how we shall react to things and situations in the world, are likewise throughout imposing generalizing restrictions on what we shall do or not do, and subjecting our future performance to rules, and it s wholly nonsensical to ask how such rules govern what afterwards eventuates, since they would not be rules if they did not thus govern what eventuates, or if the rules could be trimmed to fit any and every contingency. Rules, then, have a place in the economy of things and persons, whether we choose to reify them as immanently governing principles or not, and they can be known and decided upon in advance of their implementation. The adoption of a rule, or the mental grasp of it, or its evocation into full activity by circumstances, are therefore something that *can* occur in a flash, despite all Wittgenstein's objections, and are not to be identified with the endless class of their fulfilments. If there is, then, objection to the introduction of entities of reason, it may be counter-objected that an endless series of things and happenings unrestricted by rules is an unrealizable, illegitimate entity of unreason, which never can be a reality or a matter of experience. There is a great deal of nonsense in Kant, but his demand for restrictive rules in an existentially viable, empirical world is not nonsense. We may note further that the condensing, synthetic power of inner experience, and its retention of multiplied detail without spelling it all out, is the most characteristic of all its properties, and its very *raison d'être*: it is also a property that involves the restrictive generality of a rule, and without this we should not be able to say or know or purpose anything whatever. To Wittgenstein, all talk of predetermining rules, stretching out like a set of rails to infinity (§218) is essentially mythic, pictorial thinking (§222), but arguably it is only Wittgenstein's images that have introduced myths and pictures: the restrictive power of a rule is a far more essential, built-in feature of *all* that we perceive and perform, than any set of rails stretching out to infinity. Wittgenstein would not, of course, question the Kantian insistence on the rule-governed character of all talk about the world, and all action in it: it is only Wittgenstein's own perverse attempt to explain rule-obedience reductively that brings confusion and nonsense into the whole discussion. Whatever rules may be, they are not reducible to the series of acts that conform to them, and nothing transcendentally mysterious need be introduced if we recognize this. It is further clear, that we do have a different experience of cases where we perform correctly and according to rules, perhaps owing to good training or some instinctive aptitude, but without having any sense of these rules *as* rules which govern our performance, and which we accept as rules for us. In such cases we say that we do not really understand our own performance, and have no confidence that it is really right, though others may count it as such. Rules, it would seem, are only perfectly countable as rules when they are grasped and accepted as rules, and the experience of grasp and acceptance is an insightful act not reducible to anything in the way of performance.

VII

*(§§243–308)*

Wittgenstein in these sections is concerned with the problems of reflexive situations in which a person is related to himself, and in particular with situations where his speech is *with* and *for* himself alone, and in a language essentially private. Contrary to the *Tractatus*, where I can only understand and use my own language about the world as it is for myself, the position is now put forward that language is essentially shared and public, that what is said, even to oneself, is only significant if it *could* be understood by another, if, in short, it makes use of shareable public criteria even in the case of facts pertaining to a man's personal, private life.

Wittgenstein begins in §243 by imagining that there might be a tribe of people who spoke to themselves when alone and engaged in all their activities, but who might be heard and observed by an explorer, who would be able to correlate their language with what they did in given circumstances, and with the circumstances in which they did this, and so to learn to translate what they said into his own form of speech. Such a language would, however, only be private *per accidens*, if no one but the speaker ever heard it being used. Could there, however, be a language *essentially* private, which dealt only with sensations and experiences accessible to no one but the language-user in question, and not with anything accessible to other language-users? Wittgenstein in §258 conceives the possibility that someone might have a certain sort of private sensation that only he could experience, and that he might make use of the sign *E* to refer to it whenever it

216

occurred. He could point to the sensation, and call it *E*, only in he sense of directing his attention to it: being private, it could not in the literal sense be pointed to. He might then, the fantasy continues, recognize a sensation as being an *E* on many different occasions, and could say to himself 'There, I am experiencing *E* once more', and could have an impression of identity in regard to it. But Wittgenstein denies that such a move would be really meaningful since the test employed in identifying *E* is purely private and personal. For a man to say that he was sure it was the same, and that he had carefully examined it to make sure, would not offer him or us a genuine, additional test: it would be like buying several copies of the same newspaper in order to 'confirm' what one had read in a single copy (§267). To imagine such a purely private confirmation is like imagining that one's right hand could give one's left hand some money, and that one's left hand could then acknowledge receipt of it (§258). What all this entails is that a genuine language-game could always be played with someone else, and must conform to rules that others could agree to follow. If the use of *E* went with a publicly applicable criterion of some sort, e.g. a rise in the speaker's blood-pressure, then it would be a meaningful symbol no matter what private sensations it purported to report. But, if there were no such public criterion, or only a degenerate one which consisted in the mere fact that he experience was reported as *E*, there could be no genuine meaning attaching to the sign *E*.

It follows from this that all terms that purport to stand for private, inner experience, e.g. the term 'pain', must have external, public criteria and would not be meaningful without these, even if, in particular cases, such public criteria cannot be applied. There can be no such thing as pointing to one's pain inwardly, and recognizing it as pain: one can *have* pain, *be* in pain privately, but this is not pointing to it. And if one says 'I am in pain', this may not be very different from merely groaning and sighing *unless* one can also supply publicly accessible criteria of being in pain. Wittgenstein then in §293 introduces the celebrated image of a beetle. If each man had a box into which only he could look, and called whatever he saw in it a 'beetle', no such thing as a beetle, apart from this queer linguistic usage, would have been introduced into the use of the language. It would not be significantly determinable whether what seemed to be called 'beetle' were like, or unlike one another, nor even whether anything of the sort existed. They would be irrelevant to our speech with one another, and hence to all our speech as such, precisely as the ultimate simples of the *Tractatus* are also irrelevant to our speech. Wittgenstein then says that his aim is to get people out of all this inner-outer puzzlement, to show the flies the way out of the fly-bottle (§309). It must not here be supposed that Wittgenstein is rejecting out of hand any language-game of describing one's feelings or one's images, relating one's dreams and so forth. Only one is not then to be taken as describing or relating something in an ordinary sense of these words, since such language-games never go beyond the report-stage and can at best, if other criteria are not added, only offer themselves as their own degenerate criteria. A carefully and sincerely sketched feeling, dream, image- or memory-experience has its whole criterion of correctness in what people carefully and sincerely allege, and what others are prepared to accept as being careful and sincere. The analogies used in such reports or descriptions would, further, for Wittgenstein, not rightly be called 'metaphors', since there would be no other way of reporting or describing such matters. How we spoke of them would be how they were.

It is, of course, possible so to define a 'language' that a monologue dealing with matters unshareable by others becomes impossible, and this arguably is all that Wittgenstein has done in the remarkable sections just cited, which have, however, aroused infinite philosophical excitement and a literature of comment that practically amounts to an industry. A definition of language that has, however, such unthinkably unacceptable consequences must be one that refutes its own implicit claim to state what we, in fact, cover in our normal use of the term 'language'. For our actual use of language does not exclude the possibility (which we sometimes rate as a fact) that one person may have experiences that he cannot, except in a wholly vague and general manner, communicate to another – a mystical experience, for example, described as one of spiritual interpenetration, an awareness of a colour that others cannot see, or of a spatial dimension unknown to them, etc. – and that one could very well pick them out, and take note of their recurrent similarity on many occasions. A single person has, further, in many respects the character of a society: one of his perceptions can confirm another, and what he sees at one time can be confirmed by what he remembers at another, etc. The comparison of intrapersonal confirmation with the buying of several copies of the same newspaper is in no way apt, since different copies are not separate sources of information which could possibly disagree, and whose agreement is accordingly significant. And as regards such a concept as identity, especially in the realm of general characters, it is plainly of such universal import that the circumstances in which we were taught to use it are of null importance. We may have acquired it in conversation with our aunts, but henceforth, whether in heaven or hell or Nirvana, or immersed in our own private fantasies, we can still be adjudged to be using it properly, and in the same manner. It may further be stressed that unshared characters of experience can still always be spoken of in an *indirect* manner. Blind people certainly understand that the sighted perceive qualities that *they* cannot apprehend: they do not need to construct fantasies of mechanisms attaching their brains to other people's retinae, etc. The conception of interpenetration, of a fourth dimension, and of an ultra-violet shade, can likewise be formed indirectly by those who cannot fulfil them perceptually or imaginatively.

In an absolute sense we cannot, of course, talk a wholly private language, since it is not clear what it could be: words like 'sensation', 'experience', 'character', 'same', etc. are necessarily shareable in meaning, even if contingently unshared in some cases, and even demonstrative symbols such as 'here', 'now', 'this', and 'I' have a universal side to them, which is well understood when we hear other men use them, and on which Hegel built extensively. Descartes, likewise, in uttering his *Cogito*, envisaged his predicament and its resolution as being not his alone, but standard for *all* men: however much he might strip everything beyond his own thought of reality, it was still conceived as one thought among many, in giving voice to which he might speak for all. Language-games can, in fact, only be played and taught on the terrain of the all-comprehensive game of being one speaker or auditor among others, and of facing a world of common situations, all of which can, with sufficient penetration, come to be for all speakers of predominantly the same character. Beetle-boxes are indeed part of the human scene: there may always be things and features and relations in the world as it is for one person, and not in it as it is there for another person. It is, however, presupposed in all linguistic intercourse not only that there *are* beetle-boxes, whose contents are not in the vulgar, overt sense open to us, but also that we can to some extent see into those boxes, and that those proceedings which psychologists have called ones of empathy, and phenomenologists ones of appresentation, are the standard ways of achieving such a seeing. The feeling of ourselves into the overt reactions of men and animals, and the use of our own actual or imagined experiences as paradigms of *theirs*, are the standard ways in which the dispersed, but also profoundly interconnected, world of experience makes itself manifest to each and all of us, and which can perhaps be seen as culminating in much closer and more reliable forms of mutual penetration, mystical or scientific, but not for that reason intrinsically wide of the mark. We also employ similarity of bodily structure and behaviour to give sense and validity to the assumption that the world is largely the same, though never altogether the same, for others, as it is for ourselves. We unquestioningly place the gambolling lamb in a meadow which is as green for it as it is for us, and project the same buoyancy into its gambols as we should feel if our old bones still permitted them. Philosophical arguments based on the logical possibility that identical stimuli and responses might go with quite different feelings and sensations in different organisms, or on the supposed meaninglessness of speaking of similarity and dissimilarity where direct comparison is excluded, would then present themselves as cases of gratuitous scepticism and linguistic scruple which do nothing to undermine the perfect confidence inspired by our ordinary procedures.

Wittgenstein himself often appeals to the tissue of natural connections which make linguistic communication possible, as in §275, where he says that in speaking of the quality meant by the word 'blue', one points to the sky, which is taken to be part of a public, not a private world. If we hold, as Carnap later did, that the quality or content of experience is never linguistically communicable, but only its form or logical structure, it remains obscure how such structure can be communicated when quality is not. Obviously all that we distinguish, whether as public or private, forms one world, and its public sectors are merely those

which are more readily and directly accessible to everyone –
though even there there are differences in 'angle' or perspective.
It is arguable that Wittgenstein's extreme 'publicism' in the
*Investigations* reflects the secret working of his never abandoned,
ultimate solipsism. Solipsism makes a man's own subjectivity so
unique and all-constitutive as to deprive it of the significance that
it might derive from its contrast with other subjectivities. But
then, since speech has to be interpersonal, it has to become a
dialogue, not between subjects, but between talking and listening
animals, and must have all its criteria of meaning in the one
world public to them all. That this may be, in some transcendental sense, private to a single, empty self, is thus made irrelevant
and unmentionable.


## VIII


*(§§309–71)*

This section repeats many of the points previously made. It
begins with the famous statements of the aim of Wittgenstein's
philosophy: to show the fly the way out of the fly-bottle, to free it
from the need to answer many 'deep' questions due to a
misunderstanding of the uses of language (§309). §§310–15 deal
with the rules that govern the use of the word 'pain'. To say 'I am
in pain, but it's not so bad', could be replaced by instinctive
noises and gestures: it is in many ways profoundly different from
a declarative statement. This statement of Wittgenstein's is no
doubt true in some cases: to say plaintively 'I am in pain' may be
little different from moaning, and might even be described as
such. There is, however, such a thing as an interest in pain as a
phenomenon not unlike, e.g. the aurora borealis, but which
flashes about, not in the sky, but in some region of one's body.
This interest need not wholly vanish even when a pain becomes
agonizing, and one way of reducing the agony of certain dental
and other operations is to experience them in an agreeably
masochistic, observational fashion. It is at least interesting to
know what a certain pain is really like, and whether it is really
bearable or unbearable. Pain is, psychologically, a very interesting experience, and its association with the unpleasant very

strange and variable. There is therefore an element of the detachedly observational behind some utterances of the form 'I am in pain', and when the intensity of the pain takes over, we shall probably have recourse to pure groaning and say nothing at all. Wittgenstein, however, denies that we can give ourselves a private exhibition of a pain which is like the exhibition of a broken tooth. Wittgenstein as a child probably never stuck pins into his skin to see what the pain was like and whether he could stand it: if he had done so, he would know that such a private exhibition is not unlike a public exhibition of, say, fireworks, which may perhaps be equally unpleasant. Wittgenstein's dogmatic pronouncements may here be contrasted with the vastly varied categorizations which introspective psychologists such as Titchener have brought into the examination of pain, as well as into every other form of organic and kinaesthetic sensation, using metaphorical descriptions without stint, and often with great aptness and stylistic brilliancy. Even ordinary introspectionists can produce interesting descriptions of an electric shock.

The remainder of the section deals mainly with thinking, and tries to show that there is no special interior process which the word 'thinking' connotes. He denies that when we talk or write there is any inner process separable from the talking or writing (§318), but forgets that when we talk or write our action almost always has an inner side, in that it is 'there for us', something of which we are luminously, or perhaps only marginally, conscious, and that, when this fact is made plain, everything that we do with our·fingers or our pen or our larynx can also be said to be 'in our head'. The interior and the exterior normally go together and supplement one another, rather than pass over into one another, and while we cannot distinguish two acts in, say, pronouncing a German diphthong very carefully, we can very well distinguish certain laryngeal and sound changes from the conscious highlighting and sense of activity that attends the whole proceeding.

In §§329–21 Wittgenstein similarly denies that there is any indefinable experience of seeing something in a flash, and holds that, when we use such a phrase, we do so exactly in the sense in which we make a summing-up of something in a few scribbled words. There would seem to be little aptness in this comparison. If I am playing a game of prime-spotting in the series of cardinals, I may see in a flash that 23, 29, 31 and 37 are primes, and that the intervening cardinals are not, without having more than the naked consciousness that this is so, a *Bewusstheit*, to use the technical Würzburg term, unaccompanied by anything like the jotting down of a note. (The consciousness in question is, of course, not infallible.) Sudden understanding, Wittgenstein maintains, is not a specific experience, sensuous or non-sensuous. 'I see' is no more than an exclamation expressing a glad start, and, as we proceed, we may find that we do not see at all (§323). There is no inner experience that portends success, or is found to do so by induction. We say we can succeed, and sometimes we in fact do succeed (§§324–5). These remarks are not convincing in the case of the prime-spotter, even though it is true that a very convinced case of prime-spotting may be mistaken: one may 'see' 91 to be prime. Certainly, however, one may have the perception that 29 is prime without murmuring the word prime subvocally, and this perception has a quality of inner rightness which we do in fact profoundly trust. Wittgenstein does not fail to recognize such a felt rightness as foundational in various of his language-games. He refuses, however, to recognize any peculiar experiential *quality* in such cases, that calls for acceptance: rightness and acceptance would seem to be one and the same?

§327 denies altogether that there is an observable event known as thinking: all that is going on are certain actions and words, without any mysterious inner accompaniments (§330). Instead of saying 'This pencil is blunt, but it will do', I may substitute a gesture, but it is an illusion to think that there is an inner accompaniment common to both word and gesture. Many careful reflectors would, however, feel that this is not an illusion in all cases, and that we can, in fact, experience such an inner accompaniment without either words or gestures. 'What were you thinking?' 'I was thinking that the pen was blunt but would do.' 'Did you hear or say these words *sotto voce*?' 'I did not.' 'Did you flex muscles, etc.?' 'I did not.' 'What did you do?' 'I just had the thought.' It would seem, in fact, only the blind craving for something palpably *anschaulich*, something given to sense or intuition, that makes it hard for people to believe in sensuously unfulfilled thoughts, which none the less may be full of sense or content. Wittgenstein then goes on to deny that, having said something, we can go on thinking it without saying it, yet surely, after one has said 'You have been deceiving me', with horrid conviction, one can go on harbouring this thought for a while without expressing it in words or gestures? In §333 Wittgenstein goes on to deny that there is any specific experience of *conviction* which accompanies all convinced assertions, and in the sense in which conviction means something more than a subtly pervasive feature of the whole scene, or which attaches to part of it, he is certainly right. Noticeably specific experiences of conviction are somewhat rare, and arise mainly when something is questioned. We feel convinced, for example, that the figure in the distance is a penguin and not a man, but hardly that the people to whom we are speaking are men and not penguins. On the other hand, there *are* colourings of experience that only become manifest when we *compare* one case with another, and it is clear that there is often for us an experienced difference between what is for us a part of reality, and what is not. The living friend who actually walks beside us, and the dead friend whom we vividly remember from a similar walk, are certainly present to us differently, a difference inadequately expressed by saying we know that the living friend is *really* beside us, whereas the dead friend, alas, is not. There is no reason to doubt that a sensitive man like Wittgenstein would have had countless poignant experiences of the difference between the real and the unreal, between believing and merely conceiving: where he failed was in detecting adumbrations of such differences even in less poignant cases. But even a laboratory technician knows the difference between the reading he *ought* to get, and the reading he *does* get, and lives through the difference without saying or doing more than silently knowing what he knows. In §334 Wittgenstein similarly denies the existence of specific experiences of intending, with equal correctness and incorrectness. There are intentions as poignantly experienced as the nailing of these to church doors, and intentions distinguished only by a very faint note of 'to be doneness', as when we go up to someone and greet him. There are also intentions which reflect habits of action, conformity with which would only be accepted if such a question arose. These differences are, however, relevant and important, and cluster around a paradigm where there *are* specific experiences.

In §335 Wittgenstein denies the existence of thoughts that wholly precede their verbal expression: it would appear, however, that we experience such thoughts very frequently, as when, for example, we become aware of mockery in someone's tone, and *then* say, 'You are making fun of me.' Such pre-existent thoughts are as frequent as those that linger on for a while after we have given voice to them. §339 denies that thinking is an incorporeal process that lends life to speaking but which could occur wholly without it, as in the alleged experiences of deaf-mutes and such as Helen Keller, who have reported many complex experiences that occurred before they had learned ordinary language-uses. It is indeed hard to be sure in such cases whether later reports accurately reflect previous experience, but it would also be purely dogmatic to reject this *a priori*. Victims of aphasia, who were quite unable either to speak or to understand speech, but who are afterwards restored to their normal speech-capacity, sometimes accurately report what happened to them in hospital, in their previous aphasic state, which persons treated them kindly and which otherwise, etc., and all such reports accord with other lines of evidence. The complex inner life of an aphasic, brought to light in such wholly credible reports, in fact refutes the extraordinary stress on linguistic expression to which certain psychological types are prone. Wittgenstein says that unspoken thoughts certainly exist but are only possible in those who have learned to speak (§§345–9), and it is, of course, true that many thoughts, spoken or unspoken, reflect linguistically taught distinctions. It is only so very easy to put many thoughts into words because words have previously, we may say, been put into such thoughts. Our learned use of words such as 'terminal', 'post-prandial', 'innocent', 'elliptical', etc. has enabled us to think wordlessly of the matters first thought of in connection with the use of such words. Much thought, though not conducted in words, borrows most of its syntax, and its referential devices, from words. Ultimately, however, the traditional view is right, and all the devices employed in the use of words reflect deeper practices of thought, which, however, achieve maximum clarity and communicability when they are verbally expressed. Wittgenstein in §352 says that it is an abuse of the Law of Excluded Middle to assume that certain thoughts must be present, or not present, in someone's experience when there is simply no criterion that would establish either alternative. It is like asserting that 777 must occur or not occur in the expansion of $\pi$, even if no one ever can calculate far enough. There are some, however, who hold that something like a God's-eye view of all things is a presupposition of all significant thought and reference, and that it works better than the equally transcendental idea of the world or reality. And the notion of thoughts that might have been, but were not expressed in language, can profitably be extended to abnormal human aphasics and normal animal aphasics. An animal can show that it thinks something is edible or dangerous quite as reliably as a man, and imaginative constructions of the world as it is for animals are not necessarily sentimental nonsense: they may be as well-based as Tolman's investigations of the 'hypotheses' entertained by rats learning to get food by running mazes. The refusal to extend the word 'hypothesis' to a mere rat is not a mark of respectable scientific caution, but rather of humanistic and linguistic chauvinism. We value our differences from a rat so inordinately that we must deem them enormous even when they are patently quite measurable. The attribution of thoughts to machines and pieces of furniture is not, however, as Wittgenstein would have it in §§359–61, to be put on a level with their attribution to animals. For while computers and robots do enough to show, by their varied outputs, that the world is there for them through many varied inputs, and that numerical and logical relations are also, in some highly analogical sense, there for them, their lack of certain delicacies of response, of a welcoming or dismissive character, would make it impossible for us to attribute any conscious sensitivity to what they thus respond to. They respond selectively, but mechanically, and they cannot be supposed to feel anything. Not feeling anything, they therefore lack the very basis of anything that could be called consciousness or awareness. For while conscious awareness involves an intentionality which transcends or points beyond itself, it would without lived-through feelings and sensations, have nothing to transcend or point beyond. Animals, however, by their delicate shading of responses which welcome, avoid or prolong encounters and responses, show that they are intimately living through highly specific, qualitative experiences into which we can likewise feel ourselves, but it would be highly artificial to try to practise similar appresentations on computers. We are, however, here touching on matters of the utmost difficulty, which require a far fuller treatment than is possible at this point.

## IX

The hunting down of private experiences continues in these sections. Men, Wittgenstein holds, are obstinately persuaded that processes go on in them which are merely false pictures prompted by verbal usages. We often say that we are experiencing the *same* thing now as then. Wittgenstein says that, in default of a public criterion which other men acknowledge, there is no sense in such an employment of the word 'same' (§378). The reply to this contention is that men who accept it that other men use the word 'same' correctly in situations ordinarily called public, also license the use of the word 'same' when other men use it in connection with their private experience, and when they perhaps justify the use of the word 'same' by analogical descriptions that fit the experiences of others. ('I suddenly felt that everyone around me was an automaton without an inner life.' 'How curious. That's exactly the experience I once had in a theatre in Tangier.') The criterion of being a reliable speaker who uses the word 'same' with discretion in public situations, is therefore a publicly accepted criterion even in the case of matters of the 'inner life'. We do not demand to sit in on your last year's experience in Tangier. Wittgenstein then denies that we can use quality-words like 'red' in default of a public acceptance of our use: hence the application of 'red' to an image cannot be justified (§382), It none the less goes quite unquestioned in the language-game in which it is practised. A man's testimony to what he does 'in his head' is not, Wittgenstein says, really testimony: it is only what he is inclined to say (§386). This is not, however, what ordinary people are inclined to say. Imagining is dealt with in §§391–402. To say that imagination introduces us to private objects which resemble public ones, but are somehow different, serves no purpose: the 'visual room' that I imagine is a room that no one owns or can point to, not even I myself. But what, however, we may here ask, of the psychological experiment where people are shown faint actual pictures projected on to a screen, and are then led to imagine that they are only imagining these? This is a standard experiment to show that images are not

227

so different from sense-data as men are inclined to say. And what of after-images? Isn't it hard to distinguish them from actual sense-data? And why must we accept such physicalistic puritanism in our language? The whole attempt to purge the physical world of everything that varies from subject to subject, will obviously end in a physicalism of primary qualities, in which nothing but electrons, etc. can be talked about, and our ordinary common-or-garden things will become mere projections of our language, which ought not really to be objects of discourse at all. Such nonsense plainly surpasses any of the nonsensical forms of what Whitehead called the 'bifurcation of nature', since the time of the Greek Atomists.

In §403 Wittgenstein says that it would be quite feasible to have had different words for our own and for other people's pains. This would not do other people any injustice, but we prefer to say that their pains are the *same* sort of thing as our own. In the same manner, disputes between idealists, solipsists and realists as to the independent existence of sensibly perceived objects or of other people's pains are really linguistic disputes (§402). Very arguably, this statement stems from Wittgenstein's own inexpugnable solipsism, which was fully confessed in the *Tractatus* and still defended in the *Blue Book*. A solipsist can obviously only make sense of the existence of sensible objects, or of other people's experiences, in terms of experiences and usages of his own, so that it becomes indifferent whether he speaks of them in a realistic or idealistic or purely solipsistic manner. With the vanishing of other, independent subjects goes the vanishing of the one residual, central subject so that it becomes quite indifferent what we choose to say.

Wittgenstein further argues that, since it is nonsensical to say that I don't know whether I am in pain, it also makes nonsense to say that I know that I am in pain, except perhaps as a form of pain-expressive behaviour (§§402–8). The paradoxical ruling that one can only know what one can also doubt is, however, arbitrary, and quite unacceptable. I cannot doubt that 7 is a prime number, but I can also rightly say that I know it to be such. It further makes perfect sense to say such things as that I was in pain all the time, but that my preoccupation with certain duties led me to ignore such pain completely. Pain, as we have said, is a phenomenon, like the state of the tides, which can be noted or gnored, but which it is extraordinarily hard, but not impossible, to ignore when it is intense: one can, however, conceive of a successful Stoic suddenly realizing that he has been in pain for a long time. §412 dwells on the widespread notion that there is an unbridgeable gulf between our inner mental processes and anything that goes on in the brain. We are not in a position to observe our own mental happenings and at the same time correlate them with our observed brain-happenings. If, however, experiments uniformly connected certain brain-excitations with sensations of certain sorts, the unbridgeable gulf would be bridged, and all hitherto private experiences would acquire a public status. But to those who use ordinary methods of analogical description to explore the field of sensational and other experiences, this field is already covered by shared, public senses, and nothing very important is to be gained by such brain-exploration, which, however, confirms the rational presumption of considerable parallelism between the cerebral and experiential fields, whether or not we care to go in for a perfectly meaningful, but more widely ranging 'identification' in such a case.

§418 doubts whether being conscious is a fact of experience, a question perhaps suggested by Wittgenstein's readings of William James. Plainly, however, consciousness does reveal itself at all times in the variety of its modalities, and particularly in the variable high-lighting or conscious emphasis which is a feature of all human experience, and which cannot, despite the efforts of Ryle and others, be reduced to any behavioural accompaniments or after-effects. Some things or features are at all times very clear as to what they are, as to their indefiniteness or vagueness of structure, while others sink into a margin of unclarity, and yet perhaps afterwards come into the full focus of conscious clarity. This clearness of conscious awareness is, of course, quite different from the objective clearness of structure or intensity of sensational impact: a voice softly uttering a few mumbled but important words may be maximally clear while a vast surrounding hubbub may pass unnoticed. And a dim figure may be maximally clear, while a fully illuminated one may be ignored. It is possible to raise to maximal conscious clarity a faint pressure in one's left big toe, thereby also providing an impressive exhibition of what consciousness as such is and what it is not, and the irrelevance of its object-matter. There are, of course, countless other important differences in consciousness, and in particular that of the sensuously fulfilled and the cogitatively unfulfilled, or empty, which are equally important. So also the difference between the inwardly lived through, *felt* experience, and the objectively directed or intentional experience, or the difference between the experience passively undergone or the experience which has a note of agency or activity. Consciousness is a genuine phenomenon as well as a reality, and can be examined and studied and analysed, mainly in the light of comparisons and in immediate retrospect, and with the use of analogical language. It will not, however, reveal itself to grossly sensual men, who expect it to have the effulgence and sharp outline of a set of arc-lamps.

§420 then considers the uncanny experience of feeling that all the people around one, despite all they say and do, are mere automata without an inner life, a supposition which at least shows that the inner life of others has great reality for some of us. Wittgenstein holds that this uncanny experience is essentially meaningless, and involves no more than a queer feeling. To some of us, however, it represents an awesome, if abstract possibility which we are happy to know (in a perhaps Moorean sense of 'know') is untrue. That Wittgenstein can regard it as merely a queer feeling is yet another proof that he never took the existence of other experients quite seriously. He says in §427 that, when someone says he wishes he could read what is going on in someone else's thoughts, he is only playing with a picture. The sort of reading he is conceiving means nothing unless a public, i.e. a physical criterion, can be brought in. God himself, it would appear, could, on Wittgenstein's view, not be one to whom all hearts were open, all desires known, and from whom no secrets were hid, and yet this transcendental picture enters into the background of all our discourse with others. Somehow, we take it, our dispersed inner lives form a single, totally surveyable picture, with many profound affinities and divergencies among its severed parts, whether this can be publicly established or not. One can only hope that there may be experiences of psychic interpenetration in some phase of a life to come that will suffice to shake Wittgenstein's obdurate physicalistic publicism, which is only the reverse side of his equally obdurate solipsism.

Wittgenstein further denies that there is an inner act of

understanding that gives life to an assertion: the correct use of expressions itself imparts all this life. This recalls to me the utterance of a London colleague who was both a hot gospeller and a convinced cyberneticist. He was convinced that a robot might be so trained to make the correct verbal responses as to be capable of being saved. §436 then formulates the fascinating view that it is a philosophical dead-end to imagine that we don't know all we are experiencing, since it passes away too quickly. This evanescence is, however, quite obviously the truth and refutes any equation of what we inwardly experience with what we can or cannot say. This is, indeed, a philosophical dead-end, but only to a dogmatically exhaustive, self-sufficient linguistic absolutism, which Wittgenstein's doctrine arguably tends to be.

X

*(§§437–500)*

These sections are concerned with various types of intentional act, and with the superstition that they *contain* their objects in some queer, non-natural manner. We talk as if wishes and expectations somehow included their objects as real parts in themselves, but not in such a manner as would amount to the fulfilment of such wishes and expectations. The connection between a wish or expectation, on the one hand, and its fulfilment on the other, is, according to Wittgenstein, a grammatical connection: asked what are our wishes or expectations, we have to use the same words that we should apply to the objects to which they are directed. Wittgenstein, however, denies that there is any pre-existent or inexistent *presence* of the object in the mental act: being expectant is just being restless, etc., and ceasing to be so when a certain event transpires. It is in language alone that an expectation and its fulfilment make contact (§445). We say that, if anyone could perceive my expectation, he would automatically know what I was expecting (§453). Wittgenstein, however, denies that meaning can be attached to perceiving an expectation, whether my own or anyone else's. §455 and §457 make intentionality into a metaphor: we liken someone's meaning of something to his going up to it. §462 deals with references to the absent or non-existent: I can look for someone when he is not there, but I cannot hang him when he is not there. There is a tendency to think he must be somewhere in the former case because he is somewhere in the latter. The presence of an object in a thought is, however, for Wittgenstein a piece of disguised nonsense which he wishes to turn into a piece of patent nonsense (§464). We may hold, however, that Wittgenstein's difficulties are simply due to his refusal to understand what can be meant by the presence of an object in or to thought. This presence merely means that certain experiences are experiences *of* such and such objective matters, and would not be the experiences they are if they were not of the matter in question, and yet that their being *of* such matters is quite unaffected by the fact that what they are *of*, is actually absent or non-existent. I expect food in the cupboard even if there is no food there, and it would be absurd to say that my expectation could not be of food, since there is not food there to be expected. Intentionality or mental reference is, as Brentano classically said in an Appendix to his great work on psychology, *not* a relation in the sense in which one can only have a relation to something if there *is* such a thing – one can, for example, only sit on a chair if there is a chair to be sat upon – but rather something, which from such an existential point of view is only relation-like (*Relativliches*), since a thought or other intentional act can as readily be concerned with what is non-existent or absent, as with what actually exists or is present. 'Intentional inexistence' is therefore a wholly innocent phrase, which says no more, to talk *á la* Wittgenstein, than that being *of* some specific object or state of affairs is a part of the sense or the grammar of a great number of mental-attitude expressions, and that objects may be necessary to the adequate description of a mental attitude even if there are no such objects present in the described situation, or anywhere at all. Obviously the object of a reference may in this harmless sense be present *to* or *in* our thought, or our mental attitude, without thereby being anything contained in it in the most ordinary sense of 'contained', nor need it, in fact, in this sense, be contained in anything else. And that there are inferential pitfalls if we attempt to identify intentional objects with real ones or with other intentional objects, or seek to characterize them further than they are intentionally characterized, and so on, are pitfalls not unknown o the ordinary speaker, but explored in much more detail by the modern logician, with his interest in opaque contexts. With care, we can learn to speak of objects of mental reference in contexts which also deal with existent objects, in such a way that no absurd conclusions are drawn. To say that the non-existent has a queer sort of being in expectations and wishes may then be a piece of dangerous mystification, but it may equally be no more than a recognition of the incompleteness of any account of our experience and behaviour, or even of the powers and tendencies of physical things, which leaves out the non-existent or the counter-factual altogether. It is, further, false to hold that it is only in language that an expectation and its objective fulfilment make contact. Animals, who do not use language, often expect food where and when they fail to find it, and they also often find food where and when they expect it. Their expectations therefore make contact with objective situations, or fail to make such contact, without the benefit of mediating expressions. And we also, being animals in very much of our thought and action, can be as overtly and inwardly silent regarding what exists or does not exist, and yet be as clearly and as rightly or wrongly conscious of it, as animals are. Words and expressions are, in fact, only brought into the discussion of the whole matter out of a misguided desire to have something existent which will do duty for the ineliminable non-existences which enter into the sense of our words and expressions.

In §482 Wittgenstein considers the nature of inductive certainties, and regards them as products of a certain language-game. Nothing would induce us to put our hands into a flame, even though it was only in the past that we burnt ourselves (§472). It is senseless to ask whether burnings in the past provide good ground for expecting burnings in the present: what other grounds could one have? Obviously one is not asking for a formal demonstration. Justification by experience must in some cases be final: if it were not, it would not be justification (§485). Wittgenstein is here taking up a Moorean stance, only Moore would say that he *knew* what is thus justified, and that this knowledge is sufficient to invalidate the arguments of Hume which seek to invalidate *it*. Moore would further think that there was some remarkable property of the state he calls knowledge which coheres with its reliability, whereas Wittgenstein only sees it as a rule set up in a certain language-game, the inductive-empirical one. He at least owes us an explanation as to why it is so vastly more important and fundamental for our life than is the game of greeting or joking or the many other games that he recognizes.

## XI

(§§500–68)

In these sections Wittgenstein is particularly concerned with supposed experiences of meaning *this* or *that*. He tries to show that there are no such experiences, or none that are uniform and specific, but that we are ready to use words in various ways. When we consider what goes on in us when we use words with meaning, it seems as if there were something coupled to those words, which latter could otherwise run idly (§507). He suggests that there is no uniform way of saying 'It's warm here' and meaning 'It's cold here' (§510). Has he forgotten the various childish games in which one did precisely this, saying 'Bridget did it' when one meant that Nancy did it, or 'The pudding's nice' when one meant that it was horrid, and so on. A child has no difficulty in making anything mean anything: I once made 'Thababettlett' mean 'Uncle is boring me.' He queries our power to give meaning to the sentence 'Does the sequence 7777 occur in the development of $\pi$' (§516) or to the sentence 'After he said this he left her, as he did the day before' (§525). But the picture of a God's-eye view, which arguably is involved in all references, make the former perfectly meaningful, and the latter is only more indeterminate than the majority of our references: we are plunged into a complex situation involving two persons of opposite sex, two partings and two consecutive days. Further details are left indefinite, as in many similar utterances, and the only impropriety is the use of pronouns and articles which suggest that they should be more definite. Wittgenstein further says that the understanding of a sentence is much more akin to understanding a theme in music than is commonly supposed: it consists in being able to go on appropriately (§527). This is all right, but in both cases many report package-experiences

(*Bewusstseinslagen*) which can thereupon be unpacked: why should we reject such reports, merely because they are phrased in the analogical fashion alone appropriate to them? A few other doubts and denials may similarly be queried. Wittgenstein doubts whether we can really *see* courage or timidity in a face (§537), though in Part II of the *Investigations* he would probably have let this pass. Certainly we do or experience something which is admirably expressed in this manner, and others frequently agree that it expresses just what *they* experience, or can experience, when they look at the face in question. In such a case what need have we of further witnesses? Wittgenstein also doubts whether there is a specific feeling of hope that gives 'I hope he'll come' its meaning (§545), and certainly there are cases in which no such feeling is present, and other cases where it is very poignant and passionate. None the less there are, in the whole range of such cases, affinities more definite than any between 'I hope he'll come' and 'I am afraid he'll come': there is, we may pompously say, an orientation to the future, a hesitant placing of a certain content in it, and a welcoming of the content thus placed. If these matters are not present to us in the world as we intend it, and as we intend ourselves in it, what gives our utterance its specific direction? Not the unnumerable facts and rules that are relevant to it, but which are much more peripheral to it than the matters just mentioned.

Wittgenstein then goes on to deny the existence of any unique experience of negation and negativity. Quite clearly, since there are many different senses of negation, e.g. absence, difference, contradiction, contrariety, the negation cancelled if repeated and the negation strengthened by repetition, etc., there will have to be many distinct experiences of negation and negativity. And in this case too there will be poignant experiences of negation, as when some very confident assumption is invalidated, and ones very lacking in poignancy, as when one asserts, in contradiction of some foolish error, that someone is *not* a conservative. There will also be poignant experiences of negation as when someone uses self-contradictory language to bring out something very unusual – God is everywhere and nowhere – or a concept's very interesting interior conflicts. We may, in fact, say with Wittgenstein that experiences of negation form a family, but that there is none the less, in all of them a governing affinity that pervades their many variations. All involve the failure of a fulfilment, poignant or trivial, that there was some reason, whether strong or faint, to expect. Animals, like ourselves, must certainly experience some of the more elementary forms of negation. Wittgenstein further says that there is no special way of experiencing the differences between different senses of the verb to be, whether existential, predicative, identificatory or whatever. Plainly there are a great number of different experiences, and some near-absences of experience, attending the use of this verb.

## XII

*(§§568–641)*

In these sections Wittgenstein continues his negative treatment of so-called intentional experiences, e.g. experiences of expecting, opining, believing, hoping, judging, willing, doing, trying, intending, etc., and of the alleged mental 'atmospheres' that go with them. In all these cases he queries the existence of more or less uniform inner states corresponding to much-used psychological verbs: all that is present is a widely ranging readiness for overt responses, verbal usages, images, feelings, etc. He denies (§571) that psychology deals with psychical processes in a sense comparable to that in which physics deals with physical processes: it merely investigates certain physical reactions of human beings, including their speech-reactions. Expectation is dealt with in §572, §§575–7 and §§581–6, belief and opinion in §573 and §§578–9, decision in §§588–9, intention in §§591–2, familiarity in §596, recognition in §§602–5, judgement as to the time of day in §607, volition in §§611–621, trying in §§622–3, volition again in §§627–8, being about to do something in §§635–8. The examples chosen are often very apt, e.g. 'For a moment I was going to deceive him' (§638), a perfect example of an experience that wordlessly packs much detail into an instant package. Wittgenstein was not poor in inner experience: he had the soul of a poet, and the mind of a laboratory technician. He was only poor in the categories in which he tried to analyse and explain his rich experience. In all such cases Wittgenstein applies the slogans: 'An inner experience stands in need of outward criteria' and 'A main cause of philosophical disease is a one-sided diet: one nourishes one's thinking with one kind of example' (§593). 'When we do philosophy we like to hypostatize feelings where there are none: they serve to explain our thoughts to us' (§598). He takes the view that words like 'expectation', 'recognition', etc. do not express unique, uniform, lived-through attitudes or atmospheres, but cover a vast range of cases of experience and action held together by the use of a common word. He argues that there are no peculiar, uniform feelings of familiarity or strangeness when things are familiar or strange to us, and certainly no feelings of ordinariness when we confront ordinary things. We do not, he says, have specific experiences of recognizing the furniture every time we enter our familiar room (§§602–6). The act of intuitively estimating the hour does not depend on a qualitative time-atmosphere (§607). The notion of willing as a specific inner act is quite mythic: there is no inner mechanism which, with outer assistance, brings our actions about (§§611–17). It is hard to see on what grounds Wittgenstein can maintain all this. Voluntary action, of course, covers a wide spectrum of cases, some rich in feelings and interior experiences, others almost devoid of the latter. But the antithesis of active doing or endeavouring, on the one hand, and passive undergoing, on the other, is one that *can* be poignantly and saliently experienced, and such active doing and endeavouring fits subsequent realization in a uniquely fulfilling manner which, unless we have been indoctrinated by the infinitely passive Hume, leads us to say that activity we experience feels *productive*, at least in part, of the outcome that eventuates, that it helps to *make* or *cause* or *bring it about*. Our notions of production, causation, bringing about, all originate in this sort of context, no matter how much they may be afterwards extended to purely physical transactions, and we have no reason to bring in 'mechanisms' of any sort to throw light on them. Active endeavour is simply felt to continue itself in, and so to bring about a certain outcome: what can bringing about be but just this, though we may, of course, extend our concept to less poignant cases. Wittgenstein goes on to say, with perfect correctness, that specific experiences of trying do not exist in the majority of cases where we say that we were trying to do something (§§622–3): we do not experience active endeavour when, as we say, we try to sit down, but are impeded by some sudden disturbance. Wittgenstein briefly considers an analysis of voluntary action in terms of an absence of surprise (§628) at a given outcome, e.g. at an arm-movement, and thereby realizes the experienced naturalness and appropriateness of the realization of what we want, however much this may later give rise to sophisticated logical and physical questions. In general, we may say that Wittgenstein has established that our major intentional attitudes can all be accompanied by a wide range of inner experiences, but are not accompanied by uniform, invariant ones: what he has *not* shown is that there are not paradigms for these attitudes, by their varied degree and direction of approach to which they are best classified, and that in these paradigmatic cases certain experiences, which range over a relatively small region of difference, play a significant, central part. There are paradigms of the voluntary, the expected, the hoped for, the tried at, etc., however indefinite their outlines may be, and it is in the light of such paradigms that we extend the use of such terms to cases that only distantly adumbrate them. Aristotle said that in addition to cases where terms have a single, invariant meaning there are other cases where they rather point to a unity of goal and derivation: they apply to cases which all derive from a single, paramount case or towards which they all tend (Τὸ αφ' ἑνὸς εἶναι κὰι *pos* εν ἅπαντα συντελεῖν). Cases of categorial notions like being, good and unity are in this position, as Aristotle teaches, but so we may say are cases of psychological attitudes such as belief, volition, approval, etc. Such attitudes have dim, denatured cases with only a few aspects properly developed, and other cases in which there is full development in every relevant respect, including the inwardly experiential. There is a vast gulf between a belief which considers all grounds, feels all hesitations, and makes all practical preparations, and one that is as ill-considered and ill-derived as the assertion that the weather in the Caribbean is usually warm and fine.

## XIII

*(§§642–93)*

The trivializing analysis of alleged inner attitudes is carried on in these sections. A man reports that 'At that moment I hated him' but, if he really rehearsed that moment to himself, he would have to assume a certain facial expression, think of certain happenings, breathe in a certain way, re-arouse certain feelings in himself, and so on. He might think up the whole scene in which this hatred flared up, and might play at feelings approximating to those of a real occasion, and be helped by having actually experienced something of the sort (§642). A momentary intention subjected to such an analysis dissolves into many 'thoughts, feelings, movements and also connections with earlier situations'; if one tried to make a single sensation clear, it might prove to be no more than a particular tickle. A great number of our alleged inner experiences amount to no more than to our readiness to use certain words: it was as if we said to ourselves 'If only I could stay longer' or 'I shall now do this', etc. We ought not to think of the language-game as deriving from the inner experience, but as being the primary thing of which the inner experience is only an interpretation (§§655–6). The grammar of the expression 'I was then going to say . . . ' is related to that of 'I could then have gone on.' Both express linguistic dispositions, not unique inner experiences. §664 contains an important reference to the difference between surface-grammar and depth-grammar. The surface-grammar of an expression is what is explicit in the syntax and the semantics of the expression, i.e. the way in which it functions in the construction of a sentence, and the connections we should summon up to define its meaning or to elucidate it linguistically. The depth-grammar, on the other hand, would here, somewhat unusually, seem to involve all the obscure sensations, images, feelings and gestures which condition our use of the expression. Thus if we were in pain, and simultaneously heard a neighbourhood piano being tuned, and said to ourselves 'It'll soon stop', there might be a specific direction of this utterance to the pain *or* the piano, which direction, Wittgenstein says, would be settled by a variety of facts involving context, muscular adjustment, subsequent responses and a directed *look* which is taken to express a direction of 'attention'. What is absent from the depth-grammar in this passage is anything like the specifically directed intentionality which Brentano postulated: this is a mere reflection of the surface-grammar. Wittgenstein in this passage is taking a position similar to that of Titchener at Cornell, whose pupils introspected the contents of their minds *existentially*, i.e. only for what they *were*, not for what they meant. What they *were*, then consisted simply in the classical sensations, images and elementary feelings of Wundt, decorated with a few further differences such as that of the qualitatively clear or obscure, which did duty for the traditional degrees of attention. What they meant depended on the whole context in which they occurred: in the case of verbal meanings this would have largely coincided with what Wittgenstein called 'use'. Both Titchener and Wittgenstein wished to make meanings vanish from reported experience. They might *carry* our meanings but were, as existences, essentially meaningless. On our more traditional view, all this represents a colossal mistake. Images, sensations, feelings, words are the mere surface accidents of conscious awareness: its true substance consists of the self-transcendent acts of reference, intention, etc., which are intrinsically sense-informed ('sense' here not having anything to do with the senses) and object-directed. Reference to something is not, for Wittgenstein, a unique conscious direction to something, which thereby becomes our object: it covers bodily reactions of pointing, listening, looking, etc., which are at best its integument (§§669–70). There is, Wittgenstein says, no unique act of meaning precisely this thing and nothing else (§§669–91). The problems of conscious reference are indeed considerable, for not only must we have specifically directed conscious experiences, but we must also in some cases be able to bring their intentional objects into coincidence with real objects in the world. The new idealism of Hilary Putnam here tries to come to our aid, but we ourselves prefer a God's-eye view semantic *à la* Malebranche: we place all things, including all the digits in the expansion of $\pi$, as well as whatever is possible or impossible, in time or beyond time, in the intentional range of a paradigmatic intelligence, with which we may be presumed to have some sort of remote contact. The tergiversations of the *Philosophical Investigations* drive us to this point, so that they must, despite surface appearances, harbour great dialectical stimulus.

## XIV

*Part II*

Part II of the *Investigations* consists of an interesting series of fragmentary observations written down after the main part of the work in 1947–9: the editors tell us that Wittgenstein probably intended to work them into the earlier part of the work. We shall content ourselves with a few comments on Wittgenstein's more interesting remarks.

(i) Wittgenstein deals with the limitations of animals due largely to their lack of language. A dog can believe that his master is at the door, but not that his master will come the day after tomorrow. We may concede this, but yet urge, from actual experience, that a dog may recognize the unnatural quiet of Sunday, and slink away to avoid the impending bath. (ii) deals with the ambiguity of meaning attaching to words like 'till', 'is', and 'Scot' (as a name and a nationality), etc. Can we be said to have a parade of different meanings before the mind, as some people say they have? Wittgenstein doubts if we can, but we should assert a spectrum of cases culminating in a case where the ambiguity is patent and vividly given in detail. In (iii) Wittgenstein asks what makes the image of *him* be an image of *him*. He answers that a verbal acknowledgement suffices. It indeed does, but we should at least require the possibility, and the occasional realization of one of those package syntheses in which, without a spelling out of details, we savour a man's whole aspect and manner of being. Those who regularly pray for their friends will know what this is like.

(iv) says that to say of a man that he is not an automaton is not experienced as being informative. But it may be, by those at least who experience profound spiritual shock and horror at purely physicalistic analyses of human character and experience. The minds and souls of others are for them total worlds into which they venture in imaginative faith: these worlds are not purely imaginable in terms of people's bodies and what these do. (v) says that talking about people's experiences and about people's behaviour are different language-games with very complicated interrelations. And he questions whether there are special presuppositions in the case of the experiential language-game.

We reject, however, any complete translation of what can be said in the one game into what can be said in the other. We are going against both games if we go against their partial irreducibility.

(vi) Wittgenstein here begins with an admirable description of a package-experience of meaning, a *Bewusstseinslage* or posture of consciousness in the Würzburg sense. 'Suppose someone said: Every familiar word, in a book for example, actually carries an atmosphere with it in our minds, a "corona" of lightly indicated uses. Just as if each figure in a painting were surrounded by delicate shadowy drawings of scenes, and in them we saw the figures in different contexts.' Such an assumption would not be, for Wittgenstein, adequate to explain an attribution of an intention or an understanding to another person, since the attribution of atmosphere in question only goes for ourselves, and we cannot know if others have such an experience too. To this we may, however, reply, in Moorean vein, that while we may not know all the minutiae of other people's experiences, we do indeed know their general character, and in some cases as reliably as we know anything whatever, appresentation duly carried out being as reliable a procedure as any, and that if we did not know this, we could ignore them, or slaughter them, or do exactly what we chose with them. We know this in the sense that we are far more certain of this than of any scientific or philosophical theory that runs counter to our conviction. We must not, however, exaggerate the range of such inner experiences of meaning, or of our knowledge of them. They certainly do not invest every familiar word in a book, nor are they always present when we use the conjunctions 'if' and 'not', nor are they ever wholly uniform at all times or for all persons. If, however, they are never present, or have absolutely no uniformity of character, then we are indeed dealing with robots or demons which we can use or misuse as we like. The certainty that we are dealing with beings who can share our meanings in an experiential as well as a behavioural sense is *a priori* in the Kantian sense of being a basic presupposition for all learning by experience. There is nothing mysterious in such a situation, nor need we see transcendental subjectivity behind it, or at least none other than that which validates a belief in an intelligence such as Kant also believed in, which is as much creative as all-intelligent. To understand the grammar of intentionality in all its variations is

242

indeed to remove mystery rather than create it.

In (vii) Wittgenstein says we have to make assumptions as to whether people can be deceived by their memories or not, whether they really had dream-images while they slept, or merely seemed to have had them when they woke. He doubts whether the question has either meaning or interest, and whether we even ask it when someone is telling us his dream. He asks whether it is nonsense to raise the whole question as to whether dreams really take place during sleep, or are a memory phenomenon of the awakened, and says that this will turn on the use of the question. Presumably he means to suggest that dreaming could be validated by encephalograms, talking in one's sleep and other public criteria, or, alternatively, that, since dream-reporting is the criterion of having dreamt, we *did* dream if we report dreams with care and sincerity. He probably does not mean to identify dreaming with its criterion, since this is certainly *not* what we say. Malcolm has carried the Wittgenstein treatment of dreams much further. We, however, may prefer to hold that the reasonableness of Descartes's whole position invalidates Wittgenstein's and Malcolm's verificationistic position rather than the other way round. Dreams certainly are a part of the world as we find it, and they are not in ordinary talk or thought to be identified with the reports which purport to describe them. Wittgenstein further considers the whole evolutionary picture of an unconscious world that then evolves into a world with many dispersed centres of consciousness to be no more than a picture, which takes us in by suggesting that it already has an application and a use. We may, however, prefer to trust the evolutionary picture rather than any epistemological or semantic theory.

(viii) deals with the fact that kinaesthetic sensations apprise us of the precise position and movement of our limbs without presenting the latter, and that the location of pains, etc. occurs without the 'local signs' which the earlier psychologists hypothesized. What is essential is that we can *say* at which place we are affected, and this ability need not rest on any quality or character of sensation. It might be added that we do not judge by the *character* of the sensations in our semi-circular canals how our body is positioned, nor by the differing *intensity* of the sounds on our two ear-drums whence the sound is coming. But that our body relies on unsensed differences in stimulation in apprising us of many matters does not mean that the use of words plays an essential part in such apprisal.

(ix) says correctly that we cannot be said to observe something if our observation itself produces it: the existence of what is observed must be independent of our observation. If a fear is called into being by our attempt to observe such a state, we are not, strictly speaking, observing it. Wittgenstein seems to be concerning himself with the old problem that introspection can create or destroy or modify what it seeks to introspect. Such problems are best exorcised by relying only on introspections of the quite immediately past. Such introspections avoid an interference by observation, since even the just past transcends the observing act, but they also avoid the transformations which a longer wait might permit. The Würzburg psychologist relied entirely on such immediate retrospections: dishes hot from the oven of the inner life were, we may say, placed at once on the table of introspection. They were not allowed to lose warmth in the chilly air of dubious theorizing.

(x) deals with the use of a verb like 'believing' which sometimes refers to one's own perhaps not very poignantly experienced attitude, sometimes merely makes that attitude more emphatic: 'I believe it is going to rain' can be about our present attitude, but it can often merely mean the same as 'It is going to rain.' One can, Wittgenstein says, imagine a language in which belief has *no* expression apart from the tone of one's assertion. There is a great deal that is dispositional about believing, and a great deal that is behavioural, but the relation of a speaker to belief in himself is quite different from his relation to belief in others: one can hardly say 'Judging from what I say, this is what I believe.' There is little to object to in this section.

(xi) This section deals with a sense of 'seeing' which has been deeply studied by the Gestalt psychologists, with whose work Wittgenstein seems to have been superficially acquainted. On their view, organization into pattern, relieved from background, is a universal characteristic, not only of all sense-perception, but also of the neuro-physiology which underlies it. Wittgenstein imagines, as some of the earlier psychologists imagined, that the seeing of objects as organized in particular ways, e.g. as three-dimensional, and in a particular perspective, involves an invariant sensation resting directly on physical stimulation, and a superimposed reading that one is inclined to call an inference, or a thought, or an interpretation, if one is clear that no conscious experiences are covered by these names. The psychologist is deeply interested in the causes of these equivocal interpretations, e.g. those of a figure in a text-book which can be seen as a glass cube, an inverted open box, a wire frame or a number of boards forming a solid angle, etc. A duck-rabbit, which can be seen either as a rabbit with long ears looking right, or as a duck with a long beak looking left, is also much discussed, and has made a vast impression on many readers of Wittgenstein who would seem not to have read other books on the psychology of perception. Wittgenstein uses the term 'seeing as' to indicate this variable, superimposed sort of perceptual seeing, which Husserl recognizes as present in *all* perception, and in all thought-reference. To see or to think of anything whatever is necessarily to envisage it from a particular angle, *as* this or *as* that. Predication and description thus enter into *all* reference. Wittgenstein, however, is far from accepting such a doctrine: one does not, he says, take cutlery at a meal *for* cutlery, nor say to oneself 'Now I am seeing this as a knife and fork.' One does not indeed, but this does not affect the fact that the cutlery on the table is there for us, and there for us *as* cutlery, even though this is certainly not worth saying, and certainly not 'experienced' in any poignant, highlighted manner. Wittgenstein notes that 'seeing as' can change dramatically, in some cases voluntarily, and in such cases 'we describe the alteration like a perception, quite as if the object had altered before our eyes.' Wittgenstein, the inveterate physicist, prefers not to say this. He cannot permit talk of an inner object described in the same terms as an outer one, even though this is in fact how we do talk of it. Like Helmholtz, making three-dimensional vision a blend of sensation and unconscious inference, Wittgenstein says he would almost like to call knowing an acquaintance in a crowd 'an amalgam of seeing and thinking' (p. 197e). There is nothing wrong about recognizing such an amalgam, provided it is recognized as present in *all* conscious reference. Wittgenstein naively asks (p. 202e) 'When I see the picture of a galloping horse – do I merely *know* that this is the kind of movement meant? Is it superstition to think I *see* the horse galloping in the picture? – And does my visual impression gallop too?' Obviously the sensuously absent enters into all perception, without necessarily being represented by an image, and is rightly recognized in describing such perception

Wittgenstein goes on to deal interestingly with the psychology of coloured hearing, as when the vowels have colours assigned to them in the poem of Mallarmé, or in the oddities of what may be called conceptual visualization, as when we prefer to say, as most of us do, that Wednesday is fat and Tuesday lean, rather than the other way (216e). Wittgenstein is obviously correct in speaking of a secondary sense in such cases, and in refusing to call this sense 'metaphorical'. For the yellowness of the vowel *e* for myself, or the leanness of Tuesday, is not anything for which a more literal expression could be substituted. It is good that Wittgenstein recognizes all these interior nuances: it is a pity that he did not carry this recognition much further. Life subserves other ends than getting on in the physical world. He then goes on to say that if a man were thinking of someone as he spoke, and God saw into his mind, God would not have been able to see whom the man was thinking of (p. 217e). This denies to God the resource of seeing things as the man sees them, as a sort of secondary 'seeing as'. But since we ourselves possess this poor capacity in a great many cases, and can certainly, after long acquaintance with someone, and long practice of appresentation, see at least some things as he sees them, with much of the packaging of past experience involved, it is quite irreverent to deny such a capacity to a God. There is, in fact, no veil hiding other people's experience from ourselves, except the veil of an obdurate physicalism, which rates nothing as there which is not sensationally accessible, without any efforts at appresentation. Further limitations to the Divine Vision are set forth in pp. 225e–226e. There are no mathematical truths independent of whether human beings know them or not. But what if all human beings think and talk in terms of such man-independent truths (213e)? Wittgenstein further canvasses the possibility that there might be people who were aspect-blind, unable to read alternatively expressions into someone's face, or to see a figure as *either* a white cross on a black background or the other way round. He is not himself clear whether such aspect-blindness would be ruinous to communications, and he is plainly right in the case of many unusual aspect-seeing which some people cannot simply enter into. But if, as we have held, aspect-emphasis is a necessary feature of all consciousness, a totally aspect-blind person would be an impossible sort of idiot, who would make nothing of anything in the world or in himself, and with whom communication would be an impossibility. The rest of the section provides a great deal of material for reflection and criticism.

The last three sections of Part II (xii–xiv) are interesting. (xii) emphasizes that there is an accommodation of our basic concepts to basic facts of nature. If these basic facts were different, men would conceptualize quite differently. Obviously Wittgenstein is correct. The peculiarities of our contact- and distance-receptors undoubtedly affect the concepts in terms of which we understand the world, and the peculiarities of our motor-adjustments similarly affect our concepts and our actions, and not only these but our values. In the same way everything in our perception and action is determined by the character of our central nervous system: if this were more holistic, or more rigorously partitioned, the world as we see it, and our responses to it, would plainly be different. Speculative pictures of other-worldly existence are here of some value, particularly those which endow men with supernormal capacities, as in the writings of Swedenborg: they at least bring out the contingent peculiarities of our manner of existence. (xiii) briefly touches on the relation of memory-pronouncements to past events: man, he says, learns the concept of the past through memory-judgements which for Wittgenstein amount to a use of words. Wittgenstein plainly believes that we acquire the concept of the past by acquiring the use of the past tense, and would not be favourable to the view that there is a universal phenomenon or experience of states of things flowing away into the past, and that this is presupposed by all past-tense learning. We, however, must adhere to the traditional rather than the Wittgensteinian view. The river of time is indeed a poor metaphor, but what it represents seems beyond question, if only in the sectors of being where we ordinarily act and think. Section (xiv) deals with the confusion and barrenness of psychology, which is not, he says, due to the fact that it is a young science, but to its basic conceptual confusions. The existence of experimental methods makes us think that we have the means to answer psychological questions that trouble us, but questions and methods pass each other on the way. We agree with Wittgenstein that there is an overwhelming need for a satisfactory methodology for the analysis and explanation of personal experience, and of the linguistic and other forms of behaviour that go with it. We cannot, however, allow that Wittgenstein in the *Philosophical Investigations* has done much to satisfy this need.

## XV

We may conclude this chapter and this book with the somewhat sad admission that Wittgenstein's *Philosophical Investigations* has been very far from providing us with anything like a well-worked-out philosophy of mind on which a philosophy of language, of logic and mathematics, and of philosophy in general can be founded. Wittgenstein's account of the mind and its workings ranges almost as widely as James's *Principles of Psychology*, Stout's *Analytic Psychology*, Koffka's *Principles of Gestalt Psychology* or the writings of Husserl on transcendental phenomenology, but it cannot be compared with any of these works in regard to system and depth of treatment. It is basically unsatisfactory because it is throughout dogmatically negative. It disposes of countless attempts to analyse fundamental mental postures by refusing to admit the existence of a range of phenomena that are rightly denominated 'private' or 'interior', in the sense that a making plain of their import and content involves a sometimes difficult use of analogical language, and a demand to look at things in a certain manner whose nature is hard to characterize straightforwardly. The success of such demonstrations – we cannot call them ostensions – is shown by the deep *agreement* of many speakers in the descriptive analogies used in such inter-introspective diction, and by the regular adoption of such analogical diction in further psychological reports. Wittgenstein, however, follows no method in his treatment of most of the psychological reports that he considers. While not refusing to admit the existence of images and feelings, and other private data of various degrees of complexity, he only admits them as long as they are highly palpable and comparatively structureless. They must parade like soldiers before the senses and the imagination, and they are not to be credited with containing a rich wealth of organized detail that can only be teased out of them by questioning, and they cannot be credited with containing their objects in the very special sense in which mention and limited characterization of their objects is essential to saying what is 'there' for someone. Everything subtle or intricately structured must be sought in the words which such unsubtle, unstructured experiences evoke, and in the manner in which such words are *used*. The fact that there are no discoverably uttered or even imagined words in such situations is then counterbalanced by the words that come afterwards, and by the actions that are the follow-up of such words. There is a further difficulty in the fact that our normal use of the word 'use' involves bringing in many not publicly observable matters. Thus if I explain my use of the term 'dragon' as applied to someone's duenna, by saying that I regard her as a cross old woman whose one aim is to prevent her charge from having any men-friends, I explain my use of the expression by features of behaviour that have to be viewed in a certain light, which undoubtedly belongs to the inner life, so that the use of the expression 'dragon' involves a reference to many matters which are not uses of expressions, unless, indeed, one is willing to countenance an infinite regress in which the use of $A$ is explained in terms of the uses of $B$, $C$, and $D$, and so on indefinitely. Obviously the regress must end somewhere, as Wittgenstein would say, and it cannot end with a use. The use of the word 'use' has many advantages on account of its manifold connections with things, experiences, persons, situations and so forth, but this universal connectivity means that it can never end in complete understanding: we have to invoke other matters which are not uses. In the case of ordinary tools and instruments the regress need not go far, but in the case of words the regress has to go on into the interior, personal life of men, and the world as it appears in that interior, personal perspective. Wittgenstein, in his introduction of the concept of 'use', intended a great simplification, but the simplification simply does not come off.

Wittgenstein, we may say, practises introspective analyses, but mainly with the intention of rejecting what he regards as falsely mystifying forms of such analyses, which put into them many matters which pertain to our speech and action over a period, and to the many situations in which these latter might occur. To counter this mainly negative treatment of reported inner experiences, we ourselves must attempt to lay down a few norms for valid introspection, for statements as to how things appear to us, and as to how we ourselves are responsively oriented towards them. The first norm is that such statements must never be made, in the first instance, about our experiences in general, much less in regard to the experiences of anyone and everyone, though this may come later on. The valid introspective report must concern what has been experienced in more or less the last minute (i.e. the last sixty seconds) when, very curiously, we are able to assume a double stance, and both preserve in life the experience that is just lapsing, and yet also to distance ourselves from it, and to ask and answer questions about it, and make valid discriminations within it. And of all the valid discriminations we can learn to make within it, the most important is that between the elements that are sensuously or imaginally present in it, which consist in actual sense-data and images with no non-sensuous slants included in them, and other elements that have nothing of the sensuous or imaginal about them, though they may attach to, and be *carried* by, elements that are sensuous or imaginal. Thus if, in reading a novel, I imagine the proud entry of a beautiful heroine through a French door – the example is borrowed from Titchener – the sensuous imaginal elements include the sides of her person and clothing that it is possible imaginatively to see, and not any further bodily or spiritual features that are not capable, in this angle, of being imaginatively envisaged. That the discrimination in question is not easy is shown by the mainly silly and spurious criticisms of Moore's attempts to talk carefully about sense-data. Plainly such discriminations can be made in the case in question, and no one would say that, in such an imaginative envisagement, the woman's throat, or her rear view, or the degree of her pride, was given to us in the same intuitive manner as the erectness of her carriage, or the whiteness of her dress. This does not mean that these features were *not* given to us in another cogitative fashion, or that some of them, though not even thus given, would readily have been thus given had there been any reason to think of them. Plainly the difference between what is before us in a fulfilled, sensuous fashion, and what is before us in another genuine, but sensuously unfulfilled, manner is a genuine one, even if it is paradoxical that we can know just what redness, a sensuous quality, is, experience the feel of it, even when we imagine no instance of it. It is also clear that it is far from easy to draw a clear line between what we sensuously and cogitatively envisage: thus it is not easy to say whether the consciousness of visual depth is or is not sensuous, and the fact that it is not easy to make the discrimination in question is itself a character of the conscious experience in question. But, once the great discrimination between the sensuously and the cogitatively given has been made, the discovery will also soon be made that the immensely preponderant part of the things around us is non-sensuous, that every sensational or imaginal element is the carrier of a vastly complex and heavy cogitative burden, which vastly exceeds it in importance. One glimpse of a familiar object may also involve a cogitative package-experience which countless glimpses and contacts would be necessary to unpack, and while some of this packaged content is merely a matter of dispositional readiness, a great deal represents fully achieved conscious grasp. We are not, however, here attempting to provide a complete phenomenology of this difficult field, such as Husserl has worked out in many admirable passages. What is important is that we should recognize the many discriminations that are possible in these fields, and that some of them at least have nothing of the fictitious or mythic about them. They illuminate the use of words, and are not mere reflections of the latter.

There are other important discriminations that one must be trained to make if one is to go far in introspective analysis. The most significant are differences in attentional clarity, the differences between what is highlighted cognitively, occupies the focus of awareness, and what is marginal, is certainly there for us, but not obtrusively, luminously there. This is not the place to draw further discriminations between being in the actually present attentional margin, and being merely *ready* to come into consciousness: the careful introspectionist does not confuse these. We are not, in the normal case, marginally aware of the house next door or of the contents of our desk. Nor does the careful introspectionist confuse attentional clarity with the activity or passivity of attitude that may go with it, nor with the many remarkable consequences – ability to remember, careful performance, etc. – which Ryle and others have connected with it. Significant also are the differences in 'light' or 'angle' which Wittgenstein has studied under the rubric 'seeing as', but which affect *all* our conscious orientations. And very significant are the differences between an extraspective and an introspective orientation: we are differently oriented towards a three-dimensional picture when we are interested in the way in which we are conscious of it, and when we are interested in the scene or situation or object that it presents. And obviously we shall have to reckon among inward directions of consciousness the appresentative or empathetic directions through which we read feelings and mental orientations into other people, whether real or imagined. Important too are the great differences between the experiences of active orientation and those of passive receptivity, and between those that are fully serious, and engage the whole person, and those that are playful and aesthetic, and again between those that involve a striving towards ends, whether these take the form of precisely delimited projects or wide general policies. There is also the distinction between orientations that are cool and without emotional warmth, and those that are warm-blooded and emotional. The grammar and syntax of all these types of experience requires to be worked out, and it is arguable that this has been much better done by many of the more or less traditional psychologists, phenomenologists and philosophers of mind than by Wittgenstein. The falsifying, merely pictorial element certainly abounds in inner-life talk, but it will none the less not do to throw out the baby of inner experience with the bath-water of undisciplined diction. One can learn to use analogical language with circumspection, and we can establish as good a communication by its means as we can establish anywhere. Fundamental philosophical doubts can, of course, never be finally exorcised from any field of discourse, and it would be highly regrettable if they could be.

This book will now have to end on a general note of appraisal: what degree of philosophical significance or 'greatness' shall we attribute to Wittgenstein's *Philosophical Investigations*, and the many other works that led up to it, including the *Tractatus Logico-Philosophicus*? Our own response to all this work has been critical at every turn: Wittgenstein has offered us no adequate philosophy of language, nor of logic or mathematics, nor of mind and its conscious experiences, nor of anything absolute and transcendent, whether from an ontological or axiological or mystico-religious point of view. Wittgenstein's treatment of all these matters has itself been largely negative and destructively critical: he has rejected what seemed to him the idle pictures that men fashion in going beyond the actual uses of language, but he has given us little understanding of what those actual uses are, and what they ought to be. His general course has been to abide with what is commonly said without attempting to find ontological or interior moorings which make this adherence justifiable and profitable. Blind acceptance of the use of expressions, without a justifying ontology or experiential phenomenology, does not, however, recommend itself to even the most naive users of words: they look for a justification of use, and they seek it beyond use. Wittgenstein, however, never so clarifies his concept of use as to make plain what it amounts to, and what it demands, and why it should be valued and respected, and he has even left it to others to explain in detail why philosophical treatments that go beyond the normal use of words are mistaken and unfruitful, and how they can be corrected. Thus it was left to G.A. Paul and J.L. Austin to expose the false problematic of sense-data, etc., in a systematic manner, and it was left to such as myself to explore in some detail the false problematic of time, which Wittgenstein touched upon but had not explored in his criticisms of Augustine. (I am now far from thinking that my exposures were in all respects valid.) The Logical Positivists at least gave clarity to the concept of the use of expressions by connecting it with the anticipated verifications of sentences in which the expressions occurred by certain sense-data, but Wittgenstein has no corresponding commitment connecting use with sensation or verification. Sometimes the concept of use implies custom and uniformity: there must be a *rule* connecting the correct use of an expression with something or other, but what this something or other may be Wittgenstein fails to elucidate clearly, only that it cannot be anything private to the speaker or transcendently unobservable. Yet he does not wish to limit the conditions of use to what is purely physical: these conditions are left vague, they are simply the circumstances in which it is customary and correct for an expression to be employed. We thus have a world of usage sustaining itself by its own inherent, standard-setting power, and without deference to anything beyond itself. The correct use of 'red' is simply its utterance in the range of cases in which we agree that 'this' expression should be used, and we must not try to justify our use by appealing to the presence of a quality, or to an experience of identity. It is obvious that such a circular theory cannot shed light, and that if we are to be deprived both of the light of inner experience and of external objectivity, we must seek light from some other source. This Wittgenstein does not, however, provide, beyond appealing vaguely to the way the world happens to be organized, or the way that men are constituted.

We must, however, allow ourselves to look on Wittgenstein's doctrine of meaning as use in another regard, in which his immense importance and depth as a philosopher, which we have always felt in studying him, becomes truly evident. Wittgenstein means language not to have an absolute or self-sustaining role, on which all other objective and subjective matters are dependent, but rather to have a centrally connective role, so that none of them would be possible as it is, or connected with one another as they are connected, without the intermediation of language. There are indeed pre-linguistic, phenomenological meanings from which language takes its origin, but these would never have acquired their rich differentiation, nor their fixation and their ready communicability, without the assistance of language. Thus we certainly had *Ur-erlebnisse* and *Ur-erfahrungen*, not only of all elementary qualities and forms of pattern, but also of negation, of allness, of sameness, of affinity, of pastness, of futurity, of factuality, of probability, of activity, of passivity, of need, of delight, of ease, of difficulty, etc., long before we learned the use of expressions, and there is no reason why, *pace* all anti-sentimentalists, we should not attribute such experiences, in rudimentary form, to animals. A bitch may well be clear that *all* the puppies in her litter are there, but that *this* puppy is *not* one of them, and was not here *before*, etc. But the world partitioned and again put together in the elaborate way in which our world is partitioned and also put together would be impossible without the definite, fixed words which we connect with our partitions and syntheses. The elaborate inner life which we further attribute to ourselves and others, and which is often certainly wordless, is, however, an inner life which permits linguistic expression, and would not have the rich differentiation that it has, without linguistic differentiation. There are package experiences in which the most complexly articulated relationships are experienced in a flash, but they are packages that can be unpacked into lengthy verbal protocols, and would not be the packages they are if they could not be so unpacked. This neither reduces them to dispositions, nor removes their unifying, magisterial role: they cannot, however, be fully magisterial unless they have words, or something like words, to work in and through. The connection of men with other men, and with other conscious beings is, of course, wholly prior to language: a wordless babe can plainly appeal to a particular parent to help her in some situation, and can see that parent as willing and able to do just this. Words, however, fix the whole pluralism of persons immeasurably, and define the role of its members more clearly. Obviously the world of conscious persons taking account of one another's actual or possible attitudes, only achieves full development in and through language. And though Wittgenstein's exclusion of private language in limited fields is both exaggerated and arbitrary, it is obvious that a rich store of perceptual and cogitative differentiations, and their firm validations, are only possible when there are established and agreed linguistic uses. The possibilities of introspection are, moreover, immeasurably dependent on the language which pins down an inner state by analogies that others find acceptable in their own case: the most nebulous experiences acquire a certain distinctness when they also acquire analogical expression, and this not necessarily an expression that removes their nebulousness, only one that recognizes it fully. Through the use of language we are likewise able to have all sorts of complex attitudes and discriminations, and our wordless enjoyment of such attitudes and discriminations is rather an attenuation of our verbally expressed enjoyment than the other way round. Through the use of language, we may say, we inhabit an invariant real world and a world that is there for others as much as for ourselves: through the use of language we likewise inhabit a world that contains others, and others with whom we have varied affinities, and to whom we can make many cognitive and practical appeals. Through the use of language also the things in the world are sorted out into kinds, and discriminated into individual specimens, in a much more elaborate and constant manner than would be possible in wordless experience. Through the use of language, likewise, performances involving numbers can be immeasurably increased in complexity and accuracy, and we can pick out primes in a series of cardinals as readily as we can pick blackberries from a bush. Aspects and features of any degree of abstraction can by the use of language become counters that we can readily play with in thought, e.g. the logical paradoxes, the branched theory of types, etc., and incorporate into dazzling theorems. It is not necessary to continue this tale. Linguistic expressions are indeed the principal focus where inner comes into contact with outer, the universal sense with the particular instance, dispositions with exercises, and where men in their immensely complex psycho-physical organization come into contact with themselves and one another.

But though we thus realize the universal connectivity of language, and its overall responsibility for the intelligibility of the world and its contents and denizens, we need not therefore ignore the role of the different categories of items that are thus connected: the individualities and particularities in the world, the varied entities of reason that work through them, the states of affairs that they constitute, and the logical forms present in these, the experients that envisage the world and other possible worlds, the God's-eye view that is an overarching regulative Idea, and so on. There need be no stinting of entities of reason, or of types of individual experients and experiences, or of ineliminable Absolutes of alternative coverage and mode of operation, etc. etc., merely because language enables us to talk of them and to connect them with one another. Language requires whatever we can intelligibly talk about as much as whatever we can intelligibly talk about requires language. If this is the true message of Wittgenstein, then he is not to be taken as a reducer of all things to words and verbal uses, but as one who generously counsels us to say what we like, and to explore any realm of entities and connections among entities, whether existent or merely subsistent, temporal or timeless, subjective or objective, and so on, that can be subjected to rationally ordered discourse of some sort, and can lead to agreed conclusions or at least to acceptably alternative ones. Wittgenstein can thus be envisaged even as permitting mystifying forms of diction, as he did at the end of the *Tractatus*. There are good uses of language in which it transcends all its ordinary uses. Wittgenstein may have started his higher intellectual life in laboratories, and much of his thought reflects the highly mechanized, well-lit, clinically therapeutic arrange-

ments of such places. There was, however, always for Wittgenstein, beyond the laboratories of science and the concert-
chambers of traditional philosophy, the immense background
traffic and rumour of an ancient human city, the Vienna of
human existence, with its innumerable interpersonal transactions
and forms of life. It is on such a background that the aphorisms
of Wittgenstein's *Philosophical Investigations* must receive a
hearing. They are not so much clearly stated contributions to
philosophical theory, as essays in an attempted escape from the
fly-bottle of traditional philosophizing, which happily fail of their
purpose, but none the less contribute a new and perennially
important note to philosophy, the notion of a liquidation of
philosophical questions, not so much by finding one-sided
answers to them, as by coming to understand all the forces and
motives that incline us to speak in one way or another, and by
the choosing from them all such modes of speaking as satisfy us
best, and do the best justice to all that we do say, and that we
want to say.

# INDEX

258

# Index

# Index

# Index

# International Library of Philosophy

Editor: Ted Honderich

*(Demy 8vo)*